No Vill

Crime, violence, and infamy are not tragedy. Tragedy occurs when a human soul awakes and seeks in suffering and pain to free itself from crime, violence, and infamy, even at the cost of life. The struggle is the tragedy, not defeat or death. That is why the spectacle of tragedy has always filled men not with despair but with a sense of hope and exaltation.

-- Whittaker Chambers

No Villains,
No Heroes

Based on a shockingly true event:
the gun battle in the Carroll County
courthouse, Hillsville, Virginia,
March 1912

Thomas Moore

Pp
PROSEPRESS

www.prosepress.biz

No Villains, No Heroes
Copyright © 2012
Thomas Moore

Published by ProsePress
75 Red Maple Drive
Pawleys Island, South Carolina 29585
www.Prosepress.biz

Comments: contact Thomas Moore on his Website
www.ThomasMooreBooks.com

Comments can also be found on
Prose Press Face Book

ISBN: 978-0-9851889-0-0

Cover images courtesy of
Carroll County Historical Society.

Cover Design : OBD Art and Illustration
Contact: proseNcons@live.com

DISCLAIMER and ACKNOWLEDGEMENTS

This is a work of fiction based on true events. Except for the clearly historical people in the story, all other characters are products of the author's imagination and do not represent real persons, living or dead. Any resemblance to real persons is unintentional and coincidental.

To make the historical elements as accurate as possible, I consulted all the sources I could locate on the Hillsville story and visited the related physical sites. At the same time I found it necessary to simplify the tale to avoid overwhelming the reader in a mass of detail. I relied most heavily on *The Carroll County Courthouse Tragedy* by Ron Hall, a Carroll County native. This remains the most balanced and definitive non-fiction account. Taylor Fitchett, director of the University of Virginia Law Library, provided invaluable research material, for which I'm grateful. I'm indebted to the helpful staff of the Carroll County Historical Society and Gary Marshall, Chairman of the Centennial Commission.

Ernie and Liz Smoake offered their mountain-top aerie as the ideal place to research and write the story. The fair and tender ladies of the Draper Mercantile and New River Retreat also provided a writer's refuge, and I'm grateful to owner Debbie Gardner and her staff, especially Jackie Farr.

Writing is a solitary pursuit, but advice from discerning readers during the process is essential. My thanks to John Hall of Floyd, Virginia for insights into the culture and people of the Blue Ridge, and to my son Stuart Moore for his wise critique. Special thanks for the crucial editorial support of Kirk Sale, author of twelve outstanding books; and Virginia Amos, free-lance editor *extraordinaire*. Finally, I'm grateful to Robert O'Brien and ProsePress for turning the effort into a book which I hope will illuminate and instruct as well as entertain.

*For Ernie Smoake, Blue Ridge Mountain sage,
and his lovely wife Liz.
Friends indeed.*

Chapter One

Cheviot Hills Farm, Upperville, Virginia. June 1968.

Man is the only creature with foreknowledge of his own doom. This awareness instills a need to leave something behind, to explain himself to those who follow; and he becomes a teller of tales. How he plays his short hour on the stage, nobly or meanly, is a story; and he lives surrounded by the tales of others as well as his own. That's all we humans are in the end, a collection of stories; which confer a kind of immortality when we pass them on to our children and grandchildren.

Now the time has come for me to tell the untold chapter of my story. It's the only item of remaining business before I shuffle off this mortal coil. That won't be long, if I read the faces of the doctors correctly. I'm 89 years old and my mainspring is running down. But we all go the same way home; there's no point in fretting about it. At least I can go without regrets if I complete the circle of my life by sharing this amazing tale.

Although I've been asked many times to tell about my role in the famous 'Hillsville Horror' and often found myself besieged by writers and historians, I couldn't until now, until I knew my demise was imminent. The memories have remained a sharp knife in the soul all these years, for the tale includes Emma, who played a small part in the tale and then died young! – ah, too young! – leaving me desolate. Emma Romilly. She of the golden coloring, dark eyes, and a wistfulness that shone out from her sharp intelligence. When I think of her, or of Claude Allen, who also died untimely, and unjustly at the hands of the state, the desolation rushes back upon me with such force... Well, the only way I could live with it all these years was to push it into the background of consciousness.

My vision and my hearing are going now, but my mind isn't. When I'm fully awake, my memory's still good enough to finish the tale. Strange, how those long-ago events stand in sharper relief than the things that happened yesterday. From birth I was blessed -- or cursed – with an acute memory. I enjoyed such full recollection that some called it a photographic memory, if there is such a thing. It proved invaluable in the practice of law. I carried around in my head virtually the entire Code of Virginia and the common law and could recall at need the appropriate case law precedents. For 56 years I've also carried around a full recall of those bloody yet heady days in Hillsville, in faraway Carroll County, Virginia. Memories of such vividness, and of long-departed Emma, have become a burden. The only way to find peace is to tell the tale. Yet to tell it right, I needed distance from the event. I didn't want to stir up old passions, re-open old wounds, since descendants of the principals on both sides still live down in the Blue Ridge. But, as the ancient Greeks said, truth is the daughter of time. Facts emerge and passions cool with the passage of years. All the direct parties to the battle have passed on. Now my turn's coming, and the time has finally come to speak.

And what a story it is. There's nothing in our state's history to equal the Hillsville Massacre of March 14, 1912. According to the governor at the time, it was the greatest crime in the history of the Commonwealth of Virginia. No other such episode has occurred in the entire country before or since – a blazing gun battle inside a crowded courtroom at the height of a notorious trial. It was followed by the most intense manhunt of the time and was the most shocking newspaper story in the United States; some even say the whole world, until the Titanic went down a month later. It's got all the elements of high drama — suspense, violence, betrayal, tragedy, and pathos. If you include my part in it — redemption. Strange as it is, it has the added virtue of being true.

***

Hillsville is the county seat of Carroll County, Virginia, deep in the heart of the Blue Ridge, about 60 miles southwest of Roanoke. The combatants in the fight were members of the Allen family, a prominent clan in the southern part of the county near the North Carolina-Virginia line; and officers of the Carroll County court.

Floyd, leader of the Allen faction, was one of five brothers. The Allens were simple country people, active in the business most common to their world, extracting a livelihood from the land. We wouldn't consider them cultivated by today's urban norms, but they were literate, and the brothers had even held public office as county constables. They weren't slack-jawed, weak-eyed, inbred hillbillies like the big national papers made 'em out to be. The Allens were as a fine-looking a set of men as I ever saw. Well formed, carried themselves with a certain dignity, handsome. Almost distinguished, you might say. Claude Allen was certainly handsome, with movie star looks. They didn't go 'round in hog-washers. They usually wore dark suits and ties and looked like successful pillars of the community. Which they were, in fact. Psychopathic cretins they assuredly were not.

The county's elected leaders were Republicans; the Allens old-time Southern Democrats. County officials saw the Allens as rivals for power, as obstacles to their New South politics, and as throwbacks to an age that ended at Appomattox in 1865. The Courthouse believed the power of the Allens had to be broken if Carroll County was going to enter the new century and partake of the progress and prosperity it offered. The result of these fundamental differences in politics, culture, and interests was a long-running feud between the Allen family and the 'Courthouse Ring' that finally erupted into an armed clash.

Floyd Allen feared, not without reason, that county officers were seeking any excuse, any pretext, to prosecute him, which they eventually did. The Allens believed it was persecution, not prosecution. My view is, when you see your enemies out to provoke you, especially in the realm of politics, you ought to expend every effort not to be provoked. But such subtleties were lost on a passionate and choleric man like Floyd Allen.

There was much to admire in Floyd Allen; in the entire family, but Floyd carried those virtues to excess. He skirted right along the edge of the law; and I mean real law, the kind that's written in human hearts, that tells us right from wrong and informs us when we've failed to treat others with charity and respect. Floyd always claimed he minded his own business, and I

4

guess he tried to. He respected others, but just barely. He was an unreasonable man, basically; too quick to take offense, defending his rights and prerogatives too aggressively. He went beyond what the provocation justified, beyond what most folks had come to see as acceptable. He said on more than one occasion that he would die and to go hell before he spent a minute behind bars, which tells you something, even if you believe the Courthouse Ring had it in for him. I believe they did, in fact. But I also believe Floyd gave them cause. Can you draw a bright line and show who was right and wrong, or who was mostly right and wrong? No, you can't. This is the human complexity underlying the story. This is my theme, you might say.

In March 14, 1912 a Carroll County jury found Floyd Allen guilty of assaulting two sheriff's deputies and recommended a sentence of one year in prison. Amid the collective indrawn breath of the spectators, many of whom expected trouble, the judge ordered the sheriff to take Floyd into custody. Scowling with fury at what he saw as a rigged conviction, he stood up and announced sullenly, "Gentlemen, I ain't a-goin."

No one knows with certainty who fired first; no one ever will. But when Floyd flung down the gauntlet, a series of gunshots shattered the expectant hush. Floyd went down wounded in the leg, then came up fighting. In an instant mass gunfire swept the crowded court as Floyd's kinfolk drew their pistols and opened fire on the court officers, who blazed back with their pistols. Five people died in the crossfire or were mortally wounded – the presiding judge, the prosecutor, the sheriff, a juror, and a witness in the gallery. Seven died, if you count the subsequent executions of Floyd and his son Claude. If you believe Jack Allen's murder a few years later was connected to the case, that would make it eight dead. Seven were wounded, some seriously.

Floyd was hurt too badly to move, but after a period of confusion and indecision, the rest of the Allen-Edwards fled into the hills. The governor of Virginia called in the Baldwin-Felts Detective Agency to restore order and track down the fugitives, which we did with the Agency's usual competence, but not without stepping over the threshold of the law ourselves. For a time I led the manhunt for Baldwin-Felts, an experience that changed my life profoundly.

I was watching an old movie yesterday evening. Not much else I can do these days except listen to the radio, watch TV, and wait for the final call from my Maker. Along came that old classic, "My Darling Clementine," with Henry Fonda, Walter Brennan, Victor Mature, and Ward Bond. It's about Doc Holliday and Wyatt Earp and his brothers in the gunfight at the OK Corral. Tombstone, Arizona in the 1880's. Most Americans know the story, one of the most famous in the Old West. It's an epic, like our own Horatius at the Bridge. But just think -- how many books, movies, and TV shows have been made about the gunfight at the OK Corral? A dozen, maybe? An event that lasted all of about thirty seconds, and only three ruffians died. Some say the Earps and their friend Doc Holliday were the ruffians, but that's beside the point. Point is, it has dominated our folklore unlike any other such episode. Yet it hardly compares with the 'Hillsville Horror,' as the press called it.

The Hillsville gunfight lasted for an eternity it seemed to those who were caught in it. It took place during an actual trial, then spilled out into the street. The, ah, participants actually took time to reload. It was a genuine firefight, not just a quick-draw, from-the-hip shooting like Tombstone. All this mayhem in a crowded courtroom, not a bar room, not in a dusty Western street like in the movies. Over a hundred eyewitnesses. At the OK Corral there were only two.

Then followed the biggest manhunt in America until Melvin Purvis and his G-men came along in the 30's and took down John Dillinger and those boys. The sinking of the Titanic knocked us off the front pages in April 1912, but up till then I got my share of headlines. It felt good to read my name in the biggest news accounts of the day — for a while. Yet in the half century since it's faded from the news, few people have heard about Hillsville beyond the Blue Ridge of Southwest Virginia. And the Blue Ridge might as well be the back side of the moon to most Americans.

The tragedy ended seven lives and profoundly changed others – mine included. When the gun battle left Sheriff Lew Webb dead on the courtroom floor, the Commonwealth of Virginia formally deputized the Baldwin-Felts Detective Agency to bring the Allens to justice. Justice. Or so I thought. Yet my involvement, of which I was so proud at the time, taught me lessons about the meaning of justice which I never anticipated and transformed me entirely.

Baldwin-Felts was ostensibly a private firm but often acted as a de facto arm of the state. In its day the Baldwins were the most celebrated guns-for-hire after the better known Pinkertons. Thus Hillsville is their story, too – of the indomitable William Baldwin, founder of the firm; his intense and often vindictive partner Thomas Felts; and of Tom's lost brothers Albert and Lee Felts, who proved the old adage that those who live by the sword also die by it.

I quit the Agency at the height of the Allen trials and 'went over to the enemy,' according to Baldwin and Felts. Hanging up my guns, I enrolled in the University of Virginia law school, ending up the best criminal defense lawyer in the Commonwealth, according to many. Maybe so. But only after what I did to the Allens. That's still on the debit side of the ledger.

Later I did keep some innocent people out of jail, or worse. And I never knowingly defended anyone accused of a capital crime unless I believed they were innocent. Did well enough in the law that I had the luxury, you might say, of picking my clients. I preferred to represent those I thought would end up unjustly railroaded by the state without the best possible defense.

Sadly, there are lawyers who pull their punches. They don't want to offend the establishment because they hope to end up on the bench one day. But who knows who's really innocent? In the end, only God knows. One thing you soon learn about criminals; they're often good liars. Besides which, things like this are always messy and complicated, as much as we in the law might prefer 'em clean and simple.

The Allen clan did wrong, it's true. But there was right and wrong on all sides, the Carroll County Courthouse Ring included. Hindsight tends to regard the characters in history's pageant as saints or sinners. But real life is not so simple. In each of us lives the capacity to do both good and evil. In March 1912 there were no villains, no heroes. The Allens didn't deserve the death penalty, especially Floyd's son Claude. Prison, yes; electrocution, no. Take Sid Allen and Wesley Edwards. They did exactly the same crime, yet only received prison sentences. Why were they any less guilty than Floyd and Claude?

But then, those who died in the shootout didn't deserve it, either. That was the terrible sadness of it all. Just like a Greek tragedy, you might say. No one deserved what happened. Such a terrible result growing from such a trivial incident. After 56 years I still can't figure it all out, and not from lack of trying. It made me decide, better a dozen guilty should go free than one innocent suffer death, especially at the hands of the state. Judicial murder, in other words. When that happens, then in a way we're all responsible, as citizens of the state. I can tell you from bitter experience, the state finds it too easy to convict. Too much temptation for an ambitious prosecutor, too much trust among juries. Jurors figure — wrong, about half the time: if the state indicts somebody, then they must be guilty.

Prosecutors or state's attorneys are mostly conscientious men who love the law and want to serve the community. But sadly, many aren't. This kind of fellow gets handed a big case, sees his name in the papers, then goes all out for a conviction. The temptation is hard to escape – it's only about winning, not about truth, guilt, or innocence. Next thing you know the fellow has sailed into the governor's mansion on the headlines. When you send someone to the electric chair just because you have the power or you think it'll get you elected to high office... Well, it made me decide to become the best defense lawyer I could be. Instead of a... well, instead of a hired gun acting under color of law, which is what I was when the Hillsville gunfight took place.

I had a unique vantage point on the tragedy. Now my hope is that this perspective might temper the public's thinking about the true meaning of the law. Most folks I know like to say, 'Toss 'em in prison and throw away the key. Send 'em to the chair. Reasonable doubt? Hell, that's for Liberals and sissies.' The result of such an attitude? Too much law and order and not enough justice.

***

To understand what happened in March 1912, or more to the point, why it happened, you have to go back to the place it happened. Unless you understand Hillsville, Carroll County, the Blue Ridge, and the Appalachian Mountain culture, it won't make any sense. This culture and region aren't easy for modern urban or suburban Americans, with all their modern conveniences and plenty of money, to understand.

A man's character is formed by many influences, but certainly one of them is the place that nurtured him. The Blue Ridge is a special place, often a hard place, and it stamps its hardness on a man. In 1912 Carroll and the surrounding counties really hadn't entered the 20th Century. There were no paved roads and only a handful of automobiles. Almost everybody rode horseback or in horse-drawn carriages or they walked. Only a dozen or so telephones were in all of Hillsville. In most ways, what we're pleased to call progress hadn't yet arrived.

Life there changes slowly, memories are long, and folkways are strong. Like mountaineers everywhere, these people were — still are, in fact — fiercely independent and self-reliant, like their pioneer ancestors who settled the mountains in the 18th Century. Mostly Scots-Irish, with a bit of German thrown in. They were proud and touchy. They had a kind of freedom in their isolated hills that most folks, especially city-dwellers, never experience. Even today they may be poor, but they've got this old-fashioned sense of honor, the kind that went out with the Code Duello here in 'civilization.' They didn't bother others, for the most part; and by the same token they expected to be left alone.

To be sure, there was a lot of moonshining and a lot of drinking. Most of the crime was associated with too much corn liquor — drunken fights, mostly. Of course, the act of 'stillin' 'shine was a crime, a Federal crime, and some folks got locked up for it. Blockaders, they called 'em then. But there was no shame in it. Hardly anyone considered making blockade whiskey a genuine crime. Certainly not an act of moral turpitude. It was the only way some of them could make a living. Nor did the Federal Government care about the fact of making whiskey or its consequences. All the Government cared about was getting the tax. It was a *malum prohibitum*, not a *mal in se*, as we call it in the common law. In other words, an administrative offense against the state, not an evil in itself. The campaign against it made people hostile and suspicious of the Feds — of all government, in fact.

Unlike today, being a government official was not particularly a source of public esteem. Folks tended to solve their problems their own way instead of resorting to the law. Some call it 'taking the law into your own hands.' But that was their culture, the preferred way things were settled, and no one thought it wicked or strange.

There were informal as well as formal means of social order. We here in the Big World think that only the formal means count — laws, courts, written documents and contracts, judges, government agencies, and so forth. But at the turn of the 20th Century in the Appalachians, the informal means were more important; and the clan was a principal one. Unlike modern life, families were close and intensely loyal. You didn't have the mobility there you have today, so the clan remained physically close. Most people lived out their lives within a few miles of where they'd been born. Irrespective of the occasional black sheep, they stuck together in all other ways and looked out for one another. It was necessary for sheer survival in the early days of settlement, and the tradition remained strong. It does today in Appalachia. You stood by your people and defended the family honor and family interests, right or wrong. If it meant joining a vendetta you otherwise had no real part in, so be it.

This is one reason that even before the shooting, the country got the idea the region was violent. But it wasn't really. There was less crime and violence than in most other places, especially big cities. True, there were famous family feuds, like the clash of Hatfields and the McCoys up on the Kentucky-West Virginia border. That was a big news story for a time, too, in the late 1880's and 1890's.

Aside from the occasional feud there was little or no violence. You'd be far safer in Hillsville or Floyd or Galax than you would be in downtown Richmond or Norfolk, or especially in Washington, DC or Baltimore. That's true today; it was true then. Folks didn't lock their houses at night. Women could walk alone unmolested. Armed robbery and other kinds of theft were almost unheard of.

True, there were lots of guns. But guns by themselves wouldn't... Well, maybe I better reconsider what I was about to say. I guess if so many hadn't been armed inside the Carroll County courtroom, things might've turned out different. I say might have. The underlying conflict would've remained as bitter as ever. Floyd Allen said he wasn't going to jail upon his conviction. What other choice did he have if he wasn't armed? He meant it, and he wasn't one to back down when he'd committed himself, 'specially when he believed he was being railroaded by the Courthouse Ring. But without guns in play, folks might've had the chance to cool down. Or the gunfight might've had a change of venue and taken place in a less crowded location. Who knows?

It must seem extraordinary, even unthinkable to folks today, all those men in the courtroom with concealed weapons. In 1912 in the Blue Ridge, which was a kind of wild frontier, guns were a part of daily life. Still are, in fact. In 1912 carrying in the courthouse was allowed. It was basically up to the presiding judge. There weren't any metal detectors at the door; the technology didn't exist. In fact, it was the Hillsville shootout that caused the Virginia legislature to outlaw carrying weapons into court; law enforcement officials excepted. On some of the older Virginia courthouses you can still see the cite posted at the entrance.

The point is, Carroll County and environs were an armed society, and yet there was little violent crime. This is one reason why the Hillsville shootout, which was basically an anomaly, was so shocking. Folks generally believed an armed society was a polite society. If you were a free man and a gentleman, and by that I include the 'mountain gentlemen,' you proved it by carrying. It was a mark of pride, status, and self-regard, you might say. Just like in the Middle Ages, when the word gentleman meant someone with the privilege of bearing arms, while the serfs were forbidden the same.

Now, here's another important piece of background of the time and place you can't overlook. It was part of the political context of the shooting. The thing wasn't entirely over personal grievances as some in the yellow press suggested. And that piece of the political context was the Civil War. Or the War Between the States, as we Virginians prefer to call it.

1912 was less than fifty years after Lee surrendered to Grant at Appomattox. Lots of folks were still living who'd taken part in the nation's deadliest conflict. Memories of the War were fresh. Fortunately,

Hillsville hadn't suffered directly; that is, there were no major battles to destroy the town and county like there were in Central and Northern Virginia or the Shenandoah Valley. But, memories were still raw over Reconstruction, and many Southerner still burned with a sense of being invaded and expropriated by the Republican Party. Today people forget how hard it was after the War. The state and its economy were virtually destroyed, and there was no Marshall Plan for the South. You had to do whatever you could to survive. All you had to depend on was yourself and your kin, and it made people hard.

Virginians loyal to the old ways were Democrats, mostly in reaction against the party of Lincoln and the Radical Republicans. Even so, a number of locals joined the Republicans, mostly because it was a quick way to patronage and they had to find some way to make a living amid the terrible poverty after the War. Some were simply greedy for political power and status. Some joined out of genuine conviction. They said, "The War is over, we have to move on." They saw old-time Southern Democrats as disloyal to a re-united America — as backward and selfish obstacles to progress. These post-war Republicans believed in a New Order, and the old retrograde Southern attitudes had to be swept away if the region was to claw its way out of the 19th Century and into the 20th. Many Democrats regarded these 'Scalawag' Republicans not just as political opponents, but also as unprincipled opportunists and traitors to the South. So there was a great deal of bitterness on both sides of the political divide, more than just your usual Democrat-Republican rivalry. The impact of the Civil War didn't end at Appomattox.

I experienced this myself growing up in Rappahannock County. My father was a young private in the War with Mosby's Rangers, the legendary horsemen of Colonel John S. Mosby, the celebrated 'Gray Ghost' and one of the most famous heroes of the Confederacy. After the War Mosby became a Republican as well as friend of Ulysses S. Grant himself. He accepted a post in Grant's administration, which caused many Virginians and folks throughout the South to turn against Mosby and revile him as a traitor. I remember Daddy being upset about it, although he stayed loyal to his old commander and never joined in the condemnation.

The Confederacy was also part of the Allens' heritage. Jeremiah Allen, father of Floyd, Sidna, Jasper or 'Jack,' and the others, served as a lieutenant in the Confederate Army. The Allen clan, like most local Democrats, were loyal to the Old South and its traditions, for better or worse. The Courthouse Ring despised them for it, and the Allens returned the sentiment tenfold.

For all their flaws, I admired the inhabitants of the Blue Ridge. Still do. It's not a popular attitude, especially here and now, and especially among people of our background. People like us condescend. Well-off, educated at the best schools, socially prominent. If we take any notice at all of our Southern highlanders in their remote hills and hollows, we tend to make fun of them. Snuffy Smith. Li'l Abner. The Beverly Hillbillies. But how can you not admire a people who are brave, proud, honest, self-reliant, and independent? I've even been known in a weak moment to, ah, admire their moonshine whiskey. Of course, every virtue has its dark side, its opposite that makes it a vice. Or it may become a vice when carried to excess. I think that's what happened there in 1912. But if this story helps broader society see these folks in a more favorable light, then it's another good reason to tell it.

Frankly, our lost, confused, empty world of the city and suburb could use more of that mountain culture.

At the same time I've tried to be objective about the case. Though I was closely connected with it, I consider myself a disinterested party. Thirty years in the law taught me to see both sides of a question. The way it transformed my life would argue that I have no selfish interests to promote. I come back to what I said earlier. There was right and there was wrong on both sides. Plenty of it. In this story, truly, there are no villains, no heroes.

Now, I only had a supporting role, you might say, in the Hillsville drama. In fact, I wasn't even there for the gunfight. Baldwin-Felts wasn't called in 'til the next day. But though I'm not a main character in the play, I am the only one in the cast who's still living. After the shooting I interviewed as many participants and witnesses as possible. My report to the Governor was considered the most authoritative of all at the time. I wouldn't make that claim today. I'm a different man from that young detective, full of piss and vinegar — and insufferable self-righteousness.

I was 32. But it seems like several lifetimes from 89, which I'll be next month if I hang on that long. My investigation of the shooting took place while the details were fresh in people's minds. I even spoke to Betty Ayers before she died, not that she knew anything. She was the young woman in the gallery hit in the back by a stray bullet, and I was the only law officer to take her statement. I took the wounded Floyd Allen into custody and got his statement. So I have good grounds when I claim the Hillsville Massacre was not only the worst event of its kind in the history of Virginia, it also remains the most tantalizing mystery in the history of Virginia. For all my boast at the time of getting the best eyewitness accounts, I learned later as a member of the criminal defense bar that eyewitnesses are notoriously unreliable. For all my pride in my investigation, I began to conclude at the time, and I continue to think now, that no one can say with certainty who drew first, who fired first, or whose bullet hit whom.

* * *

It was not my original plan to become a detective, which in the case of the Baldwin-Felts Detective Agency was a euphemism for hired gun. As a young man, I dreamed of becoming a professional soldier, influenced by Daddy's adventures with Mosby's Rangers and the fireside stories of relatives who fought with Lee, Jackson, and Stuart. In my impressionable mind they were epics, like the Greeks before the walls of Troy. Later I saw military glory up close and personal. It's not at all what it seems on the surface. Things are seldom as the authorities tell us. That lesson stood me in good stead years later during the Hillsville case and the pursuit of the Allens. But before I reached this self-awareness, and under the spell of my Confederate kin, off I went to the Virginia Military Institute in 1895, set on a military career.

After VMI I ended up as a newly minted second lieutenant and commander of a rifle platoon in the First Marine Regiment in the middle of the Philippine Insurrection, as it was called. It wasn't an insurrection, however. It was a war of independence, in principle like the one we Americans fought against the British Empire in 1776. Only this time we were the imperialists. But I cared nothing about that. It was my generation's war and I was determined to prove myself and sup deeply of glory.

In the summer of 1901 the war had been going on about two years. We'd defeated the Filipino regular forces, but then along came the *Insurrectos*. They went guerrilla on us, and that's when things really got ugly. The cycle of atrocity and reprisal became appallingly brutal as the natives fought back with unconventional tactics we'd never encountered. Occupying soldiers always end up hating the natives in a protracted guerrilla war, just like today in Vietnam, because you can't tell the combatants from the non-combatants. We ended up doing things that I'm ashamed to recall after all these years, things that would be classified as war crimes today. It wasn't military glory but mass murder. Even today at the end my life when I ought to unburden myself, I can't bring myself to summon up the gory details.

If the experience made me ashamed, it also made me hard. I thrived on danger and excitement, living on the edge, you might say. With a knack for combat, I made good decisions under pressure and didn't get rattled when all about me was chaos. Despite the shame I gave myself over to a kind of bloodlust. That's the way we humans are, full of complex and imponderable motives, where contradictory feelings exist side by side.

I also received my first and only wound. A rifle round from an 8-millimeter Mauser passed through the fleshy part of my right thigh, fortunately missing the femur. It was painful as hell, but could've been a lot worse. In that tropical environment it could've gotten infected and I might've lost the leg. But it was a clean wound and an honorable one. I was able to go home without having to take part in such terrible things again. The leg healed, though slowly. But I had been wounded in the soul, and that never healed. And thereby hangs the tale.

Chapter Two

I warned I'd be making a wide detour through my early years, but it was necessary to bring the tale to my decision to become a Baldwin-Felts detective. Without that decision I'd never have been drawn into the Hillsville case. I'd have just been another credulous reader of the sensation-mongering newspapers.

When I returned to Virginia, the Philippines seemed more than half a world away. It was more like returning from another planet altogether. It was... how can I put it... disorienting to be back here amid the familiar, clean, and comfortable after all I'd seen and done. It took a while to pull myself together. Since the thread of the story has brought us back to the scene of the crime, you might say, now's the proper time to tell what was happening in Southwest Virginia and Carroll County, since that has a direct bearing on the events of March 14, 1912.

By the early 1900's far-sighted businessmen had begun to discover Appalachia, until then a backwater culturally, politically, and economically. The United States was a rising imperial power, creating an insatiable appetite for natural resources to feed the maw of all the new industry — coal, lumber, construction stone, minerals. Suddenly civilization began to thrust its snout into the Blue Ridge, disturbing a settled and placid way of life. But no one asked the residents. The outsiders brought in a new dynamic, new energy; new forces to be reckoned with by a very conservative people who were not only unaccustomed to change, but actually resisted change for the most part. Of course, there were many folks in the South still suffering from the War Between the States and Reconstruction and eager to jump on the bandwagon of industrialization, even if they had little real share in it. They were too blind or too greedy to recognize they were merely the hewers of wood and drawers of water for the big Northern capitalists, and were fouling their own nest in order to do it.

I got drawn into the enormous national engine of production and consumption in 1905, when I went to work for my father's lumber business. We were headquartered in Sperryville, east of the Shenandoah Valley and just on the flank of the Shenandoah Range. Specializing in hardwoods, our staple was the American chestnut, a natural resource the value of which can't be overstated. The largest and best specimens grew in the Southern Appalachians. But at the end of the century when I was a VMI cadet, a terrible blight, some kind of fungal infection, began to kill off this great national treasure. It spread at the rate of two dozen miles a year, and by the time I got home from the Marine Corps in the fall of 1904, the chestnut tree was fast disappearing. The family business had to search farther afield every month looking for stands of chestnuts and the other species we needed. I was at loose ends, still suffering a kind of stress from the war, and had nothing better lined up.

Daddy and I had begun to have our differences, mostly over the Philippine war, over my future, and over why I wasn't living up to his inflated idea of me. He complained that all I did was hunt — deer, foxes, and young women. I was becoming a wastrel. His solution? Working for him scouting for timber. The job took me deep into a region I knew little about and had always regarded with the condescension of my time, place and, class. The hills and hollows along the New River and its tributaries were prime country for hardwoods. There I discovered a place of surpassing beauty and majesty. In the process I got to know the highlanders of southwest Virginia quite well.

It was soon clear I wasn't cut out for business. I was good at the scouting. Loved getting back into the hills and chatting with the mountaineers. But I was poor at negotiating for timber rights. Those folks were almost always hospitable, but also shrewd and tough. They had to be to survive, and they hid it behind a camouflage of down-home simplicity. The so-called hicks from the hills took this college boy to the cleaners every time. Dad complained we weren't making any money on my deals, which was no doubt correct. He kept wiring me to 'stick it' to the locals, until one day I'd had enough. I wired back and told him where to stick it. So he wired back and said he was coming down to Hillsville and to meet him at the rail station. I wasn't happy at all, but there was nothing I could do to prevent his coming.

I was staying overnight in Roanoke, and the next day I happened to spot an ad in the paper. The Baldwin Detective Agency was looking for "a few proven, able, and stout-hearted men seeking good pay and adventure." I'd heard of the Baldwin agency in passing, like most residents of Virginia. They were the local franchise. William Baldwin, the founder, was born in Tazewell, Virginia and was a now resident of Carroll County. Thomas Felts lived in Galax, Virginia, about 15 miles west of Hillsville. He was an early employee and then went into partnership with his boss. Their head office was in Roanoke, the biggest city in the southwest part of the state. Four years later they added Felts' name to the billing, and it became known to the world as the Baldwin-Felts Detective Agency. To avoid confusion, I'll call it that from now on.

The Baldwins as the agents were known, were either reprehensible or praiseworthy, depending on where you stood. The two founders had formed the agency to provide security for the Norfolk and Western, the Valley railroad, then expanded their operations to offer security for the mine owners in southwest Virginia and the state of West Virginia. This translated on the ground into strike-breaking or union-busting, which is what the ad meant by 'adventure,' as it turned out. If you were a mine owner, investor, or part of the social and financial elite, you saw Baldwin-Felts as the epitome of modern, enlightened policing, a necessary defense against anarchy. If you were a coal miner or a poor mountaineer, you saw them as armed thugs, the enforcement wing of a callous, greedy establishment.

I was born into the state's social and economic elite. Like most upper-class Virginians of the day, I abhorred labor violence, strikes, outside agitation, and whatever else we conveniently chose to call anarchy. If I looked down on my fellow Virginians in the Blue Ridge, I looked down on the denizens of West Virginia even more.

I went 'round to the Baldwin-Felts address and filled out an application. The prospects didn't appeal to me entirely, but I felt in my bones I had to leave the lumber firm, had to free myself of Daddy's domination and strike out on my own. How exactly I didn't know; no other options had occurred to me. But I needed to prove myself to myself. Surviving the Philippines with a commendation and an honorable wound hadn't done it for me as you might expect, mainly because of I'd acquired such deep doubts about the rightness of America's dirty little war.

The local staff man told me William Baldwin was especially interested in combat veterans of Cuba and the Philippines. That should've given me pause, but at the time I wanted – needed -- to think of myself in heroic terms. I was glad somebody else put a value on my killing experience. Above all, I believed this was a way out of the family business that my father would approve.

The same morning I got a call at the hotel from William Baldwin in person. He said he was particularly impressed with my application and arranged to have supper that evening at the hotel. I have to say, despite my later views, that he was an impressive individual. It was easy to see why he'd succeeded so well in his chosen line of work and inspired such loyalty from his agents. In his mid-forties, he was a well-set up fellow, handsome in a severe-looking way. Blonde hair going gray and a walrus moustache. I especially remember his confident and authoritative air, yet not overtly aggressive. You could feel a kind of power emanating from him, from his piercing brown eyes.

After the meal, he leaned back a little and lit up a cigar, offered me one, which I politely declined. We chatted a while about my background. He was glad to learn I knew the area and the people, insofar as a flatlander can know them; and appeared duly impressed with my family background and VMI credentials. Then he turned to questions about my wartime experience. His voice was quiet and businesslike, yet he was personable and smiled easily. Then he explained the history and mission of the Agency.

"Mr. Hayne," he said at last coming to the point, "the Baldwin Agency needs good men like you. You can shoot, you can ride, and you've proven yourself in combat. We provide a vital service, but it needs special men. If we weren't on the job, there'd be no coal to heat people's homes and run the factories. No safety for our vital railroads. No law and order in the hinterlands. And as you may know, the Commonwealth has no state police force, so we are often called upon to fill that role when an urgent public need arises. With us you have the opportunity to do well by doing good."

We discussed salary for a while. It wasn't as much as I might make were I to prove a success in the timber business, but neither was it insignificant. Baldwin's air of purpose and self-assurance began to thaw my skepticism. He had a psychological advantage that asserted itself silently – he was clearly plagued with none of the self-doubts that assailed me. Still, I needed more to be convinced.

"Yes, sir, you may be right," I said. "Fact is, I haven't been able to settle down since I got back from the Philippines. My family has a prosperous timber business, but I don't seem to fit in. Frankly, it just doesn't interest me. Although the money does," I added quickly. "I'd be making a financial sacrifice to join the Baldwin Agency."

He replied, "Only for a while, until we see how you work out, as with any new position. In your case I have no doubts you'd increase your earnings in no time."

"Well," I said, the uncertainty still in my voice. "I'm just not sure. Becoming a policeman, even for a fine private firm like yours, is not ..." I left the thought unfinished.

He nodded and smiled with evident understanding, and changed tack. "Tell me," he said. "How do you spend your non-working time?"

"Well, I hunt a lot," I said. "Deer and grouse, mostly. Whatever's in season. And I ride to the hounds -- foxhunting. I'm a member of the Rappahannock Hunt."

He said, "Mr. Hayne, I've never fought in a war, although my other armed encounters might come close. But I find that some men, once they've had a taste of it, of the action and danger, that is, never lose it. They're never good for anything else." He gave me a penetrating look. "I think you're one of those men."

I said nothing but squirmed slightly in my chair, discomfited by his perception.

He continued, "I think we can promise you all the hunting you can handle. By that I mean man-hunting, the greatest sport there is." He smiled. "And the money will come. Let's not forget that."

Toying aimlessly with my bread knife, I stared down at the damask table cloth. And suddenly, unbidden, something dark and deliciously disturbing stirred inside me, a repressed memory of the Philippines. Appalled at myself yet helpless to block the images, I looked up to meet Baldwin's mild gaze of perfect understanding.

For an instant I glimpsed why there will always be war and violence; the seeds lurk unseen in all of us. I sensed rather than thought that the wolf rising in the heart must be restrained, or at least re-directed into positive acts. This is a primary role of the father – and of course, of the Father. In that instant I found a father figure, something I needed at the time without realizing it, someone authoritative yet without the caprice and judgmental harshness of my own father. William Baldwin seemed to see into me and accept me for myself; indeed, to value me for myself. Later I encountered another less appealing side to the man. And even worse, his alter ego Tom Felts – a prim and pitiless policemen always self-righteously on the side of the terrifying confusion called 'law and order.'

Finally I said, "Mr. Baldwin, I believe I just may be your man."

He nodded, and his smile widened. "I knew it before you did. When can you start?"

"Why not right now?" I smiled back.

***

As I look back it seems as if Fate or some hidden hand was preparing me specifically for my role in the Hillsville story. For before joining Baldwin-Felts I actually knew the Allen family. At least I felt I understood them and how to deal with them, far more than any other Baldwin man was likely to, at any rate.

Floyd was born in July 1856, five years before the War Between the States began, and was nine years old when it ended. His father Jeremiah, or Jerry as he was known, served in the Confederate army. Jerry had seven sons and three daughters. Not only did Jerry have a big family, he was somewhat old for active service. He volunteered anyway and was elected a second lieutenant in his regiment. Late in the War, Jerry's oldest son Anderson -- Floyd's oldest brother -- also went off to the War. Both father and son served until it ended in April 1865. Another brother, Washington, evidently died during the War from an accident on the farm. Counting Anderson, Floyd had five surviving brothers. But only two, Sidna and Jasper or 'Jack,' are part of our story, so I'll skip the details about the rest. Don't want to confuse you with too many characters. There are enough people as it is to keep track of.

Floyd grew up with his family's stories of the War and in the shadow of that terrible conflict. He faced the same struggles that all Southerners faced getting back on their feet after 1865. Even though the Blue Ridge of Southwest Virginia suffered less from actual combat than other places in the state, the Allens were nevertheless deeply affected. If Floyd grew up into a hard case, it's no wonder. He wasn't the only hard case in those hills, not by a long sight. Doesn't excuse his bouts of temper and occasional violence, but it does help explain them.

The Allens had some schooling, but the country schools of the day were pretty basic, usually one-room affairs with few books or learning materials. And the kids generally didn't attend the full term. Everybody had to help on the farm; it was a matter of sheer survival. When harvest time came in the fall, they'd be home working instead of poring over their slates or their McGuffy Readers. So I won't say Floyd Allen was an educated man, but he wasn't illiterate, either. He could read and write well enough to function in his society, which was all that was expected.

Floyd and his brothers came up like most everyone else in their time and place. Tough, individualistic, self-reliant mountaineers, with the old Scots-Irish loyalty to kith and kin. Known for their hospitality, though somewhat suspicious of strangers at the same time. Floyd was said to be the best friend you could have in a scrape and the worst enemy. He was a man of action, not introspection. Yet he had enough self-awareness and basic honesty to admit he did fly too easily into an angry passion.

I met Floyd Allen before the shooting, back in my Hayne Timber and Millwork days. I didn't remark much upon the encounter at the time, although he did make an impression. It was roughly a year before I went to work for Baldwin-Felts, which would have made it the fall of 1906. As I mentioned, part of my job was to get to know the influential people in the area, and the Allens certainly fit the bill — Floyd and Sid in particular.

Returning from surveying the hardwoods down in southern Patrick and Carroll Counties, I was riding back up the mountain to Hillsville from Cana, which is down near the Virginia-North Carolina line, about half a dozen miles north of Mount Airy, North Carolina. You pass through the south wall of the Blue Ridge by way of Fancy Gap when you come back that way. It's one of the most beautiful spots in the Blue Ridge, in all of Virginia, actually. The Blue Ridge drop off very sharply there. From Fancy Gap Mountain, looking out over North Carolina below, on a clear day you can see Pilot Mountain rearing straight up from the plain and staring back at you from the distance. It's a marvelous place, especially in the fall when the leaves turn red and gold, which is when the encounter occurred. But on this occasion I wasn't enjoying the view. My horse had bowed a tendon and I was walking him lest he go completely lame. It was slow going in the cold and dark. It got darker and darker and I got colder and colder. Then damn if it didn't start to rain.

I'd been told that a prominent citizen name of Floyd Allen and some of his family lived right off the Fancy Gap Pike just below the crest, and I knew that the mountaineers would usually help folks in trouble. I stopped at the house that had been described, a prosperous-looking two-storey frame house with brick chimneys, and rapped on the door with the handle of my crop.

A handsome but austere-looking woman in black, slightly stooped, opened the door a crack, peered into the gloom, and said, "Yessir?"

"Ma'am," I began, "I'm terribly sorry to trouble you, but my horse has 'bout gone lame and it's still fourteen miles to Hillsville. I was hopin' — "

A voice boomed out from within. "Cordelia, who is it?"

Mrs. Allen opened the door wider to reveal a trim but muscular man in his early fifties approaching in the hallway. He was dressed in dark trousers and galluses over a white shirt, with the collar opened and black tie loosened. To my not great surprise he held a six-shooter in his right hand, with his right arm crossed over his chest to display the weapon prominently. Taking no undue notice of the gun, I took off my felt campaign hat. I was startled to feel icicles forming along the brim.

"Mr. Allen, I'm Carter Hayne, from over t'other side a the Blue Ridge." Without being aware, I had a tendency to slip slightly into the vernacular when addressing these folks. Evidently it never came across as condescension, which was certainly not my intent. Otherwise they'd have treated me far less cordially. They knew condescension from flatlanders when they met it, and they resented it. "I work for Hayne Timber. My father's Caldwell Hayne from near Sperryville. You might've heard of him. My mount's gone lame and I'm way late gettin' back to Hillsv'lle. And now a freezin' rain's startin' to fall. I was hopin' you might have a barn or shed where I could take shelter for the night."

He scrutinized me carefully with a steady — I would say discomfiting — gaze, then motioned me in and stuck out his hand. Glad to have passed inspection,

I stepped inside the warm entry hall, nodded again respectfully to his wife, and shook his hand.

"We don't put up guests in no barn," he said almost scornfully, thrusting the handgun into the waistband of his trousers. It looked to me to be a .44 Colt Peacemaker, the classic cowboy pistol. "Fetch yore traps and come on inside. Me an' the wife was just about to eat supper. Yore welcome to join us and stay the night. You set there by the fahr and warm up some. While she sets the table, I'll stable yore mount and rub her down."

I was about to protest this extra courtesy, but he raised his hand. "Won't have no argyment, now. Yore our guest." There was something commanding in his voice and manner. Floyd sported the common walrus mustache, which gave him a certain gravitas, along with his blue eyes and six feet of height. Taking off my soaked mackintosh, I obeyed gratefully and settled by the glowing cast-iron stove to thaw. Half an hour later I sat down to a sumptuous meal; plain country cooking, but ample, hot, and delicious. We made desultory conversation for a while, with Mrs. Allen remaining mostly silent as she attentively heaped our plates with seconds of turnip greens, cornmeal johnny cakes dripping with fresh butter and honey, and potatoes roasted with the tenderest venison I'd ever put a fork to. Everything appeared to have been produced locally.

A small earthenware jug of 'squeeze' materialized from I know not where. Floyd and I each took a glass and pushed back after we could eat no more.

"Mrs. Allen," I said. "Can't say when I've had a better meal, if ever. I'm much obliged. For the supper, and a warm, dry place on such a night."

She smiled a wan smile. "Yore right welcome." I got the impression she was not in the best of health.

Cautiously sipping the fiery corn likker, also doubtless produced locally, I said, "Mr. Allen, if I was to eat like this every night, I sure wouldn't stay and fit an' trim like you. How d'you manage it?"

"Well, like most folks 'round here, I stay active. I work hard for what I earn — huntin,' farmin', loggin', some freightin.'"

As he catalogued his various occupations, my eyes were drawn involuntarily to the jug of moonshine on the table. He followed my stare. Then we both looked straight at each other and burst out in deep, simultaneous laughter.

"Active indeed," I said. "A lot of runnin' about these hills, I reckon." Running from Revenue agents remained unsaid. His eyes twinkled merrily as he chuckled, though with a touch of bitterness, no doubt at the dangers of avoiding the Revenue. But still, I was glad to see there was a softer side to this rather forbidding character. I was also glad to see that I'd evidently won his trust, even though nothing overt was ever said about moonshining.

"My boys help me out. That makes things easier." He spoke of his sons with pride.

"Tell me 'bout your boys," I said.

"I got three. Oldest is Jeremiah, named after my Pa. Then there's Victor, who lives next door to us here in the Gap. And finally there's Claude. He's got mosta the brains in the family. He's down in bidness college in Raleigh."

He proceeded to tell me about the rest of the clan, and seemed proud of them as well. No question, the Allens were a force in the lower county, socially and financially. His brother Garland was a Primitive Baptist minister, a calling which Floyd didn't seem to hold in the highest regard. But Jasper, or Jack as he was called, did quite well at farming and ran a sawmill.

Sidna was the wealthiest in the family. He operated a store and sundry and supply business farther north toward Hillsville.

I knew Sid Allen's home well. Everyone did. It was the finest in Carroll County, a sprawling two-storey Victorian affair with turrets and wrap-around porches and ornate trim, about eight miles north of Floyd's up the Pike. That's now U.S. Route 52, and it's still there, a local tourist attraction. Sid was not only the most successful, but in some ways the most unusual of the brothers. The others were deeply rooted in their mountain soil, but Sid had contracted a case of the wanderlust when he was a young man. During the Yukon Gold Rush, he went off adventuring in Alaska. Didn't find gold, but he made a fortune selling supplies to the miners. Then he went to Hawaii, foreseeing the land rush that started there in the 1890's. He had vision, all right, and came back with ample money to pay for his lavish home.

His place and Floyd's, and the fine furnishings in Floyd's house, were not the hallmarks of backwardness. It struck me then that the Allen clan had an unusually strong drive to succeed, stronger than most of their neighbors, perhaps. And that could lead to envy and resentment. It's just human nature. Furthermore, Floyd was appointed at various times as a special constable for the county. His reputation as a fighting man lent him a lot of credibility as a peace officer, and that no doubt caused some to fear and resent him, too. But whatever you care to say about them, the Allens were not a gang of outlaws that some Northern newspapers made them out to be.

Floyd went on to tell me about his Edwards kinfolks. His sister Alverta had married John Edwards and they had six children. Two of Floyd's nephews figure prominently into the story, Wesley Edwards and

Sidna Edwards. Don't confuse Sidna Allen, Floyd's brother, with Sidna Edwards. Back then Southern families often re-cycled given names, naming the second generation after those preceding. As I said, these people lived by the clan. They were bound together by blood, and the shared names were a way of showing it.

As the night deepened, the corn loosened our tongues and Floyd began to unburden himself, providing a glimpse of the molten spirit seething below the surface. One thing we had in common was timbering, and he paid me a compliment. "Mr. Hayne, yore firm's pretty well thought of 'round these parts. Folks respect how y'all are content to buy the timber and not try to take folks' land. And you pay fair prices, I've always heard tell." No doubt this reputation was an unintended result of my lack of business acumen Dad had complained about, but I kept that to myself.

I said, "Mr. Allen, I'm not from your community, but I am a fellow Virginian. My Pa, like yours, wore the Gray. He rode with Mosby." Floyd seemed duly impressed. "I was brought up to respect all the folks and ways of our state, just as I'd demand from others."

"Damn right," he said, pounding the table. "It's them outsiders that's causing the trouble 'round here in these hills. Them big companies come in with their money, they buy up local land, and they clear-cut it or mine the guts out of it. Don't care nothin' about the balance a nature, just gettin' their profit. They leave an ugly mess a jumbled deadfalls and cause erosion, run-offs, and floodin'. They also run off the game, and we depend on game for the table. They suckin' the life out of us."

His diatribe wasn't altogether unjustified in my opinion; I'd seen with my own eyes the outside exploitation he objected to. But what seemed to anger him most wasn't the economic exploitation itself but the blatant disregard for the welfare of the locals it displayed. It wounded his pride more than his pocketbook.

He continued, "Them railroads and big companies with their money, they buy up these turncoat Republican politicians in the county. Then the county runs up the taxes on folks, knowing the pore folks 'round here they got no cash income to pay it. So they got to sell out or lose ever'thing. The bought-'n'-paid for politicians got a willin' sheriff to run folks off if they don't go peaceable, and a bunch a toadies for deputies. And that opens the door to the big timbermen and mine owners. They come in and commence to steal ever'thing that ain't nailed down."

I had no way of verifying the truth of his claims about local politics, though it wasn't inconsistent with what I'd heard elsewhere in the county. I had no way of knowing at the time, but I was getting a forewarning of Floyd's violence in the Hillsville Courthouse. His strong sense of independence, his feelings of grievance against the county government and the unwelcome changes to his world, and his violent temper created a volatile mixture that inevitably exploded five and a half years later. It was just waiting for the right spark.

In the early 1900's Southwest Virginia was a kind of frontier. The word implies more than just a geographic boundary. It's also where different cultures meet — and clash. Here in the once-overlooked Blue Ridge the last of the old ways were encountering the new: progress, big city capitalism, the money power, and a new kind of politics. Politics that was impersonal and remote rather than intimate and personal, as they'd known it. Politics that served power more than the people. Local government no longer belonged to them, but to outsiders with checkbooks. It was the tail end of the 19th Century fighting a losing rear-guard battle against the onset of the 20th. One local folklorist put it this way, "Law and order come on 'em kind of sudden."

What happened to the people of the Blue Ridge Mountains in those days — and Floyd and Claude Allen are a dramatic symbol — is parallel in many ways to what happened to the Indians in the Far West, the destruction of their culture and once-proud way of life. And just as tragic.

At the risk of getting ahead of myself but to further illustrate, a year after his murder trial, after quitting Baldwin-Felts, I interviewed Floyd in prison, just before his execution. He tried to explain his pent-up violence, of which the Hillsville shooting was simply the culmination. He told me, "Guess I didn't take too well to what was hap'nin' in Carroll County, and things just built up inside me. It was the place of my blood, where my great granddaddy settled after the Revolution. I saw that the folks gettin' rich didn' do nothin' useful. They didn' deal in goods but in political favors. I saw that folks was gettin' ahead more by graft and pull than by honest work. And the law? I'm in here 'cause a the law, they say. But what is the law? Is it only what them that has the power says it is, and to suit theirselves? The Good Book says that rulers are not a terror to good works but to the evil. But what do you do when the law don't protect the people from the crooks but protects the crooks from the people? I saw corruption bein' rewarded and honesty made into somethin' to be ashamed of. Ain't the law 'sposed to prevent that? Well, in Carroll County it didn't, and I just wadn' goin' to take it."

Self-serving perhaps; but also hard to argue against.

For what it's worth, I remember one of the last things Floyd said, and it might serve as a lesson to officeholders everywhere, at all levels. Especially those politicians, who believe that government is above the law instead of subject to it, like the rest of us. He told me, "They say you cain't fight city hall. Well, I guess I showed 'em, if ya got the brass, and when it's the only way that's left, you can shore shoot hell out of it."

***

It may appear I've been pleading the Allens' case as their defense counsel. That's not my aim, although I concede they did win my sympathy. When I said life was complicated and not a matter of black and white, I meant it. But now the time has come to balance the scales, time for some perspective from the other side. I never lose sight of the fact that five people died in the shootout and seven were badly wounded. Even if you were a staunch partisan of the Allens and could show the courthouse officials somehow 'had it coming,' you'd still have to admit that the juror Gus Fowler and the spectator Betty Ayers were innocent bystanders, and their deaths were totally unnecessary and tragic. Wrongful deaths, no small matter. I'd include Judge Thornton Massie with them.

Long before that fatal day I'd gotten to know Judge Massie while working with Baldwin-Felts. He was a good, decent, and fair-minded judge. He was not a dedicated enemy of the Allens, which you might construe about some of the others. In fact, he was so fair and high-minded that he turned down a request to search the Allens when they came into the courtroom that day. It's sad. I can't prove it, and he's long gone; but I believe it was because he knew, or suspected, that Sheriff Webb and William Foster had it in for the Allens. I think he wanted to avoid a visibly punitive act by the bench to satisfy the personal antagonisms of the anti-Allen faction. You might even say Judge Massie died for his vision of judicial fairness. That's my opinion, anyway. I've got no hard facts to support it. That's the difficulty in arriving at a conclusion. Everybody's got an opinion but few provable facts.

Over the years, as I delved deeper into the tragedy, I learned that when anybody started questioning the conduct of the Allens, and by that I mean their history of violence before the shootout, Allen partisans would complain it was all a case of bias against them or even a conspiracy, by the so-called 'Courthouse Ring' in Carroll County. Well, there was a courthouse ring, no doubt about it. But every county seat has a courthouse ring. Unless there's deep rivalry or political enmity among them, it's natural for people who work together for the county to talk about the county's needs and coordinate in solving its problems. That doesn't indicate a government conspiracy against a citizen. It's only when officials get too much power or use it for their own personal aggrandizement that you've got a serious issue. Was this what developed in Carroll County in 1912? Were the Allens and Edwards really a threat to public order, or did they incur the hostility of the Courthouse simply because of their political opposition? Maybe yes, maybe no, or somewhere in between. Once again, the ever-present human ambiguities assert themselves.

Now, I'm relating this next episode ahead of the actual sequence of events. My purpose is to provide some insight into the other side of the dispute, as revealed by a Carroll County deputy sheriff, Eliahu Gillaspie. There are always two sides, aren't there? Well, almost always.

When I arrived in Hillsville the day after the shooting, Floyd Allen was laid up at a local hotel. He'd been hit three times and was unable to flee like the rest of the clan. Tom Felts arrived soon after and we took Floyd into custody. Then William Baldwin ordered me to begin the hunt for the other fugitives. I conducted a quick preliminary investigation and a number of hasty interviews while organizing our men for the pursuit. Among the people I interviewed was Deputy Gillaspie. However, he was no longer deputy sheriff, which bears on why Baldwin-Felts got pulled into the case.

There was an old provision in the Virginia statutes at the time going back to posse comitatus in English common law. The principle was that deputies did not hold an independent office. Their authority was literally deputed to them by the sheriff, who in turn derived his authority from the sovereign people. That's why they're called deputies. If the sheriff was removed from office for any reason, sudden death included, the deputies' authority ended simultaneously. Though not unheard of, losing a sheriff in a gun battle was an unusual circumstance. Carroll County found itself without a police force just when they feared they needed it most. Hillsville officials claimed the Allens might re-arm, come back, and finish the job. They wired the Governor in a panic to do something, and he called in Baldwin-Felts.

Deputy Gillaspie might've been an Allen enemy or not. I had no way of knowing, though I had to assume some bias on his part. Certainly he was torn up over the deaths of Sheriff Webb and the others. He'd just been in the thick of, and narrowly survived, the blazing gun battle with the Allens and was still shaken. It was not an everyday event even for a deputy sheriff. Furthermore, he'd now lost his job, and no doubt he blamed that on the Allens. But he didn't strike me as a man lacking integrity, by any means. He related some things "to put me in the picture," in his words, so I'd have a good idea of the desperate character of the men we were about to hunt down. What he told me was more or less in accord with what I'd heard over time from others, and with what I was able to verify later as I dug deeper into the case.

For all their virtues, the Allens were not a jolly clan. Deputy Gillaspie had this to say when I interviewed him the day after.

"Mr. Hayne, I can show you from the court records, the Allens and their kin are almost always in some kind a trouble with the law. Now, these are proud people and these are hard times. I can understand them gettin' in a few scrapes now and then. After all, I'm one of 'em. I was born and raised in these parts. But there's too many things you just cain't ignore, settin' aside what I just been through with 'em." He added, "You should've been there. It was like all the devils from hell was unleashed."

I nodded sympathetically; truly glad I hadn't been there. "Can you give me the details from the records?"

"Yes, sir." He was a slow-moving, heavy-set fellow in a brown tweed suit a size too small, but his mind didn't seem slow in the least. Without hesitation he consulted a file, one that struck me as distressingly full. "I'll start with what folks gin'rally know about the Allens. A lot of it's hearsay and wouldn't be admissible in court, but anyone 'round here will tell you Floyd Allen is a nacherly violent man. Why, he even tried to shoot his own brother oncet in a fit a temper. Jack, his own blood kin."

"I thought they were such a close-knit family," I said.

He replied, "They are. Like most a the families in the county. That's just my point. You have to really break bad to shoot yore own brother. Fortunately, neither one of 'em was kilt." He paused thoughtfully.

"But I got to be honest 'bout this. Floyd's brother Jack has a reputation, too. Folks say he's as mean-tempered as Floyd, if not worse. Thing is, nobody knows who started the fight between 'em. It was over settlin' their pa's estate. Was Floyd tryin' to shoot Jack, or vice versa? Was they tryin' to shoot each other at the same time? I don't rightly know. And them that do know ain't talkin'. No one ever filed any charges."

Either way, it appeared the Allen temper was sufficient to trump brotherly love. I was glad Floyd was safely locked away in jail and I wouldn't have to face him across the muzzle of a gun.

"And there's a lot more in the hearsay department," Gillaspie continued. "All I can say is that when there's this much smoke, there's also gotta be fire somewhere."

This all sounds pretty bad. But you have to remember the context, the time and place; and look at it through the lens of 1912 in Appalachia, not 1968 in downtown Richmond. It was like the Old West. Similar social conditions and economic hardship, plus the collision with the old and new I mentioned.

"Now," he said, opening the file, "here's the formal charges."

There was a charge entry for assault with a deadly weapon, nol prossed for lack of evidence, when Floyd shot a man in the leg in 1904.

"Rumor was Floyd threatened to shoot him again, this time in the head, if he testified," Gillaspie explained.

Then Floyd got in a brawl with Revenue officers because they got drunk and abused his hospitality; charges dropped. Floyd shot a black man in North Carolina. Again, no prosecution, this time on grounds of self-defense, although I found this one highly dubious. Black men normally didn't go around starting fights with white men in North Carolina.

Trying to inject some levity into the heaviness, I said, "My goodness. The family seems to've spent so much time feudin' and fightin', I wonder how they had the time to succeed in farmin' and tradin'."

Gillaspie didn't smile. He continued. "And we haven't even gotten to Sidna Allen. He's a case, too. He was charged with counterfeitin'. Had an employee name of Preston Dickens who was usin' an electro-plating machine Sidna owned to make counterfeit coins, then passin' 'em off down in Nawth Car'lina. Everybody figgered Sidna was the brains behind it, but Dickens confessed. Took all the blame on hisself, and Sidna got off."

I laughed and said, "Thank God. At last we got an Allen crime that didn't involve a shootin'. If I have to chase one of 'em down, I'm glad it's Sid. He sounds like a stand-up fellah." Which, strangely enough, is how he turned out when my Baldwin colleagues finally caught him. By then I had left the Agency. But I'm getting ahead of myself again.

Gillaspie didn't get the joke. He said, "Well, they all been charged at one time or another — the Allen brothers and the sons — with makin' illegal whiskey."

"But, Deputy," I said. "Some of the best people 'round here make blockade whiskey. That doesn't mean much."

"Yes, sir, that's true. Most a the folks hereabouts don't hold with the Revenue. People in this mountains been makin' whiskey hundreds a years, all the way back to Scotland and Ireland. But, the law's the law; an' we're sworn to uphold it."

I was to hear that often in the next few months: the law's the law. Invariably I would nod in solemn agreement. Only later did I really begin to reflect on what it meant, when Floyd Allen asked his plaintive question in prison two nights before he died: "But what is the law?"

"And the Edwards boys?" I wondered. "The nephews. Some of them took part in the gun battle yesterday, didn't they?"

"Ah, the nephews," he said. "They got the Allen temper, but they ain't never been in trouble with the law."

I still remember the sad, stricken look that came over his face. He and I and many others who followed the case were struck that this terrible loss of life, which wasn't over yet although we didn't know it then, flowed from a seemingly minor episode involving Wesley and Sidna Edwards, sons of Floyd's younger sister Alverta. Generally well-behaved boys, they unwittingly set in motion the train of events that would become the most dramatic criminal case in Virginia history and wreak havoc on their extended family.

Chapter Three

Earlier I suggested the Hillsville story was like a Greek tragedy, in that such awesome consequences flowed from a trivial cause. When the triggering episode occurred, the players began to act out their roles according to their respective natures, seemingly driven by forces they couldn't control. Any one of them might have turned aside to a different end along the way, yet they hurtled inexorably toward their doom as though it was all foreordained. Yet it only seems foreordained because that's the way it happened. What if you were standing in front of the tragedy and not behind it? Nothing has happened yet. From that perspective it doesn't seems inevitable, and you have the chance to direct the flow of events this way or that by your own sovereign choices.

When I think about the Allens and the other victims of Hillsville, any sense of the capricious death and suffering eludes me. Even now, as I tell the story, I find myself somehow hoping it'll end differently; that if I could tell it in a different way I could make it end differently and avoid the anguish and the loss. But that can never be. The events must unfold again and again in every re-telling as they did between 1911 and 1913, and the characters must go on playing the parts written by Fate.

It all started at a shuckin' bee in the autumn of 1911. Better known as a corn-husking bee, it was one of those old-fashioned social rituals that enriched life in the mountains, which could otherwise be austere. Nowadays mountain folks have TV and radio and paved roads and automobiles. They can drive into town for supper and a Blue Grass jamboree. Since they don't need to provide their own entertainment as they once did, many old communal country customs have passed out of style.

But in an earlier day people got together in someone's barn at the end of the summer harvest when the corn had dried in the fields and stripped off the husks so the corn could be taken to the grist mill. Shuckin' is the local word. It was a major social event. Typically there'd be live music and dancing. Unfortunately but inevitably, someone would show up with a jug, and there'd be drinking. When there was drinking white likker, pretty soon there'd be fighting.

The shuckin' bee included an old custom dating back to the colonial settlers and their first encounter with corn or maize, which they got from the Indians. Evidently they got the old custom from the Indians as well, because the Indians believed that red kernels on the ear of corn were big medicine, conferring a kind of sexual potency. The settlers in Appalachia adapted the belief to their own circumstances. The tradition evolved that anyone finding a red ear or red kernels in his ear of corn could freely kiss the girl of his choice. This was Indian corn, not the beautifully uniform hybrid varieties we plant today, with white or yellow kernels in geometric precision on the cob. The kernels of the heirloom varieties ranged from yellow to dark brown. Red kernels occurred, but were relatively rare.

As fate would have it, it was Wesley Edwards, nephew of Floyd and Sidna Allen, who stripped off a husk to find the red kernels. He waved the ear and whooped in triumph. He'd had his eye on Lorna McGraw, one of the prettier girls of the neighborhood, although he was Maude Iroller's regular fellow. You'll hear more about Maude later. She played a key role in the last part of the story, an incredible episode of thwarted love and betrayal suitable for any melodrama.

Amid a chorus of cheers and laughter from the revelers and perhaps a little envy, Wesley grabbed Lorna, whirled her around, and kissed her. Another young man, William 'Billy' Thomas, watched with hatred, because Billy claimed Lorna as his girl. Not that Wesley would have paid any attention. After all, he'd rightfully won the prize. This was a culture in which custom and tradition were the unwritten rules. Nor was he one to be intimidated, as we'll see.

The offending kiss ought to have been the end of it. The story should have died a-bornin' right there. Billy Thomas should've let the matter pass in honor of the old custom, while Wesley went back to being Maude's regular. But it didn't end there. The corn shuckin' took place on a Saturday night in the late fall, 1910. The next morning Wesley Edwards and his brother Sidna Edwards, another of Floyd Allen's nephews, gathered for church service at their Uncle Garland Allen's congregation on Fancy Gap Mountain. Garland was, among other things, a Primitive Baptist preacher and one of the six surviving Allen brothers.

Knowing where the Edwards worshipped, Billy Thomas barged into the church, which was actually a schoolhouse, and called out Wesley Edwards. Clearly not in a forgiving mood over the stolen kiss, Billy had arrived with his male pride all swollen up, you might say, wanting revenge. He brought a number of the Thomas clan with him.

Wesley and his brother were singing in the makeshift choir loft behind the pulpit. Facing the door, they readily saw Billy Thomas when he stepped inside. Billy leveled an accusing finger at Wesley and then motioned him outside. Without a word and in the middle of the hymn, Wesley went out, perhaps unwisely. But then, he had his male pride, too; and the culture he was raised in wouldn't permit him to retreat from the challenge.

Billy Thomas said, "I got a bone to pick with you, Edwards."

Wesley saw the four Thomases waiting, frowning. He said, "Must be a mighty big bone. I see you brung the whole family."

"You insulted my girl," said Billy, stepping forward a few paces.

Wesley stood his ground. "Wasn't no insult. I found the red ear."

"Don't matter," said Billy. "You shoulda kissed your own girl instead of forcin' yourself on mine."

"Wasn't no force involved." Wesley laughed, derisively. The taunt was too much, for the report was Wesley's kiss had been vigorous, and Lorna had responded with enthusiasm. In fact, I believe a seed of jealousy was planted at the time in the heart of Maude Iroller, to flower later with such poisonous effect.

One of the other Thomases growled, "Did we come here to palaver or to teach this fool a lesson?" The four advanced on Wesley.

Brother Sid Edwards had followed Wesley out of the congregation and was standing behind him in the door, listening. As the enemy phalanx advanced, Sid stepped up to Wesley's left shoulder. The six men — two Edwards and four Thomases — commenced to brawling right there in the front yard while services were still going on.

It was hardly a fair fight. In my view the Thomases were very much to blame. You might even say they're the ones who lit the fuse on the whole tragedy. If Billy Thomas wanted to call out Wesley Edwards man-to-man, that's one thing. But to show up with four against one or even two is shameful. Among the Southern mountaineers of the period — and remember we're still basically in the 19th Century — discretion was seldom the better part of valor. It simply wasn't possible for the Edwards boys to walk away and keep their self-respect. A whuppin' would have been preferable.

In the event, it wasn't the Edwards who got whupped. It was the Thomases, no doubt to their enormous surprise. The battle is not always to the strong, but to the most resolute. As the four Thomases approached, Wesley and Sid launched into them with a kind of fierce joy, yelling the rebel yell, fists flying furiously. Most of the combatants were armed with handguns, as was common, so it's fortunate no one was shot. In any case, guns were drawn by both sides but used to pistol-whip their opponents, not discharged with lethal intent. After a very few minutes the Thomas crowd fled in bloody disorder, leaving the field to Wesley and Sid.

That's all we can say with certainty about what happened — the Edwards ended up thrashing the Thomases, even though outnumbered. There are different versions, but they're all self-serving and designed to put the other party in the worst possible light. None of the eyewitnesses let alone participants offered stories that match. But my investigation, including interviews with witnesses who were present, gave me an accurate picture of what happened. The salient fact ignored by the Carroll County officers of the law, perhaps deliberately, was this: the Edwards brothers were the attackees, not the attackers.

Needless to say, folks who don't fight clean don't take defeat with good grace. The wretched Thomas gang had violated the custom of the red ear, started a grossly unfair fight, and proceeded to get beaten up. Then they compounded the dishonor by swearing out a complaint as if the Edwards boys were at fault. As Wesley and Sid saw it, they'd won fairly and that was the end of the matter. It was a private fight. Family pride and honor dictated they didn't run whining to the law. It never occurred to them or to the Uncles Allen to go to the hated Courthouse, a known unfriendly venue, to place their version of the fight on record.

The terrible what-ifs started to accumulate. We see the first indications of the stacked deck, the bias in the law system against the Allen clan, which included the Edwards boys. The sheriff or Commonwealth Attorney should have investigated, should have looked for impartial witnesses, should have at least tried to get the Edwards' side of the story. Instead, they accepted the Thomas' version at face value. With what looks like gleeful haste, Commonwealth Attorney William Foster rushed to the grand jury and got an indictment on several charges against Wesley and Sid, including felony assault, and attempting to kill William Thomas by aiming and discharging a firearm, even though no shots were fired; and disturbing public worship. Disturbing public worship. Ha! The rest of the indictment is bad enough, but that final stiletto in the ribs makes me mad even after all these years.

When prosecutors pile on the charges, the so-called 'kitchen sink' indictment, it says to me they've forgotten their job is to seek justice, not just win cases. Justice is truth in action. Or should be.

Warrants for the boys were issued but weren't acted on right away. The Edwards lived out in the country a good twelve miles south of Hillsville. Before a deputy could ride out on horseback and bring 'em in, the whole family had heard about the impending arrests. The boys appealed to Uncle Floyd, who was the titular head of the clan and in their minds at least, a power to be reckoned with in Carroll County. He was a sometime county constable, a man of influence, and had a number of family and friends to back him up. All of them, Allens and Edwards, were under the illusion that Floyd might somehow intervene to get the indictments quashed. After all, the boys were innocent. All they'd done was defend themselves.

Floyd promised to go to town and see what he could do. If nothing else, he'd post bail so they could remain at liberty until the matter was resolved; or at worst, until they came to trial. But he was either sick or pleaded sick and failed to go. From what I learned afterwards, I think it was the latter. Floyd began to realize he was facing unfair odds with the county's justice system. But he was too proud or too self-delusional to admit it, because then he'd have to acknowledge that his stature in the community was fading.

He tried to buy time to figure out what if anything he could do. In the meantime, he advised the boys to disappear. It turned out to be bad advice. Nevertheless, in early 1911 they high-tailed it across the Virginia-North Carolina border to Mt. Airy, about 25 miles south of Hillsville.

Mt. Airy, county seat of Surry County, North Carolina, is not especially airy and it's not on a mountain. The name comes from a Scots Gaelic word of the original settlers -- àirigh, pronounced 'airy,' which means 'shieling,' a hill pasture or grassy level between the hills. It's a nice town, not far from Hillsville, a convenient place to hole up.

The boys got jobs and rooms in a Mt. Airy boarding house and were told to lie low until Uncle Floyd could use his influence to calm the situation at home — maybe get the true facts on the record and quash the indictments. That might've worked in a community where justice was often handled informally. But in Hillsville the Courthouse Ring proved indifferent to Floyd's approaches. Moreover, having nothing firm to pin on the Allens Senior, the authorities must have seen this as a chance to get at them though their nephews. Sheriff Joe Blankenship, who was in office at the time of the Edwards affair, often boasted openly on the streets of Hillsville that he was going to show the Allens they were not above the law — the law as he saw it, that is.

I met Sheriff Blankenship a few times before the tragic day in March 1912 and thought him a strutting martinet, treating everyone he met to a menacing glare. His bias was passed on to Sheriff Lew Webb who succeeded him at the beginning of 1912, and who was killed in the courthouse battle.

The Allens saw this as an attack on them though their nephews, who were innocent of anything except for thrashing those who'd threatened them. The attitude of the Courthouse convinced the Allens that the law was being perverted into a vendetta against the clan.

A few weeks later the word filtered back to Sheriff Blankenship that the Edwards boys were lying low in Mt. Airy. In those days and in that culture it was impossible to keep such a secret for long. Blankenship wired Cape Haynes, sheriff of Surry County, to please go and arrest the two violent fugitives — a professional courtesy, you might say. That's Haynes with an 's;' no relation to me. The boys were living more or less openly, and Sheriff Haynes knew right where to go. He sent his deputy to pick up Wesley, and he arrested Sidna Edwards himself.

Sid had a close call. He was armed as usual, and not wanting to be arrested with a concealed weapon in North Carolina, pulled out his pistol and dropped it between two sacks of oats where he was working in a feed store. Sheriff Haynes observed the action, and thought the lad was drawing on him. He pulled his own piece and came within a hair's breadth of gunning down his subject.

The episode, innocent though it was, further heightened the law's fear and suspicion of these two desperadoes, which had a critical bearing on what happened next. Still, the incident in Mt. Airy passed peaceably. The two boys went quietly to jail to await extradition back to Virginia.

Sheriff Blankenship ordered one of his deputies, a man called 'Pink' Samuels because of his complexion, to ride to the state line, link up with Sheriff Haynes, and bring the Edwards back to Hillsville. Samuels proceeded to follow orders. By this time, the presumed ferocity of the two boys loomed large in the imaginations of the Carroll County lawmen. The boys had beaten up four of the Thomases, and Sid Edwards had reportedly tried to draw down on Sheriff Haynes.

Samuels thought he'd better enlist some help. Stopping near the state line, he asked a neighbor, Peter Easter, to come with him. Easter was a mild and amiable man, but also a blacksmith of intimidating musculature. Though reluctant, he agreed to help his friend. Pink Samuels 'deputized' him on the spot, something Pink had no legal authority to do. On Thursday morning, April 23, 1911, the two men drove in Samuels' buggy to the North Carolina line at Cana and took custody of the Edwards.

The two boys had come unresisting to the rendezvous with the North Carolina lawmen. They'd not been handcuffed or restrained in any way, other than by the presence of the armed Surry County sheriff and deputy. But when Samuels took them into custody, he insisted on handcuffing them. Trouble is, as the only official deputy, he had only one set of cuffs. He used them on a protesting Wesley and put him in the front seat of the buggy. To add to the indignity, he tied an angry Sid's hands with a length of rope and put him in the back seat with Peter Easter. Just to make sure, he trussed their feet as well. These young men had never before been in trouble with the law and hadn't resisted arrest. Protesting being cuffed and tied, they gave their word to come along willingly. In that world, your word is your bond. But their pledge was unavailing. Pink Samuels wouldn't listen.

In those days, unlike the procedure in cop shows we see today on TV, it was not mandatory; it wasn't 'policy' to handcuff an unresisting prisoner. Pink Samuels didn't have to bind them. But either Pink was unusually afraid or he'd been told to humiliate the Allen nephews. We'll never know. Off he went with the boys trussed up like Christmas turkeys, up the road from Cana toward Hillsville — and through Fancy Gap.

I recall how astonished I was when I learned the deputies — or I should say, the deputy, because Peter Easter had no legal authority — took the road directly through the Allens' community with their nephews, whom they regarded as innocent and unjustly persecuted, tied up ignominiously like hardened criminals.

The shame of it was more than a man like Floyd could tolerate. It was such a blatant provocation that it raises the question: was it deliberate? Pink Samuels was something of a thickhead, but not a complete fool. Did the Courthouse tell him to travel this way in order to goad the Allens into a rash act? He could have taken the road though Ward's Gap just as easily. Well, there's no proof, although in light of other evidence, I believe it was deliberate. But I have to distinguish fact from opinion, or at least what we accept as fact. This is only my opinion. Informed opinion, you might say.

There's another unanswered about the episode, and Floyd knew to ask it. He may have operated on the very edge of the law, but he knew the law. The vital question was, did Pink Samuels have an extradition order? The two fugitives were arrested in one state and delivered to another, and due process of both states required a formal extradition order. But Pink Samuels didn't have one. I could never find a copy or even a request for one from Sheriff Blankenship when I went through the courthouse records some months later. I was thorough. It just doesn't exist. Not only were Floyd's nephews being treated disgracefully, in his eyes at least; but also their arrest and transport were clearly illegal. It's no surprise that he'd refuse to stand by idly while the outrage passed in front of him. But, if it was a trap laid by the authorities, Floyd leaped into it with both feet.

Floyd didn't actually encounter the deputies near his home. He'd ridden into Hillsville that morning to retain a lawyer for the nephews. He'd also met with Commonwealth Attorney Foster to arrange a personal appearance bond for the boys, and he promised Foster to bring them in himself the following Monday. Heading south toward home, he'd stopped to speak to his brother Sidna at his dry goods store on the Pike.

Sidna lived further up the road, that is, closer to Hillsville, than Floyd did in Fancy Gap.

Sidna Allen, another nephew named Barnett Allen, and a handful of customers were on the front porch of Sidna Allen's store chatting when Pink Samuels' buggy came into view from the south. Floyd was still sitting his mare, speaking to the folks present. Two of the customers were Betty Ayers and her brother. Eleven months later Betty Ayers will be mortally wounded in the shootout and die soon after. She was unlucky enough be in court as a defense witness for Floyd Allen, because she'd seen firsthand what was about to happen there on the Hillsville-Fancy Gap Pike.

Well, then, here's the scene. The lawmen approached and suddenly folks realized who they were and who was in the buggy. The Allens and the others peered at them, edgily. Floyd turned his mount, rode into the middle of the road and sat stone-like, hands folded on the pommel of the saddle, just watching. The buggy came to within a few yards and stopped, since Floyd was blocking passage. Pink Samuels turned and looked at Peter Easter in the back seat, as if to reassure himself of the big man's presence. Brother Sid Allen and the witnesses remained on the porch; but they saw the back of Floyd's neck flush red with anger at the sight of his kinsmen bound hand and foot.

"I'd hate to see his face right now," murmured Sid.

Floyd rode a few paces toward the deputies. Peter Easter said in a low but audible voice, "Pink, I told you we shoulda gone the other way."

Pink answered bravely, "Officers of the law oughta be able to go any way they want in the p'formance of their duty." But the onlookers could hear the tremor in his voice.

Sid whispered to the group on the porch, "Them Courthouse Republicans may be the power in Hillsville proper, but it's the Allens who rule in this part a the county, and they're in our territory now."

With visible effort Floyd restrained his temper and hailed Pink Samuels, calmly, almost civilly.

"Howdy, Pink. I see you got my nephews with you. But have you got a lawful requisition to bring 'em back from Nawth Car'lina?"

Pink squirmed uneasily. His two buggy horses snorted impatiently, tossing their heads. Pink took up the slack in the reins and said, "Well, no, I ain't, Floyd. Sheriff Blankenship told me to ride down and pick 'em up. I'm just followin' his orders."

"Now, Pink, you know you cain't extradite someone without a proper court order. What you done is illegal," Floyd said.

Pink said, "I tole you, I'm following the Sheriff's orders." He started to sweat a bit despite the coolness of the early spring. "Now git on out a the way and let me pass."

Floyd remained preternaturally calm. The witnesses remarked later how self-controlled he seemed — and in control of the confrontation. He said, "Deputy, even the Sheriff has got to obey the law. 'Specially the Sheriff. And that means you, too."

Pink twitched up the reins. "Walk on," he said to the eager horses. But Floyd rode another few feet forward and held up his hand. The buggy stopped, the horses hoofing the ground. Peter Easter sort of half stood in the back seat to look grimly at Floyd, then sank back.

Now Floyd's voice rose dangerously. His mare pricked up her ears and raised her head, pulling at the bit. "Pink, why have you got them boys trussed up like that? I been a law officer in this county for years. I've arrested some hard cases and I didn't never have to tie 'em up like hogs with rope like you done. You cut them boys a-loose and start a-treatin' 'em like gentlemen."

Pink said in a shrill voice, "They tried to excape. And yore nephew Sid pulled his piece and threatened to shoot Sheriff Haynes in Mt. Airy. We had to truss 'em up — "

Sidna Edwards shouted, "That's a damn lie, Uncle Floyd! We didn' try to excape and I didn' pull on anybody. We come peaceable — "

Peter Easter shoved a beefy elbow into Sidna's side. "Shut up, you," he growled.

That was too much for Floyd. He dismounted briskly and marched toward the buggy. "I said to cut 'em loose and treat 'em like gentlemen. If you won't, I will."

With a look of fright, Pink dropped the leads and reached inside his coat for his sidearm; but with the tension off the leads, the impatient horses lurched forward. Reflexively Pink tried to grab the reins and continued reaching for his pistol at the same time. He performed neither action well, and the effect was almost comical. Then he evidently decided his first task was to get the buggy under control and had to use both hands. When the horses were still he transferred the leads to his left hand and reached again for his gun. But by this time Floyd, advancing boldly, had reached his side. As Pink brought out his pistol and aimed at Floyd, Floyd grabbed it as if the whole act were one fluid motion. He deftly plucked the revolver out of Pink's hand, flipped open the cylinder, and ejected the cartridges. Pink leaned down from the buggy as if to strike Floyd with his free hand. Floyd smacked him hard across the temple, once, twice with the now empty gun. Groaning, Pink sank down in the buggy seat, holding his head with both hands.

Peter Easter had remained passive in the few seconds required for all this to take place. In fact, it takes more time to tell it than it took to transpire. Thoroughly alarmed, Easter brought out his pistol, stood up in the back of the buggy, and aimed down at Floyd. It was point-blank range. Even a poor shot could have nailed Floyd for certain, and probably with fatal effect. This story could've ended right there on Fancy Gap Road. But just as Easter pulled the trigger, Wesley Edwards threw himself backwards and knocked the would-be deputy off balance. There was a loud boom as the gun fired. The horses leaped forward again at the noise, throwing Easter off his feet and back into the buggy seat. His shot went wide, but not by much, striking Floyd in the little finger of his left hand, which he'd thrown up instinctively.

Enraged and finally out of control, Floyd tried to scramble up into the buggy, clambering over the prostrate Pink Samuels, who was still moaning and holding his head. The horses again bolted a few paces, dragging Floyd along as he grabbed the rear seat. In the back, Sid Edwards started kicking Peter Easter with his bound feet as Floyd flailed at him with Pink Samuels' pistol. He managed to land a few ineffectual blows. Though Easter was still armed, the pummeling from two directions was too much. He jumped from the buggy, fired two wild shots, and fled down the road toward Fancy Gap.

In anger or disgust, Floyd opened the cylinder on Pink's .38 and beat the weapon against the steel rim of the wagon wheel until he was satisfied it would never shoot again, then tossed it with a look of contempt into Pink's lap. Whipping out a pocketknife, he cut the ropes binding the boys and helped them down from the buggy.

"Pink," he ordered, "Give me the key to these here handcuffs or I'll thrash you again."

Dumbly, Samuels reached into a vest pocket with a bloody right hand and passed over the key. Floyd unlocked the cuffs on Wesley Edwards and tossed them after the broken pistol. Then he swatted one of the horses on the rump and shouted, "Git!"

The animals, eager for their feed and stall, trotted home up the road to Hillsville. Floyd called after them. "Pink, you tell the Sheriff and Bill Foster that I'll bring these boys in on Monday, just like I promised. And I'm a man of my word."

***

In retrospect, the whole train of events, from the shuckin' bee to the encounter with the deputies, seems almost comical. But later on, people suffered, people died. It's not a comedy, or even a tragic-comedy. If it has its share of absurd elements, it's only because people do crazy things. We all have a little madness in us, I suppose.

The harmless red kernel leads us to the essential Floyd Allen; in fact, to a glimpse into all the Allens and the impulses that led to the climatic shootout eleven months later in which many of the clan took part. Floyd's confrontation with Pink Samuels and Peter Easter wasn't just over the arrest of the Edwards boys. He'd already taken steps to surrender them to the Commonwealth Attorney or Sheriff Blankenship. True, the unlawful extradition did add fuel to the flames. But what sent his volcanic temper out of control was the unnecessary humiliation, the shame and indignity imposed upon his blood kin, and thus by extension upon himself. Can a man live without honor? It's a question Floyd asked himself -- implicitly, anyway. We in the middle of the 20th Century seldom think of asking it. Yet to Floyd, essentially a man of the 19th and not the 20th Century, honor was life itself. It was the essence of his identity, his manhood, his sense of self-worth and standing in the community.

I don't excuse what he did to Samuels and Easter. But he did have provocation. In the same circumstances I might've done the same. Call him an anachronism even then, but don't think of him as a mere hothead. There was more involved on the road from Hillsville to Fancy Gap than mere pride, anger, and self-will.

Sadly, Floyd's sense of honor helped his nephews not in the least. True to his word, Floyd delivered them to Hillsville the next Monday after the violent encounter on Fancy Gap Pike. State's attorney Foster prosecuted 'em to the full extent of the law. A few weeks later they were convicted of felonious assault on the Thomases, fined $50, and sentenced to six months in jail.

Fortunately, it wasn't 'hard time.' The Edwards had a fair amount of freedom as trusties, and Hillsville folks sympathetic to the Allen faction brought them excellent meals. Still, Floyd burned with indignation, as did his brothers, at the rank injustice and the loss of family prestige.

Time and again in connection to the Hillsville case I heard it said, 'The law's the law.' As an attorney and former officer of the court, I'm committed to this proposition more than most. Yet the Thomases were never prosecuted for their far greater culpability in the 'red ear' brawl. This favoritism undermined Floyd's respect for the formal process of law, at least as practiced in Hillsville. He came to regard the Carroll County Courthouse as a place of injustice instead of justice. His anger fastened on the building itself as well as its occupants.

Chapter Four

The conviction of the Edwards boys infuriated Floyd Allen and his brothers. But let's not forget what it did to the nephews. If before they'd only gone along with their uncles out of family solidarity, from then on they had real grievances against the Courthouse. They learned what it meant to suffer indignity and injustice. They'll be heard from again.

When the iron fist of the law grabbed the two boys by the scruff of the neck, Floyd finally began to realize he couldn't defy the county with impunity, even if its officers were biased. Or should I say, especially if they were biased. He saw he'd better start playing a different game, especially if the legal deck was stacked against him. Sadly, it was late in the game for such circumspection. Pink Samuels immediately filed assault and attempted murder charges against Floyd and the other Allen by-standers. I can't explain why Floyd wasn't arrested on the spot the day he brought the Edwards boys in to Hillsville following the fight on Fancy Gap Road. All those who could answer the question died later in the shootout. I can only speculate that the Courthouse wanted to be sure of their ground. They took the needed time to develop a case, to get hold of Peter Easter and nail down his version so the prosecution wouldn't rest on the sole testimony of Deputy Samuels.

In law the first one to tell his story usually gains an advantage, and the advantage went to Pink Samuels. Hoping to correct the problem, Floyd and his brothers Sidna and Jack rode into Hillsville a few weeks later on the first days of scheduled court when they knew the circuit judge would be in town. Jasper or 'Jack' Allen was the father of Barnett Allen, who'd been present at his Uncle Sid Allen's store the day Floyd beat up the deputies and released the Edwards brothers, Barnett's first cousins.

First thing Monday morning, they called on Judge Thornton Massie in chambers and explained their side, putting forth a case for the illegality of the nephews' extradition and making sure the Judge knew it was the deputies who'd drawn weapons and fired. All Floyd had done was defend himself. In the Allens' view, the fact that the aggressors were lawmen didn't alter the fact that it was self-defense. They asked Judge Massie for a grand jury, hoping — unrealistically — there were enough sympathetic folks in town and they might be exonerated.

As it happened, there was at least one person in town who was sympathetic to Floyd. That was me.

Yes, me. Remember, by this time I was a chief detective for the Baldwin-Felts Agency, so I was always going in and out of courthouses in the region. Not the chief detective. It was just a title given to us staff of a certain seniority.

I'd traveled to Hillsville with Tom Felts' younger brother Lee to pick up the notorious pickpocket Leo Constanza. This character had been victimizing customers traveling on the Norfolk and Western, our main client. Leo wasn't dangerous so much as he was slippery. He'd escaped twice from the law, including a Baldwin-Felts man. So the Agency sent two of us — their best, you might say. Ironically, it was deceptively slow-moving Eliahu Gillaspie, the Hillsville deputy sheriff, who had collared Leo thieving in the town's Elliott Hotel. Once Gillaspie had a bulldog grip on him, he never let go. Lee Felts and I had gone to bring Leo back to be arraigned in Roanoke.

Naturally the possibility of indicting a potential volcano like Floyd Allen had the whole town on its ear. Some credulous folks were even spreading the rumor that Floyd was going to bring the clan into town and shoot up the place if he was indicted. I knew that was buncombe. Floyd had a temper, to be sure. He could be violent. I'd even say his too-passionate nature was the character flaw from which this Greek tragedy flowed. But... a bad temper didn't justify a political vendetta by the Courthouse Ring. I had an inkling of that, too, from things I'd picked up from fellow lawmen. Knowing he was the target of the vendetta only made Floyd's temper worse.

I've talked about Floyd's passionate nature, how he skirted along the permissible edges of the law. However, from what I'd experienced, he could also be a gracious gentleman and generous friend to many at the same time. He was loyal to his ailing wife and devoted to his boys. Dangerous, yet a man of integrity. Perhaps it's noteworthy I don't use the word love in connection with Floyd. A hard man raised in a hard time and place, he simply didn't know how to express it. The better word is loyalty, extreme loyalty. It's clear he loved Cordelia, yet his kin spoke only of his loyalty to her. In fact, his devotion to this sickly woman was legendary; and him a handsome, successful man who might have had any number of women. A year later, when I visited him in prison on the day he was executed, his love — and grief — for his son Claude was heartbreaking. I was a hard man myself, and it stirred me to the depths. Ah, what a predicament we're in, all of us. It's called life. And none of us gets out alive.

This forces any reasonable person to ask, why poke a man like that with a sharp stick? By this time I understood the Courthouse had decided to take him down a few notches. True, they had a duty to enforce the law, but like Floyd they went right up to the edges of their authority – then beyond. They certainly didn't enforce the law with the same rigor against the wealthy and powerful, the politically favored. It wearies and depresses me that this abuse of power is universal in mankind, this lust to control and rule over others. Yes, even here in a small town in the remote mountains of Virginia you find it. It's universal. Instinctively, temperamentally, Floyd recoiled against it, which put him in more of a hair trigger mode than usual. His nature permitted him no other course.

All in all, it made for a volatile and highly interesting situation. Because I knew the Allens slightly — I'd also met Sidna Allen a few times — I was naturally curious about the court proceedings and about Floyd's possible reaction. I wanted to see if all the lurid tales about the Allens were in accord with my own experience. So I persuaded Lee Felts to tarry, and we hung about a bit to see what would happen. Grand jury deliberations are secret, so we just loitered about on the street waiting.

Lee had little sympathy for the Allens. He saw things in simple black and white, like most policemen. He told me, "If Floyd thinks he can get away with attacking peace officers, he's dead wrong. And one of these days he'll be just plain dead." Lee didn't foresee his own death from a similar confrontation and by a peace officer, Sid Hatfield, Chief-of-Police of Matewan. But in Floyd's case, Lee was a prophet.

The judge also took a dim view of an assault on
peace officers, no matter what the provocation. Yet
Judge Massie had no part with the Get-the-Allens
Gang. He was a decent and fair-minded man. He gave
the Allens what they asked, in spades, and the same
day. Turned the matter over to the clerk of court
Dexter Goad. But perhaps unbeknownst to the judge,
Goad was the bitterest enemy of the Allen clan. Goad
and Sheriff Blankenship handpicked folks from the
waiting jury pool who could be relied on to produce
the desired result. After Pink Samuels and Peter Easter
testified and Pink displayed the scabs on his head, in
short order the grand jury returned a true bill against
Floyd on three counts, felonious release of prisoners in
custody, criminal assault, and maiming. Since they
were all in town, they went through arraignment the
same day.

***

This is when I met Dexter Goad. I've mentioned
him already, a key player in the drama. By then I'd
heard a lot about him, but this was my first face-to-face
meeting.

Lee Felts and I were in the dining room of the
Texas House Hotel just about to pitch in to a noon
meal of steak, fried potatoes, and beer when Dexter
Goad came in with Woodson Quesenberry, his deputy
clerk. Wearing a well-tailored tweed suit and his
trademark bowler hat, which he neglected to remove
inside, Dexter strode in among the diners with a lordly
air. It reminded me of royalty dispensing boons, the
way he gave a condescending nod of the head to his
left and to his right. Quesenberry followed him like a
loyal man-at-arms.

Smothering a grin at the spectacle, I glanced at Lee Felts, who rolled his eyes. Now I hadn't just fallen off the turnip wagon. I'd been around, seen something of the wide world, you might say. Frankly, I wasn't impressed with a mere small town clerk of court, although I held no prejudice toward small Virginia towns. But Goad was clearly impressed with himself, with his little bit of authority; and it showed in his lord-of-the-manor airs.

His glance settled on us obvious strangers in town, and he eyed us warily as he walked toward our table. Lee laid down his napkin and stood politely, as did I.

Dexter was a clean-shaven, heavy-set man of about 40; not fat exactly, just imposingly solid. There was something about his sharp features and squinty eyes that I disliked immediately. He stopped in front of Lee and extended a fleshy hand.

"How do? I'm Dexter Goad, Carroll County Clerk a Court. This is my deputy, Mr. Quesenberry. And you are?"

Lee shook hands. "Glad to meet you, Mr. Goad. I'm LeGrande Felts of the Baldwin-Felts Agency. This is my colleague, Chief Detective Carter Hayne."

Goad's manner changed instantly from suspicious to obsequious. "Well, well," he blustered, taking off his hat. "This is a surprise, an honor. Why, indeed it is."

"The honor is ours. Won't you and Mr. Quesenberry join us, Mr. Goad? Mr. Hayne and I were just about to have a little dinner," Lee said. He was always selling the agency and he knew that building ties with the local law establishment might bring in future business.

"Oh, no, gentlemen," said Dexter. "I wouldn't want to disturb yore dinner."

"Not at all," said Lee cordially. "We're new in town and couldn't help noticin' all the excitement. As fellow officers of the law, maybe you can explain what the ruckus is about. Let us play host. Please, I insist." He motioned to the two empty chairs. With ingratiating grins, the two men sat.

Dexter said, "Why, as to the ruckus, today's the day Floyd Allen is to be indicted for felonious assault on two deputy sheriffs in the performance of their duty. Pistol-whipped one so bad he could hardly stand up in court. When I saw you gentlemen sittin' here lookin', well, sort of dangerous, if you'll pardon me sayin' so, I couldn't be shore you weren't some a the Allens' hired guns come to town to make trouble. I'm glad to learn you're on the right side."

By now you can tell the chemistry wasn't good between me and Dexter, right off the bat. There was something in his combination of swagger and obsequiousness, in his self-importance, that just hit me wrong.

In spite of myself, I blurted, "Come now, Mr. Goad. I know Floyd Allen somewhat. Sure, he's a hard case. But I can't imagine him hiring outside gunmen to make trouble. If he wanted to make trouble, he's got enough kin to do it themselves. But I can't see a proud man like him doing anything like that to besmirch the family name, at least not without major provocation."

Dexter seemed taken aback, but recovered. "Proud? Why, you don't know the half of it. Mr. Hayne, is it? Floyd has told plenty a folks in this county that he won't ever serve a day in jail; that he'll go to hell first. Now he's gone an' beat up two officers of the law, an' the law says he has to pay."

"Well, I agree that citizens can't go 'round assaulting peace officers," I said. "But really now, Mr. Goad, isn't there more to this story than that? Isn't it

67

true that the two deputies brought the Allen's nephews back to Carroll County illegally, without a proper extradition warrant, and had 'em tied up like violent desperadoes, which they clearly weren't, as Sheriff Blankenship demonstrated when he made 'em trusties and let 'em work in town while serving out their sentence?"

Lee frowned at me, but I was carried away by a rising anger.

I plunged on. "And weren't there witnesses to the incident who'll testify that Floyd was simply trying to get the deputies to untie the boys and that they assaulted him first?"

Dexter's eyes narrowed with his customary suspicion. "I'm surprised to hear this, Mr. Hayne. I'd a thought a Baldwin-Felts man would be on the side a the law, not of the most notorious outlaw in Carroll County."

I noted that he didn't actually address the issues I'd raised. But we were momentarily interrupted by the arrival of sizzling platters of steak, and paused briefly to tuck in. The pause was welcome because it allowed my temper to cool. I didn't want to needlessly antagonize the man.

After a few bites and a swallow of beer, I continued. "Mr. Goad, you're quite right. Baldwin-Felts is on the side of the law, and I'm not takin' Floyd Allen's part."

Here I confess I might've gotten professorial, but I wanted to impress a few things on him. Somehow, even a year before the shootout, I sensed where this collision was headed, though neither I nor anyone could have imagined what eventually happened.

"I love the law, Mr. Goad," I said. "Without it there's no civilization and we sink back into the law of the jungle, each against all. The basic principle of America is that all citizens enjoy equal protection under the law, and the law applies equally to all citizens. That means Floyd Allen. If he goes against it, then you're right; he must pay the penalty. But, Mr. Goad, it also includes public officials, sheriffs and judges and prosecutors. They're not above the law. Since they have life-and-death enforcement powers, their duty to follow the law is higher than anyone's. They have to set a good example if they expect the rest of us to respect the law and their office. Don't you agree?"

"Of course," said Dexter unctuously. "But that isn't the question at hand. Floyd Allen thinks he's a law unto himself. He's got to be taught a lesson to the contrary or this county will never prosper. Nobody wants to bring outside bidness into a county full of lawlessness and mob violence."

I could tell I wasn't getting through, and he seemed oblivious to the fact that the big corporations weren't bringing prosperity. All they did was to extract the local wealth and take it north. But I knew when to quit. I said, "Well, I reckon you know your own county better'n I do. But just remember what our fellow Virginian Thomas Jefferson once said: 'Law is often but the tyrant's will, and always so when it violates the right of an individual.'"

We finished the meal without any more controversy and on more or less cordial terms. The two men left as Felts and I lingered over a final beer. I could tell Lee was put out with me.

Finally he said, "Carter, I wish you hadn't gone out of you way to offend the man. We may need him one day." I sighed. "Lee, I didn't have to go out of my way at all. It was just the natural order of things. Floyd Allen may be a hothead, but that fellow isn't much better. Only he hides his ambition and personal animosities behind the protection of the law. He reminds me of a line from Shakespeare, 'False face must hide what false heart doth know.'"

"Maybe so," Lee replied. "But Shakespeare also said, 'We must follow close the rigor of the statute, to make him an example.'"

By 'him,' I knew Felts meant Floyd Allen. With a strange sense of brewing trouble, I finished my beer and went outside.

***

Lee and I left the hotel and walked across the muddy street to the courthouse to learn the outcome of the grand jury. In the late afternoon the proceedings ended and a stream of folks began to depart the courthouse. I approached Floyd at the bottom of the steps after he emerged from the upstairs courtroom. His jaw was working laboriously and his eyes held a faraway look. He was startled as I held out my hand.

"Mr. Allen," I said, "Maybe you remember me. I'm Carter Hayne. You and Miz Allen kindly took me in one cold rainy night down at Fancy Gap when my horse went lame. And we've run into each other a few times since at Sid Allen's store. How's Miz Allen doin'?"

Floyd seldom smiled, but at least the grim line of his lips shifted a little. He gave me his hand. "Why, shore, I remember you. Yore the timber man. Glad to see you again. Miz Allen's in a state of decline, I'm sorry to say. But good of you to ask."

I cleared my throat, nervously. "Actually, I'm not in the timber business any more. The company said you folks in these parts were always takin' me to the cleaners. I had to find other work." I essayed a rueful smile.

"Honest work, I hope," said Floyd.

70

"Yes," I replied. "I'm now a chief detective with Baldwin-Felts." I knew I had to say it straight out, knowing his dim view of the law, and was apprehensive about his reaction. Trying to justify what really didn't need justification, I added, "I mostly take care of thieves and train-wreckers for the Norfolk and Western."

He looked at me long and hard, like he was searching my soul, but didn't frown or remonstrate. "They shorely need takin' care of," he said noncommittally.

I had an idea of being the peacemaker, of somehow bridging the chasm between the Courthouse and the Allens. A foolish delusion, as it turned out. But now, feeling the ice thawed if not broken, I told him, "Mr. Allen, I'm quite concerned about these charges and court proceedings. Truly, I'm sorry 'bout what happened to your nephews. Seems like a gross miscarriage of justice."

He nodded, looking a little less stiff.

"Do you mind if I ask you what went on in there?" I tilted my head toward the courtroom.

"Well, partly what I expected, Mr. Hayne. But then there was some things none of us counted on," he said with a flash of anger.

"May I ask what?" said I.

"Well, they've charged me with felony release of prisoners, criminal assault on the deputies, and maiming. Wadn' but one of 'em a real deputy," he said.

"I see," I answered in a commiserating tone. None of this was a surprise, so I asked him, "Ah, what was it you didn't count on?"

I could see the blood rise in his face. "They gone an' indicted my brother Sid and my nephew Barnett Allen, too. 'Interferin' with an officer in the p'formance of duty,' Bill Foster said." He scoffed. "They had nothin' to do with it." His voice rose. "All they done was stand there on Sid's front porch and watch. The whole thing didn' last half a minute. It was over 'fore they could of interfered, even if they'd a-wanted to."

I was shocked, and later learned a lot of the townspeople were, too. "I'm truly sorry to hear it, Mr. Allen. I concede it don't seem fair. What will you do? I urge you not to start anything right here in town, right here at the foot of the courthouse."

He gave me a strange look and then evidently decided I was in sympathy. "We posted $500 bail and are free to go 'til trial. As for the rest, we'll just swaller our pride, I guess."

He nodded and without shaking hands again, stalked off down the street toward the livery stable. Lee Felts had moved off chatting with several acquaintances. As is typical on court days, the paved area was crowded in front of the two curved stairways that sweep up on either side to the courtroom level. It served as a kind of Athenian agora, a public place to socialize and do business.

Then I spied Jack Allen across the street, hitching up his horse and buggy. He seemed upset and was muttering to his son Barnett and shaking his head back and forth.

Suddenly Jack saw Pink Samuels leaving the courthouse. He couldn't restrain himself. Though he and Barnett were about to get into the buggy for the ride home, Jack left the rig with his son, motioning him to stay put, and strode over to confront Pink Samuels on the street. I edged to within earshot.

Jack positioned himself right in Pink's path and said, "Deputy, I'd like a few words with you."

Pink replied, "Anything I got to say to you I already said inside." He inclined his head toward the courthouse.

Jack said, "Well, I believe you lied. What did you tell 'em my boy done at Sid Allen's that day when you come into town and swore out a warrant against him?"

Pink turned pinker yet. "Don't nobody call me a liar," he fumed. "I told 'em what happened. Barnett threatened me if I didn' release the prisoners."

"Deputy," Jack answered, just as firm. "That ain't what four eyewitnesses are sayin', all honest folks. Now Barnett's sittin' right over there in my trap. Wait here and let me bring him over, and then you tell him to his face what you just said. If he's broken the law, then he ain't too good to pay for it, just like you and me. But if he didn' do nothin', then what you done is wrong and you need to make it right."

Pink snorted. "Hell, I ain't a-waitin' on nobody, 'specially you Allens. Y'all been throwin' your weight around in this county and abusin' folks long enough. But now you're gonna git what's comin' to ya."

Jack Allen's temper was as explosive as his brother Floyd's. His face turned crimson and he advanced on Samuels. Samuels backed away awkwardly and reached for his gun — a new one, presumably. Before he could extract the weapon, Jack rushed closer, drawing his revolver smoothly from a shoulder holster under his coat. With the others in front of the courthouse, I watched all this unfold in seconds, shocked, and trying to decide if I should intervene.

This was the second time an Allen beat Pink Samuels to the draw. If Samuels was going to be a full-time deputy, he'd have practiced his gun handling a little more.

Jack aimed right at the deputy's florid face and ordered in a tone of menace, "Pink, you take yore hand off a that gun or I will kill you." There's no doubt he meant it, too.

Although it seems anatomically impossible, Pink blanched and threw up his hands. Jack walked the last few feet separating them and placed the muzzle of his Army .45 — a revolver, not the 1911 automatic — right on Pink's forehead and spoke in a tone so low that few of the transfixed bystanders could hear. But I could.

Jack hissed, "Pink, you ain't fit to shovel shit in a hog fac'try, much less serve as an officer of the law. You did lie to the jury 'bout Barnett and Sid. Yore lucky I don't gun you down right here an' now. But I'm givin' you one chance for yore life. You git outta the county and don't never come back. The day I see you agin — on the street, on the road, anywhere, don't matter — I'll shoot you down like the dog you are. Now git!"

Well, Pink got. As Jack kept his pistol trained on him, he turned and fled. Went into hiding in North Carolina, near Mt. Airy. Jack Allen's threat worked. Or maybe it was a guilty conscience. At any rate, Pink Samuels really and truly disappeared. When it came time for him to testify later against Floyd and the others for the assault and release of his prisoners, he was nowhere to be found; and he failed to answer a subpoena.

Peter Easter was made of sterner stuff. When the first trial date came in December, he duly reported to testify. He seemed oblivious to any intimidation from the Allens, if such there was. But the state knew he'd be a less than ideal witness. First, he'd acted without legal authority. Second, he'd fired the only shots and had hit Floyd in the finger. Easter had argued before the grand jury that he'd acted in self-defense, fearing for his life at the hands of Floyd Allen. But still, if anyone was seriously maimed as per the indictment, it was Floyd, not the deputies. Prosecutor Foster decided not to go to trial on the strength of Easter's testimony alone. The Courthouse had to produce Pink Samuels to make the charges stick, but they couldn't. The case was on the docket twice and continued twice; that is, postponed. And still no Pink Samuels. Finally the 1911 term of court ended, and the trial of Floyd, Sidna, and Barnett Allen was scheduled for the opening of the next term — mid-March 1912.

***

I must repeat that I wasn't there for the Allen trial. Most of what I'm about to relate I learned second-hand and after the fact. But it's based on a thorough investigation I performed for Baldwin-Felts when the state brought us in to restore order and track down the fugitives. How do I know what to believe, you might ask. Well, living in the Blue Ridge, in and among real, honest people, I'd learned to detect the sound of integrity — and the sound of its absence. But I concede there are some things we'll never know for certain.

One fact beyond dispute is that Pink Samuels never did show up, despite Dexter Goad's best efforts. A month before trial Dexter traveled to Mt. Airy, North Carolina and met with the man to cajole him to return and testify. He failed. But he did succeed in fueling the flames of Floyd's sense of persecution. "Deck Goad's been pokin' under every rock in the Blue Ridge tryin' to find a snake that'll testify against me," he reportedly said. The grievance quotient went up another tick.

After two continuances because of their missing star witness, the Commonwealth decided to proceed anyway. Floyd's case finally came up on the trial docket for Monday morning, March 11, 1912.

Trial day was a typical March day in the Blue Ridge, wet, windy, and cold; when winter hadn't quite retreated into spring. The Allens displayed an almost casual attitude toward the whole affair, and the raw weather provided a reason — or pretext — for some of the clan not to show up.

There were three defendants, Floyd, his brother Sidna Allen, and their nephew Barnett Allen, brother Jack's son. Floyd and Barnett arrived that morning and took a seat in the gallery, but Sid Allen called in sick, you might say. Complained of pneumonia, which was more likely what we'd call the flu today. He was worried that the raw weather might make him worse. I have to say that a horseback ride seven miles to Hillsville in such conditions probably would have made him worse. Jack Allen, father of defendant Barnett, decided that the presence of a crowd in town on a court day would also make it a good day to sell livestock, so he and his other son Friel drove in a herd of cattle and some draft horses.

Claude Allen, Floyd's son, stayed home Monday to cut firewood. If only he'd stayed home the whole week. Strange, isn't it, how life and death can turn on such seemingly minor decisions. Floyd's other son Victor was a mail carrier, and he couldn't get off work until he arranged for a substitute, which he did later in the week, to his own harm. The Edwards boys, Sid and Wesley, had served their six months for the fight with the Thomas gang, and were to be called as defense witnesses. But Sid Edwards was also down with the grippe and couldn't appear. All in all, it was pretty confusing. It must seem like herding cats, trying to get all the players assembled in the telling. At any rate, presiding Judge Thornton Massie didn't open court until late Monday afternoon. Since there were other matters on the docket ahead of the Allen case, Floyd's trial didn't come up that day at all.

As I recount this strange and confusing part of the tale, the question recurs: why was Floyd, as Clan Allen chief, so oddly cavalier about the proceedings? Some locals said 'arrogant,' and some said 'them Allens only got what was a-comin' to 'em.' I knew Floyd about as well as anyone outside the family, and I don't think so. His trial finally opened the next morning at 10:00 AM, Tuesday the 12th. I can see him in my mind's eye; jaw set, a hard, unforgiving face, yet clouded with a look of uncertainty, as if he doesn't quite grasp this legal business or at least how it had come to this. It was far removed from the daily matters of survival that concerned him most — the harvest, cutting wood, curing meat, putting up produce in the root cellar. It seemed, well, artificial compared to the warp and woof of his life. A pre-modern man, he didn't really understand it, though he did understand it had the power to change his life profoundly, and for the worse.

At least Floyd had enough gumption to retain defense counsel; the best available, he believed -- two retired circuit judges, David Bolen and Walter Tipton. And he sat patiently as the legal mill ground out its grist, starting with selection of the jury, reportedly watching the procedure with great interest. His chief worry was that his archenemy Dexter Goad would pack the jury with Republicans, retainers of the big corporations, or other Allen enemies. Though many claimed Goad did just that, I found to the Clerk's credit that he didn't. The jury was evenly divided between Democrats and Republicans, with no obvious Allen haters. All men, by the way. Women didn't serve as jurors in 1912. Aside from the mores of the time, the main reason was that jurors were drawn from the list of voters, and this was eight years before women got the vote under the 19th Amendment.

The trial began and Floyd pleaded not guilty to all charges. Commonwealth Attorney William Foster then launched the state's case. His opening statement hit hard.

"Gentlemen of the jury," he said, "this is a simple matter and should require no agonizing and soul-searching on your part, only an honest appraisal of the facts. The Commonwealth will prove beyond any doubt, not just a reasonable doubt, that the defendant Floyd Allen did willfully threaten, assault, and maim two deputy sheriffs of this county, Thomas F. Samuels and Peter D. Easter; and did unlawfully free their prisoners, his nephews, from the custody of the said law officers.

"We will ask you to convict this notorious outlaw, this man of violence whose hands have dripped with the blood of the innocent long before he took it upon himself to assault and maim two honest public servants in the performance of their sacred duty on the 23rd of April, Nineteen Hundred and Eleven.

"The question before you gentlemen of the jury is not merely the just penalty due to Floyd Allen, but whether law and order or mob violence will reign supreme in Carroll County."

Pretty effective, I must say. Foster was said to be a good prosecutor, a man who knew the power of oratory to sway a jury, especially if his case was weak on the facts. He'd been waiting a long time to get Floyd Allen in his sights, and now he gave it his best shot.

For a hothead and man of violence, Floyd remained calm during the opening statements and subsequent testimony. Pink Samuels still hadn't appeared, despite the bench warrant issued by Judge Massie for his arrest as a material witness. The judge had decided to go ahead with Floyd's trial anyway, urged on by Bill Foster, who assured the court ex parte that Floyd wouldn't be able to mount much of a defense. In the event, he turned out to be right, more's the pity.

Faux-Deputy Peter Easter's testimony was naturally the most damaging, clouded only by his admission that he had fired at Floyd — in fear of his life and self-defense, of course — and then had run away. He also claimed the bystanders at the Allen store had threatened to aid Floyd in releasing the prisoners, and that hurt the defense considerably, including the cases of Sid Allen and Barnett Allen. Floyd's face darkened, but he held his peace.

Then another onlooker at Sid Allen's store, George Washington Edwards, took the stand for the state. As far as I know, he was no relation to the Edwards nephews. And certainly "Wash" Edwards, as he was called, proved no friend to the Allen clan.

"Mr. Edwards," Foster began, "tell us where you were on the morning of April 11, 1911."

"I was on the front steps of Mr. Sid Allen's gen'l store, north of Fancy Gap. I was buyin' some seed for spring plantin'."

"And did you observe the defendant, Floyd Allen at that time and at that location?"

"Yessir, I did."

"Did you have occasion to hear any remarks uttered by Mr. Allen?"

"Yessir, I did."

"Please relate the details of that conversation for the court."

"Well, sir, Floyd was sittin' his gray mare outside the store, and his brother Sid says, 'Floyd, why doncha get down from thar and come on in and warm by the fahr, have a cuppa coffee.'"

"And what reply did the defendant offer?"

"Sir?" said Wash.

"What did Mr. Allen say to his brother?"

"He says, 'Nope. I heard that Pink Samuels is bringing the boys back this-a-way from Nawth Ca'lina this mornin'. I'm a-stayin' right here on my hoss 'til they come, and then I'm settin' them boys a-loose, if'n I have to shoot me a deputy to do it.'"

A hubbub arose in the courtroom, and Floyd shouted, "Wash Edwards, that's a goddam lie, an' you know it!"

Tipton and Bolen tried to shush their client, who looked for a moment like he was going to come out of his chair and go after Wash Edwards.

Judge Massie was unperturbed. He said, "Now Mr. Allen, you know better than that. You'll have your chance." He peered at the defendant's table and said, though not unkindly, "Counselors, you're going to have to restrain your client's outbursts, or he'll finish the rest of his trial in the county jail."

Judge Bolen whispered to Floyd, but loud enough for some to overhear, "Now, Floyd, you cut that out. You're just goin' to hurt your own defense by that kind of thing. Like the Judge says, we'll put you on the stand and then you can call out this lie, and let the jury decide."

The court adjourned for the day, and on Wednesday, March 13, Floyd testified for himself. Since I've already related the episode, I won't repeat it here. Floyd's version was pretty close to what I've told, except in one particular. He claimed that he hadn't actually freed the prisoners, only cut their bonds to 'save 'em from the shame,' and that the deputies had abandoned their prisoners, who then went home on their own. It was a disingenuous argument, a distinction without a difference; and it convinced no one. Frankly, it's surprising that two experienced lawyers like Bolen and Tipton allowed it. But then, they didn't have much to work with. I also have to fault them for not orchestrating testimony that the County had brought back the Edwards boys without a proper extradition order. It wouldn't have been the linchpin of the case, but it would've thrown some doubt on the claims of the prosecution.

Under cross-examination, prosecutor Foster went after Floyd like a terrier shaking a rat, but he made little impression. Floyd had obviously been warned to keep his legendary temper under control, and he succeeded. In fact, he showed a trace of mountain humor in one exchange that was highly significant, although no one grasped its significance until well after the fact.

Bill Foster asked, "Mr. Allen, what did you beat Deputy Samuels with?"

Since Floyd had already admitted the attack but was pleading extenuating circumstances, there was no point in dodging the question. "With a pistol," he answered.

"With whose pistol?" Foster demanded. "Yours?"

"No," Floyd said with a grim, fleeting smile. "Deputy Samuels'."

"How did you happen to have possession of his pistol?"

"Well, sir, he pulled it on me when there wadn' no need, so I kinda borrowed it from him for a spell."

The courtroom erupted in laughter. Even the Judge was observed suppressing a smile.

Then Foster asked, and this is the part that was significant, "Well, where do you keep your pistol?"

Floyd reached around to his back — to his back — with his right hand around his right side and said, "Right here. Where do you keep yores?"

Floyd's time on the stand ended without any major setbacks, but no obvious points scored, either. He vehemently denied the testimony of Wash Edwards, but it was basically his word against that of the witness. When nephew Sid Edwards came in from his sickbed and testified, he supported his uncle, naturally; but couldn't refute the claims of Wash Edwards.

Lawyer Bolen called Betty Ayers for that purpose. She basically supported Floyd's version of events, but as she was a timid and unassertive witness, prosecutor Foster tied her in knots and nullified whatever value she may have been to the defense. She wasn't able to refute the testimony of Wash Edwards, either.

Finally all witnesses had been heard, and the two sides made their closing statements. The Courthouse Ring had every reason to be confident in the outcome and pleased with Bill Foster. In fact, a few weeks later, Dexter Goad, in a rare statement about the shootout and the events leading up to it, said in a newspaper interview, "Commonwealth's Attorney Foster tried the case with vigor, and many in court said that the prosecution had never been excelled at this bar. His closing argument was masterly, admonishing the jury to have courage do their duty in relieving the County of mob violence, which had plagued our community for twenty years."

At 4:30 PM Judge Massie charged the jury and they retired to begin their consideration. As it was still wet, windy, and cold; and since some of the clan complained of the flu, the Allens lingered in the courtroom hovering around the two wood stoves. Court normally adjourned at 5:30, but the hour came and still no jury, no verdict. Finally, a little before 6:00

the jurymen filed back in and took their seats. The participants resumed their places. Tension was high until the jury foreman indicated they hadn't yet reached a decision and asked the Judge for a clarification on the crime of assault under the state code.

Massie clarified the issue, and then asked, "Gentlemen, if this instruction satisfies your concerns, are you close to reaching a verdict?"

Charles Howell, the foreman, replied, "Yes, your honor. I believe we are close."

"Then, ladies and gentlemen," said the Judge, "I declare this court in recess until 8:00 AM tomorrow morning, at which time I hope we can conclude the matter and proceed with the rest of the court's business." He gaveled the session to a close.

Dexter Goad smiled at Sheriff Lewis Webb, who had replaced Blankenship in January 1912, and both smiled in triumph at Bill Foster. They were proud of their two days' work, full of their own rectitude, and untroubled by doubts. They only saw that they'd begun to win Carroll County for the rule of law and order. The Allens and Edwards, subdued and uncertain, scattered to different abodes for the evening, no doubt anxious about the morrow.

Chapter Five

Now we come to that deadly 14th of March 1912, a Thursday. The weather hovers at the stage where it can't make up its mind to remain winter or change into spring. Typical of the Blue Ridge in March, it's cloudy and cold. A light rain had fallen in the night. The clay roads are muddy and barely trafficable. In short, it's a miserable day.

Sheriff Lew Webb leaves home on horseback, riding toward town at first light. I haven't said much about Sheriff Webb. He's only assumed office in January and has made scant impression on the community. He's not known as a hardliner in the anti-Allen faction. But he is eager to prove himself and get re-elected when the time comes. That means going along with the powers in the county, and especially the Courthouse Ring. No doubt he's pondering what he might have to do if Floyd is convicted today, which seems all but certain.

He pats his coat pocket and is reassured by the heft of the .32 Colt automatic pistol. It's not a weapon he's familiar with. In fact, automatic pistols — well, they're really semi-auto — are somewhat new in 1912. By far, most people who carry a gun favor revolvers, the traditional 'six-shooter.' The Sheriff prefers the old six-round revolver. It's far more dependable and less complicated to use. But there's a funny thing about gun people: they always want the latest thing, whether it's really better or not. Also, the automatic holds three rounds more than the six-shooter, so in that regard it is better. Rumors are swirling, thanks mostly to Dexter Goad and Woodson Quesenberry, that Floyd Allen might try something crazy. Dexter is a forceful man, smart, educated, soon to be called to the bar, someone he ought to heed. Webb takes comfort in the extra ammo capacity of the Colt.

The Sheriff's gelding changes its gait, favoring its right foreleg. He dismounts to check, fearing it might have thrown a shoe. Sure enough, the horseshoe is loose. Cursing the inconvenience, the mud, and the weather, he walks the animal a half-mile to his cousin Allan Webb, who fortunately lives on the road to Hillsville. Allan Webb, a farmer and carpenter, is already in his workshop, and gladly stops work to put some nails into the loose shoe.

He bends over with the horse's bent foreleg held firmly between his knees, tacks down the nails, and says, "Lew, what's happ'nin' in the Floyd Allen trial? I ain't been to town or got any news lately."

Lew tells him, "All the evidence is in, the testimony's done, and the jury's 'sposed to bring in a verdict this mornin'. It's open an' shut. I don't see but that they'll find him guilty."

His cousin files down the nail heads and the edge of the horse's hoof, plants it back on the ground, stands and stretches his back. "Well, you be careful now. I hear tell them Allens are crazy and liable to do 'most anything."

Lew chews on that for a moment and says, "I don't think they'll make a fuss. I think they're just huffin' and blowin' and tryin' to buffalo folks. After all, it wasn't no capital crime. Most Floyd can get is a year. Even less for the other two."

"All the same, you watch yoreself," says Allan. "They're liable to kill you if you don't."

The Sheriff laughs, but there's an edge in it. "Well, they can kill me but they cain't scare me." He pats the handgun under his clothes. "Besides, I got me this new automatic gun."

He thanks his cousin for the shoeing, mounts the gelding, and rides the rest of the way to Hillsville, arriving in time for breakfast at the Texas House. He swallows a few quick bites as the jurymen assemble in the lobby of the hotel where they've been impaneled for the evening, and prepares to escort them up the street to the courthouse.

***

About the same time Lew Webb is eating a hasty breakfast, Judge Thornton L. Massie has finished his and has already left the same hotel. He walks the few dozen yards to the courthouse and up the steps through the retaining rock wall that surrounds the elevated courthouse lawn. He climbs the nearest of the two curving stairs to the second floor and enters his chambers. Yesterday he'd given orders to begin an hour earlier than usual, at 8:00 AM. Today he wants to dispose of the Allen case quickly and move on to the crowded docket. He hopes that by starting at 8:00 he can pre-empt a large crowd, maybe keep any disturbances to a minimum. Except for the early start, it's just another day at the office.

Former Sheriff Blankenship knocks on the door. Massie is an amiable man, but he's slightly irritated at the interruption. Nevertheless, he welcomes him in.

"Good morning, Joe," he says. "Got court here in a few minutes. What's on your mind?"

Blankenship says, "Judge, I'm worried 'bout the Allens, 'specially Floyd. He ain't goin' to take his conviction lyin' down."

"Well," says the Judge, "if he's convicted, he'll just have to now, won't he? Every citizen has got to submit to the authority of the law."

"Beggin' yore pardon, Judge," says Blankenship, "but I don't think you take my meanin'. I'm worried he won't submit, not peaceable anyways. He's liable to make trouble. I wish you'd get Sheriff Webb an' his deputies to disarm ever'body that comes into court this mornin'."

The Judge ponders that for a moment. He looks at the man and says, "Joe, you don't think too well of Floyd Allen, do you?"

Blankenship looks surprised, but answers honestly. "No, sir, I reckon I don't. Mosta us here in the law don't cotton to th'Allens. But we got good reason."

"Now, Joe," says Massie, "maybe that's part of the problem. I'm not saying your reasons aren't valid. But maybe Floyd Allen feels he's being persecuted, and that only stirs him up. My duty is to see that justice is done. That means to prosecute, not persecute. And I have to say, I'm not too happy with the way this case has been handled by the Commonwealth from the outset. I mean, just look at the number of indictments brought against the Allens because of nothing more than a schoolhouse row between a passel of boys. Fourteen counts, and most of 'em felonies. No wonder they feel the law's out to get 'em."

"And it may be the law's been too easy on 'em in the past, and now the bill's finally comin' due," says Blankenship.

"Yes, you could be right about that," muses the Judge. "But if Floyd Allen sees he's getting a fair shake from the bench, and that's exactly what he's getting from this judge, then he'll be less likely to make trouble."

Unconvinced, the ex-sheriff remains silent.

"Anyway," continues Massie, "it's too late to start disarming folks. The courtroom's half filled already. If we tried that now it would just make things worse," he says.

"Yessir," Blankenship sighs. "Have it yore way, Judge. It's yore court."

The judge gathers up his papers. The jury has begun to file in and it's almost time to convene. "Yes, it is my court," he says.

***

By twos and by threes, the Allens and Edwards have begun to converge on the courthouse from the various places where they've spent the night. The courthouse draws them, darkly, as the spider draws the fly. Their usual banter is subdued, though a few words of bravado occasionally break through their somber mood.

Claude and Victor, Floyd's sons, have spent the night at the Elliott Hotel with their cousin Sidna Edwards, Victor having managed to find a substitute for his mail route. Shortly before 7:00 the two Allen boys arise, get dressed in their best dark suits, and head for the stable to feed their horses, thereby saving on the livery fee. Then they return to the hotel to feed themselves. Sidna Edwards stays in bed a little longer, still feeling poorly from the flu.

After breakfast, they go back to their room on the second floor to check on Cousin Sid, who's slowly getting dressed. Assured that he's coming along, Victor leaves again, this time to water the horses after their hay. Claude is about to follow when he notices

Victor's revolver, a Smith and Wesson .38 Special left on the nightstand. As a U.S. Mail carrier, Victor is allowed by law to go armed, not that the law prevents his fellow mountaineers from carrying if they choose. Claude isn't armed, but he doesn't want to leave Victor's pistol unattended, so he clips it in its holster to his belt. That simple happenstance, the unthinking act of negligence by Victor, will cost Claude his life. He and Cousin Sid follow Victor out of the room, stopping by the stables for a final check on their horses, and then head over to the courthouse.

Their cousin Friel Allen, the other son of Floyd's brother Jack Allen, arises at the home of a friend, John F. Moore, where he spent the night, having felt too ill to make the long ride home to Fancy Gap. Friel is a brother of Barnet, who was also charged in the altercation with the two deputies at his Uncle Sidna Allen's store. But Barnett has already been tried and acquitted and is not in Hillsville today. Friel's first cousin Wesley Edwards stops by the Moore place a mile outside of town, and together they plod the muddy track on horseback into Hillsville. They stop at the Cochran Restaurant just across the street from the courthouse for a plate of eggs and fried trout.

It's a few minutes before 8:00, and they're barely into their meal when the bell begins to ring to convene court. Surprised by the early summons, Friel Allen leaps to his feet.

"Wes, I got to git on over to the courthouse. I need to be there for Uncle Floyd," he says. "Pay for my breakfast, will ya?" And he dashes across the street. Wesley gulps down his breakfast and follows a few minutes later.

***

Wearing a dignified charcoal suit and stiff-collared white shirt, Dexter 'Deck' Goad, Clerk of Court, reports to his station in the courtroom with a sense of anticipation — and two weapons. In a shoulder holster he carries a .38 automatic and in his side coat pocket, a .32 automatic. He has also brought along some spare ammunition.

He nods at Commonwealth Attorney Bill Foster who stands nearby by the prosecutor's table at the bar. Seemingly tense, Foster is speaking in subdued tones with Floyd Landreth, a newly-minted lawyer who assists him. Landreth glances around the courtroom and licks his lips nervously. Equally well dressed, Foster has tucked in his vest a .32 Colt automatic like the one Sheriff Webb carries. No words pass between Goad and Foster, just a long, tight-lipped look. Dexter turns to his desk and his files.

He glances up briefly with a satisfied expression as a number of deputies begin to enter and congregate, standing and talking quietly behind the enclosed bar, on the side nearest Bill Foster. Woodson Quesenberry, Deputy Clerk, emerges from the petit jury room in the rear corner and joins his boss at the clerks' raised platform. Goad touches his coat pocket while fixing his subordinate with a questioning look. Quesenberry pats his own side and nods silently.

The jury is coming in, edging past the clerks' station and taking their places in the middle of court below the bench. The courtroom begins to hum with the buzz of expectant conversation and the tread of muddy boots as more spectators enter and take their seats for the conclusion of the trial of the decade in Southwest Virginia.

Precisely at the last stroke of the bell, a punctual Judge Massie emerges from his chambers in the left rear and walks to the dais. He wears a dark suit, not a black robe, a custom not yet introduced into these rural courts.

"All rise," intones Sheriff Webb.

Amid a shuffling of feel and scraping of chairs, the Judge surveys the audience, glancing once at the defense table, and he settles into a large leather swivel chair. Massie peers over the half-glasses perched on his nose at Bill Foster, who nods that he's ready. Then he stares again more pointedly at lawyers Bolen and Tipton. They shrug with embarrassment. Their client hasn't yet made an appearance.

"Oyez, Oyez, Oyez," says Sheriff Webb in his gruff voice. "The District Court of the Commonwealth of Virginia for the 12th Circuit is now in order, the Honorable Thornton L. Massie presiding. God save this honorable court. Be seated."

***

As the bell in the courthouse cupola begins to ring, Floyd Allen and his brother Sidna Allen are just riding up Main Street under gray, lowering skies. Quickly they turn their horses down an alley off the street to Tom Burnett's stable, which is situated just south of the courthouse and next to the county jail.

Tom Burnett pops out when he sees them and says urgently, "Y'all better git on up there to court. I'll stable yore animals. I got two empty stalls."

Floyd and Sidna dismount, and Floyd says, "No thanks, Tom. Just hitch 'em there to the rail and loosen the girths. I don't 'spect we'll be that long."

Was Floyd so sure of being acquitted that he was willing to leave Mary, his prize mare, saddled and bridled and tied to the hitching post? I believe one of his lawyers, Judge Bolen, had assured him the day before he'd be acquitted, or at least allowed free on bail if he wasn't. Or maybe he was planning a quick getaway. I concede you can argue it either way.

Floyd and Sidna march quickly up the alley, turn on Main, and trot up the steps to the courthouse. Sheriff Lew Webb has already called the session to order. They're the last of the family to arrive inside. Floyd's sons Claude and Victor are already there, as are the two Edwards boys and Jack Allen's son Friel, who sits at the front wall next to the grand jury room.

Five minutes late, Floyd takes his seat at the table with his defense counsel. Judge Massie frowns down from his high place. Does he regard this tardiness as a deliberate affront to the law and to himself? Does it unconsciously influence a fateful decision he's about to render? Probably not, but then... we'll never know.

Sidna Allen joins family friend John F. Moore at the left rear corner of the courtroom, on a seat near the judge's chambers and next to his nephew Claude Allen. Wesley Edwards and Victor Allen have taken places a few feet apart from each other, toward the left front, near the north entrance and a good distance from where Uncle Sid and Claude Allen are located. Sid Edwards, arriving late in the crowded chamber, has taken one of the last available seats at the front of the courtroom, just to the right of the north entrance.

Except for Floyd, who is more or less in the center of the room at the defendant's table, the rest of the clan are spread out along the left or north side of the chamber. Opinions can vary, but it doesn't strike me as the way you'd position yourself — well, tactically — if you were planning to attack the court. For one thing, where the Allens and Edwards are seated means their own kinsman Floyd Allen and his lawyers are in the line of fire. Second, they're too spread out. Having been in combat, I know that men about to go into battle instinctively bunch together, mostly for a feeling of mutual protection. If the Allen-Edwards had gone in planning a gunfight, I think they'd have sat together, massing their fire; and they'd have wanted a direct line of sight to Sheriff Webb and the court officers, who were basically grouped in the right rear corner of the courtroom.

Of course, I can't say precisely what the Allens were thinking. Their enemies claimed they'd been plotting a massacre all along. I don't believe it. There was no evidence of it, no overheard conversations, no sightings of them all huddled together conspiring. They're all dressed in their best go-to-meetin' clothes, not what you'd wear to go on the lam in the rugged hills and hollers. They've even taken off their overshoes that protected their Sunday brogues from the mud. Both their characters and their actions that morning are inconsistent with men who're planning mass murder. No one has withdrawn his money from the bank; no one has made any apparent plans to escape afterward.

But I do feel they'd gotten spun up into a state of high tension, overlaid with worry and anger. The long train of perceived grievances against the Courthouse churned up their pre-disposition to violence. A year later, when I saw him in prison, Floyd actually shared his frame of mind on the day of the shooting. Facing his Maker, I don't believe he was inclined to lie. Floyd had grievous flaws, but he was not a liar.

He told me then, "Mr. Hayne, there's just some things a man cain't bear, cain't be asked to bear. Things like injustice and dishonor and shame. Don't matter how young you are or how old you have got. Not for yore picture in the papers nor money in the bank, neither. That's all I could think of when the jury come in that mornin'."

To me that state of mind doesn't suggest cold-blooded, pre-meditated, mass murder. There was no Allen plot, no. What happened was simply the spontaneous outworking of the man's character confronted with an intolerable situation. As the Greeks believed, 'A man's character is his fate.'

***

The cast of characters is now assembled on the stage for the climactic act, but I haven't said anything about the stage itself. I need to provide some details about the layout of the courtroom, a mental image of the geography of the place so the chain of events makes sense. What's about to happen is chaotic and confusing enough as it is.

The Carroll County courthouse is a two-storey red brick structure facing Main Street and typical of local government architecture after the Civil War. Main Street is an unpretentious, unpaved track through the center of town boasting no town square or meeting place. Its relative width compared to the town's other streets is its only virtue as a place for the public to gather. Looming over this stretch of Main is the front portico of the courthouse, supported by four massive Doric columns, painted white. An octagonal cupola surmounts the front end of the building, toward the portico. Two curved concrete stairs sweep up from the ground level on either side to the second floor, where the courtroom is located.

Try to visualize the floor plan as I describe it. Don't get confused by my use of 'front' and 'back.' The courtroom is still pretty much as it was then, a large open rectangle about 40 feet wide and 50 feet long. When I say the 'front,' I mean the end of the courtroom facing Main Street. It's where you enter from the two stairways. But since it's where most of the spectators sit, it might seem like the 'back.'

Looking all the way forward as you enter, you will see the petit jury room, where the trial juries meet and deliberate. In the opposite corner — the left rear — are the judge's chambers. Inside the courtroom itself are the judge's dais and the 'bench', located in the center rear and elevated about two and half feet above the rest of the room. Immediately to the left and adjacent to the judge's dais is a rail-enclosed platform about eight feet square for the clerk of court. It's also raised, but only about a foot high.

Down in front of the judge's rostrum and clerk's platform is where the jurors sit. I won't call it a jury box because it's an open area; it's not enclosed. The jurors sit in swivel chairs side by side in a row that makes a shallow curve as it extends to each end.

Coming forward from the rear of the courtroom, next you see what they call the 'bar.' This area is surrounded by a rail and encloses the tables and seating for the defense and prosecution. The enclosure, about twenty feet long and ten feet deep, is almost in the exact center of the court. There's an opening in the rail facing the judge and jury so that counsel can walk forward and address the court. The defendant and his counsel are seated on the left side of the enclosure; that is, on the left as you're facing the judge. The prosecution sits on the right. On either side outside the bar is a cast-iron, wood-burning stove for heat, and aisles that run from front to back.

Immediately behind the bar enclosure are chairs for deputy sheriffs, then an aisle for people to walk from one side of the room to the other, and then three rows of plain backless benches for spectators. This public seating fills the remaining space in the front or Main

Street end of the courtroom. Similar spectators' benches line the walls along both sides of the room.

That's the layout, a picture of the battlefield, you might say.

***

As I related, the jury has already met for some time the day before, and they've received clarification on points of law from the judge. Now they've filed in and taken their seats, awaiting the judge's charge to the jury. They swivel around in the creaky wooden chairs and look up to the bench as he instructs them.

Judge Massie, a scholarly-looking man with a receding hairline, a wispy mustache, and wearing half-glasses, begins. "Gentlemen of the jury, now comes the moment for which civic duty has brought you here. You have heard all the testimony. You have seen all the evidence."

He pauses and looks down at Floyd Allen, then turns to the jury and continues. "You jurors have been selected as men of standing in the community and because you are conscientious. Your fellow Virginians have reposed a special trust in you to ensure that justice prevails in Carroll County. It rests with you to decide the guilt or innocence of the defendant Floyd Allen; and if you find the facts warrant, to have the fortitude to declare him guilty, without fear or favor.

"Under the laws of the Commonwealth, it also rests with you the jury, not the bench, to fix punishment if you should bring a verdict of guilty. A guilty verdict carries a penalty of not less than one year nor more than five years of penal servitude." He pauses to let that sink in. "You are now excused to begin your deliberations," he says.

These men in their Sunday best, and some in suit coats worn with denim overalls, are just ordinary folks, like all the others in the courtroom on this Thursday, which will turn out to be the most un-ordinary day in their lives. They rise in that slow-moving, almost languorous way of the mountaineers and thread their way past the bar and the public seating to the jury room. If they seem remote in time and especially place, they really aren't. They're not much different from us today. They have the same worries about surviving in a world of scarcity and human fallibility. They work hard and struggle to raise their families, to make their community a decent place. Some have formal education, some possess only folk wisdom, which is not to be despised. I think above all, they have a basic sense of fairness. They want to see justice done. But they're not used to ambiguity, to extenuating circumstances, to shades of gray. In their world, things are mostly black or white. Already deep in thought, the jurymen stand and begin to shuffle off.

"Good luck," says the judge, somewhat incongruously as they edge around the bar and head toward the jury room.

Deputy Sheriff Elihu Gillaspie follows and locks the door behind them.

Now occurs a strange interlude as the court goes into informal recess, waiting on the jury. No one can anticipate how long they'll take or what they'll decide. A low hum fills the room as the 200-plus occupants discuss the case sotto voce. Some are no doubt placing bets on the outcome.

Judge Massie remains at the bench and confers with Dexter Goad, who hands up some routine legal papers for him to sign. Floyd Allen leans over to speak briefly with his two attorneys. Wearing a dark suit and a red cardigan sweater vest, he gets up from the table and sidles over to the nearest wood stove to warm his hands, which he wrings tensely. Floyd usually dresses formally, in dark colors. Many witnesses remark later on the unusual blood-red sweater vest, as if it signified something special. In any case, it draws attention, like a bullfighter's cape.

Floyd walks over to speak briefly to his sister Alverta Edwards, and resumes his seat inside the bar, his fingers drumming on the tabletop. Alverta is the mother of his nephews Sid and Wesley Edwards. Sidna Allen stands in the left rear corner chatting casually with John Moore about some work to be done at the Allen home. Puzzled by his nonchalance, the Edwards and Allen cousins study him for a time, wondering why he's so unconcerned, then they search out each other with increasing worry written on their faces.

***

After half an hour, although it seems far longer, the room hears a sharp rap on the door inside the jury chamber. Sheriff Webb goes over and unlocks the door, holding it open while the jurors exit. The buzz of conversation falls to a deep silence and every pair of eyes studies their faces for a clue about the verdict. But the twelve are impassive as they file back to their swivel chairs. Jury foreman Charlie Howell casts a quick glance at Floyd as he finds his seat, but his face reveals nothing.

A deeper stillness settles over the courtroom once all parties have taken their places. Judge Massie peers down at the jury over his spectacles and asks, "Mr. Foreman, have you reached a verdict?" Obviously they have, but the ancient ritual of the court must be observed.

Charlie Howell, a clean-shaven, well-dressed man in his early 40's, a school teacher, answers in an educated voice, "Yes, we have, Your Honor." He hands up a slip of paper to the judge, who reads it and nods silently. With pursed lips, he passes the slip down to Dexter Goad.

"The defendant will please stand," orders the judge. "Mr. Clerk, will you read the verdict?"

At the defendant's table, bulky Judge Bolen motions Floyd to stand, and struggles to his feet. His jaw clenched, his fingertips resting on the table, Floyd stands with him. Co-counsel Walter Tipton remains seated.

Dexter Goad rises on his little platform like an actor coming center-stage to deliver a soliloquy. Barely concealing a tight-lipped smile, and with a barely concealed note of triumph he reads, "We, the jury of Carroll County duly constituted under the Code of Laws of the Commonwealth of Virginia, find the defendant Floyd Allen guilty as charged in the within indictment..." He pauses for effect. "... and fix his punishment at confinement in the state penitentiary for a period of one year."

"So say ye all?" asks the Clerk.

The jurors assent with nods of the head, and all eyes turn to Floyd Allen. He remains rigid, unblinking, expressionless, as if he hasn't heard. But his ice-blue eyes remain fixed on Dexter Goad.

"Hold on just a moment," says the Judge, holding out his hand for the verdict form. Dexter passes it back.

Frowning, he reads it again, then says, "Mr. Foster, will you come here a moment, please?"

Prosecutor Foster steps through the bar railing and goes up to the bench.

"Counselor," says the Judge, "I think you'll agree the verdict has not been worded correctly, in accordance with the statute. Will you please confer with the Clerk and see that it's rendered properly to be filed."

Guilty as charged. We have a term in common law, *res judicata*, which basically means that's it, game over, the thing has been settled by competent authority. But there's an old proverb in the Blue Ridge, also born of experience, which trumps the legal precept: 'Don't never corner somethin' you know is meaner than you.'

Dexter Goad joins the other two in deep conversation below the dais. During the hiatus in the proceedings, while the conference at the bench is going on, Floyd huddles with his lawyers. Judge Bolen seems relieved. He whispers to his colleague Walter Tipton and to Floyd, "Well, at least we only got the minimum sentence."

Floyd's face darkens and he shakes his head slowly. "I hate to think they can do this to a man jest for standin' on his rights. I shore hate for my boys to have a felon for a Pa. It's a stain on their good name. Cain't you do somethin'?"

Bolen looks at Tipton, then at Floyd and says, "Yes, we can ask for a new trial. But we got to have grounds."

Floyd motions to his son Claude in the far left corner with his brother Sidna. "They's some new witnesses we oughta call." He reaches into his sweater vest and pulls out a sheet of paper with a list of names and shows it to his counsel as Claude walks over to join them at the bar.

Lawyer Bolen looks perturbed. "Well," he fumes, "now's a hell of time to find this out. Sure you're not just clutching at straws, Floyd?"

"Just get me a new trial and you'll see," Floyd says confidently. "I'll have Claude round 'em up and get 'em into court." He's about to hand the paper to Claude when the Judge gavels the trial back into order. The colloquy at the bench is done. Floyd stuffs the paper back into his shirt pocket, under his red sweater vest. Claude remains just outside the bar near his father, ready to ride for the new witnesses. Floyd sits down with his chair back tilted against the bar rail, balanced on its two hind legs.

Judge Bolen immediately stands and says in a loud voice, "May it please the court!"

Surprised, Judge Massie turns and asks, "Yes, Counselor. What is it?"

"Your Honor, the defense moves that the verdict be set aside and that a new trial be granted," says Bolen.

"On what grounds?" Massie replies.

"On the grounds that new evidence has emerged since the proceedings began. We have new witnesses that will shed additional light on the case," Bolen says, waving a subpoena form in the air dramatically. "If the court will indulge me, I have affidavits I intend to file in support of the motion."

Judge Massie seems taken aback, annoyed. He must wonder why this so-called new evidence is just now appearing. But he's clearly making an effort to be fair. He says, "Very well, Judge Bolen. When can you be ready to argue your motion?"

Bolen answers, "I believe we can have our witnesses and the affidavits ready by tomorrow morning."

Massie sighs; obviously sick of the Allen case and wishing it disposed of. "All right, then. I'll set your motion to be argued tomorrow morning at nine o'clock." He turns to Sheriff Webb and is about to open his mouth when Bolen pre-empts him.

"Your Honor, in that case, I request you grant bail to the defendant, pending action on the motion," says Bolen.

Another moment of deep, expectant silence settles over the courtroom. Massie purses his lips and frowns. He pauses for what seems like an age; rubbing his chin, looking first at the Commonwealth Attorney, whose frown is even deeper, then back at Floyd.

Finally he answers, "I'm sorry, but that's not the rule in Virginia, Judge Bolen. You should know that. I can't grant bail after the defendant has been found guilty and sentenced. But if your motion is granted, then I'll bail him pending the appeal."

"Forgive me, Your Honor," Bolen argues, "but technically speaking, sentence hasn't actually been passed. All we have is the jury's recommendation of sentence."

"Your Honor!" Bill Foster stands and almost shouts, but Judge Massie holds up a restraining hand.

"No, I'm afraid I can't do that, Judge Bolen."

At that point, Walter Tipton, seldom heard from, stands with an open court journal and says, "May it please the court." Massie nods and he continues. "Thank you, Your Honor. I can show the court several precedents, including cases in which your predecessor Judge Jackson granted bail in identical circumstances in this circuit. And there are other instances in the Commonwealth where the court has not deemed sentence to have been passed until — "

"Your Honor!" Bill Foster tries again.

But he needn't bother. Judge Massie has clearly made up his mind. He says, "No, that's neither the law nor the custom in Virginia."

Judge Bolen, still standing, turns and leans over to Floyd. He says wearily, "I've done my best for you, Floyd. Now you're just going to have to accept it.

We'll get your witnesses in here tomorrow and hope for a brighter day."

Floyd shakes his head, whether in anger or resignation, and says, "I'll take it calm, but I shore hate it on account of my boys."

Judge Massie asks, "Counselor, is there anything further you wish to offer on behalf of your client?"

"No, sir, I don't reckon there is," Bolen replies and sits heavily in his chair.

With a grim expression, Judge Massie turns again to Lew Webb and orders in a solemn voice, "Sheriff, take charge of the prisoner."

Webb comes forward with Deputy Gillaspie a few paces behind him. At the same moment he looks at the Clerk's platform where Dexter Goad sits smiling. Some say later it's more of a sneer than a smile. Some also says that Goad winks at Sheriff Webb. Woodson Quesenberry, Deputy Clerk of Court, also steps toward the bar with a look of satisfaction.

Suddenly a loud thump resounds in the room as Floyd comes forward in his tilted chair and the two front legs strike the wooden floor. He stands erect and says to no one in particular, "This ain't right. I still got witnesses." He reaches toward his shirt pocket for the list.

Sheriff Webb, Deputy Gillaspie, and Woodson Quesenberry all observe the action with alarm. The lawmen go for their weapons.

"Take hold of him there!" the Sheriff shouts to his deputies, reaching into his coat pocket for his .32 automatic. The unfamiliar weapon, larger than his customary piece, hangs up in the fabric.

Still fumbling in his red sweater, Floyd stares at the approaching officers with a deepening frown. Then he growls in a low voice but loud enough for the whole courtroom to hear, "Gentlemen, I ain't a-goin'."

Chapter Six

Now we come to the crescendo.

"Gentlemen, I ain't a-goin'," said Floyd Allen. I can't tell you how many times I've reflected on those words. To me they still resonate. Sometimes when I'm feeling uncertain at the approach of my own end, I say, "Lord, I ain't a-goin'." But of course, we all go in the end, whether we want to or not. And I'll go willing when the time comes, which won't be long now.

People look on death as a tragedy, but it's not always. Maybe a cruel or untimely death is tragic, like Claude Allen's execution. But Socrates, that wisest of men, said, 'Death may be the greatest of all human blessings.' Think of it as God's final mercy, a release from an existence grown too burdensome, an escape from the world-weariness that besets us all at the end. Floyd's challenge to the court brings us to a sudden shattering moment of violent death -- the high point of the story; or the low point, depending on your point of view.

I wasn't there for the actual gun battle, but the account that follows is based on my thorough investigation. By the time I got through interviewing folks who were in court that day, I felt like I'd been there myself.

First I need to review a vital point. On the first day of Floyd's trial, when he was on the stand prosecutor Foster asked him where he carried his gun. Floyd indicated it rode at the back of his right hip. But now here's Floyd reaching to his front, inside his coat, into his sweater.

Then what was he reaching for inside his coat? I'm convinced he spoke truly afterwards, that he was going for his list of new witnesses. Of course, his lawyer Bolen said it: Floyd was clutching at straws, especially in that particular moment. But, and this is an important but, the lawmen didn't know what he was doing. They were 'spring-loaded,' you might say, convinced by their own anti-Allen propaganda that there was going to be trouble. Remember the first standing rule in a gunfight — whoever shoots first has a tremendous edge. They knew this, and they weren't about to let Floyd get off the first shot.

Ergo, it's my firm belief that the law fired first. Now, who fired first may not be the only measure of blameworthiness in this sad affair; there's enough blame to go 'round on all sides. Nevertheless, it's significant. It has a direct bearing on the subsequent murder trials of the Allen family for their role in the gun battle. And I'm persuaded it was one of the two court clerks, Woodson Quesenberry or Dexter Goad. Probably they both fired simultaneously. A case of a self-fulfilling prophecy, you might say, except they were the ones who fulfilled it. But what followed was absolute chaos, so it's impossible to say for sure who fired first.

***

Well, the fateful moment has arrived. Floyd stands up and flings down the gauntlet — "Gentlemen, I ain't a-goin'" — while reaching under his coat. The pregnant silence is shattered. Blam! Blam! Shots ring out.

For an instant, the unexpected blast stuns everyone into immobility. Time is frozen. Aghast, all eyes are on Floyd as he rocks backward, half turns, and goes partly down from a hit in the right hip. But he regains his footing. Dexter Goad is shooting his .32 semi-automatic from the vantage point of his raised platform. Then more gunshots, the pop! pop! of Woodson Quesenberry's feeble .25 caliber automatic, which he fires at Floyd through the slats of the bar, kneeling.

Though wounded, Floyd is full of fight. He reaches to his back and hauls out his .38 and pumps out two quick shots, but they fly high because he's half-leaning, half-standing against the defense table from the impact of the blow to his pelvis. He's using a compact, five-shot revolver. As is common practice, he keeps the gun's hammer resting on an empty chamber to prevent an accidental discharge, so he only has four rounds — none to waste. Further evidence against a pre-meditated act, by the way.

More shots follow from the deputy sheriffs on the right side of the room. Defense attorney Bolen, suddenly agile for such a portly man, plunges under the table. The other defense counsel, wide-eyed Walter Tipton, is already there.

Seeing his father's life in jeopardy, Claude Allen rushes up to Floyd until blocked by the bar railing. He pulls his brother Victor's borrowed gun and opens fire toward the right rear of the courtroom. Soon the firing is general, a crash of volleys from both sides.

By this time, Sid Allen has drawn and opens fire at the clerk's station from the left rear of the room. Claude Allen, crouching down behind the railing in the center, aims two rounds at Dexter Goad, then shifts his fire to the lawmen who're shooting at him and his pa.

The booming gunfire in the enclosed and crowded space shocks the senses. Females scream and males bellow amid the jarring reports of the guns. Pandemonium erupts as jury, witnesses, and spectators drop to the floor or rush for the two exists.

Along the court's left wall and in the left front near the entrance, Wesley Edwards and his brother Sidna see their two uncles in mortal danger, under attack from the court officials whom they hate with a still-burning grievance. To them it doesn't matter who's right or wrong or who started it. All they know is to help their kin. Drawing his weapon, Wesley jumps up on a bench for elevation and a better aim and joins the fray. Sidna Edwards brandishes his gun but for some reason never fires, perhaps because he can't get a clear shot. Not to be outdone in his defense of the clan, Friel Allen, Floyd's other nephew and son of Jack Allen, pulls his pistol and snaps off a few hasty shots in the direction of Dexter Goad, who's already emptying his second pistol at Claude and Sid Allen.

Near the center of the court, Sheriff Webb struggles desperately with the foreign .32 automatic, which hangs up in his coat pocket as he tries to draw. Finally, it comes free and he triggers a few random shots just as he's hit three times. Grunting and spinning as the rounds strike, he collapses in mid-stride and dies at the foot of the bar.

Prosecutor Foster pulls his piece and shoots on the move, side-stepping toward the front of the courtroom outside the rail. He pops off a few rounds until the converging fire from the Allens and Edwards finds him. Dazed, bleeding, and mortally wounded, he stumbles back to the petit jury room for shelter, where he sinks to the floor and expires.

Gus Fowler, an elderly juror, is either too shocked to move or too slow. He's not a target; he just has the bad luck to be in the line of fire. A misaimed round slams into his skull. He's dead before he hits the floor, where he lies in a spreading pool of crimson.

Woodson Quesenberry has some protection from the railed enclosure of the bar, while Deputy Sheriff Eliahu Gillaspie overturns a bench for cover. Just as Gillaspie completes the action, a bullet plows across the top of his exposed left hand, causing a painful wound but doing no severe damage. Crouching low, he returns the fire with his good right hand against the onslaught from Sid Allen and Claude.

Judge Massie has been regarding Floyd's defiant words with consternation when the shooting starts. Caught in the crossfire between the Allens and the court officers, he's hit by three bullets from both sides. Little puffs of dust fly up from his black coat as they strike. A round bores in from his right — evidently from the Allen side — piercing his right arm and plunging into his chest cavity, where it severs vital arteries and collapses his right lung. He groans, slumps in his chair, and subsides to the floor. His left hand clutching feebly at the air, he soon breathes his last.

Floyd is struck again, this time in the right thigh. It's one of Quesenberry's .25 rounds. It lacks the power to hurt him fatally but hits hard enough to take him down. He falls on the mammoth form of Judge Bolen, who bawls, "Floyd, for God's sake, get away or they'll kill me shooting at you!" Oaks chips fly from the defense table and chairs as more rounds from the lawmen impact with a lethal thud.

In a panic Bolen shouts at Floyd's assailants, "Don't shoot over here any more! Don't shoot over here!"

A few spectators near the cast iron stoves have ducked behind them for protection, but most in the gallery stampede for the nearby doors. Desperate folks pile atop one another, yelling and clawing a passage through the press in the narrow exits.

Varina Ayers, one of the few women in the room, screams, "Lord have mercy, you men, let us out of here!" In the pile-up a bullet hits her daughter Betty in the lower back as she and her parents struggle to escape. The rush of adrenaline enables Betty to flee the blazing hell under her own steam, only to die a few days later.

Stuart Worrell, a spectator on the left side near the defense table, takes a round in the right hip fired by one of the lawmen. He sprawls painfully on the floor behind a bench, covering his head with his arms from the fusillade emanating from the deputies bunched together on the right.

Deputy Sheriff Frank Fowler is a first cousin of juror Gus Fowler who's just been fatally hit. He draws his pistol and manages a few hasty shots at the Allens before he's bowled over by the stampeding crowd.

Juror Frazier Faddis picks up a chair and holds it over his head as he struggles to escape. His colleague Henry Lindsay, sitting next to him, has a narrow brush with death when a bullet clips off a lock of hair above his ear as he flees toward the south door.

Two rounds graze Dexter Goad's left thigh on either side. Then a slug pierces his cheek, passing through the fleshy part but missing teeth and jawbone as it travels around the curve of his neck. He may be the luckiest man in the courtroom that day, for the bullet also misses his jugular vein, spine, trachea, and everything vital. It exits the back of his neck, ripping through his shirt collar and shearing off his rear collar stud. In the heat of the fight he scarcely notices the wound as he continues the battle with his second handgun.

At the first hint of trouble, Andrew Howlett, a spectator, has rushed toward the rear of the chamber and the petit jury room, seeking shelter. He's quick, but not quick enough. A stray round fired from the front, probably by Friel Allen or Wesley Edwards, catches him in the fleshy part of his back below his shoulder blade, lodging near the chest wall, and spins him to the floor.

Christopher Columbus Cain, a juror on the left end of the row, has the same idea. He, too, makes a dash for the petit jury room, but not fast enough to outrun two shots that strike him from behind. One slug passes through the small of his back, missing spine and pelvis, and exits his left midsection. The second strikes his left thigh, hits bone, and turns ninety degrees the way speeding bullets often do when meeting resistance. It travels all the agonizing way down to his ankle, shearing muscle and tendons. Screaming in pain, he plunges to the floor alongside Andrew Howlett.

Ex-deputy Gurvis Hall is standing in the far right corner when the melee starts. He's armed, too, but takes no part in the fight. With him discretion is the better part of valor. Leaping out the second-floor window, he dislocates his shoulder on impact. Likewise, Sid Allen's neighbor John Moore and witness John Farris exit the window on the other side of the room.

Five people are killed outright or mortally wounded, another six wounded, including Floyd. But the extent of the carnage isn't yet evident. Everyone is too focused on his immediate survival to notice the appalling number of dead and wounded.

Mere words can't capture the scene — the panic and the bedlam, the screams and moans of the injured, the stench of death, the wooden floor suddenly slick with blood. People are yelling and rushing about in panic. Smoke obscures their vision. Even though the ammunition of the day contains an early form of smokeless powder, there's still plenty of smoke. The deafening noise and muzzle flashes light up luridly in the haze and gloom. And it's all happening too fast for anyone to think or plan or do anything but react instinctively.

Now, here's the thing. In the telling of it, you have to imagine the suddenness of the firefight, the horror, the surprise, even though folks said later they'd anticipated some sort of trouble. I can't adequately convey the chaos and terror unleashed, made even more shocking by the location. Nothing like this has ever happened in an American courtroom. I'm relating the battle in orderly sentences, coherently; or trying to at any rate. Yet paradoxically that defeats the purpose of conveying what it's like, because there's nothing orderly and coherent about it. I can only describe it sequentially, yet all these things are happening simultaneously, not sequentially — all together in the same confused few moments, a minute or less. The phase of the gunfight inside the courtroom is over in less time than it takes to tell. But it doesn't end in the courtroom.

***

Somehow, despite two bullets in hip and thigh that would've disabled a lesser man, Floyd Allen vaults the railing around him and limps to the door. In the process he drops his empty revolver, but wounds prevent him from bending over to retrieve it. He's followed by son Claude, who sort of backs out, keeping his weapon trained on their adversaries as the two men retreat. His other son Victor, who's unarmed, has already made his way out of the chamber and is waiting on the ground below, hapless and uncertain, at the foot of the north stairway. Sid Allen and the nephews Friel Allen and Wesley and Sidna Edwards have also fled the second floor and are milling about anxiously below. They obviously have no pre-conceived plan, which you think would include an escape plan. Initially they're as confused and rattled as everybody else. If there is a plan, they're making it up as they go along.

The combatants have fired a total of 57 rounds, an average of about one per second. In retrospect, that may not sound like a lot. But compared to a typical police gunfight that lasts about two seconds and consumes a handful of rounds, this is a major battle. Of course, it seems much longer than a minute. Many of those present later said it lasted a full five minutes. That's a wild exaggeration, but understandable. When you're under fire, it feels like an eternity.

By this time both sides have emptied their weapons, so there's a momentary lull as everybody reloads and recovers from the shock. Most of the spectators have fled. The Allens and Edwards follow out the left hand door and down the north stairway.

Dexter Goad, bleeding from his neck wound, follows them. Both his pistols are empty. And then he spies Deputy Sheriff Fugate Dalton with a fully-loaded .38 revolver.

"They're gettin' away!" he yells. Momentarily deafened by the din, he's unaware that he's shouting at the top of his voice. He motions toward the door, indicating the deputy should pursue the Allens. Deputy Dalton is having none of it. He stands there dumb, motionless.

"Well, if you aren't goin' to use the damn thing, give it to me," Goad orders. He commandeers the weapon and heads for the door. Whatever you can say about Dexter Goad, good or bad, he's no coward.

Woodson Quesenberry has paused in the Clerk's Office where the ammunition reserve is kept to reload Dexter's two guns. When he sees his boss in pursuit of the Allens, he joins him. Goad, Quesenberry, and Deputy Gillaspie emerge cautiously from the door onto the south stair landing, weapons extended and ready to resume the battle.

Floyd has regained the composure lost when the surprise opening rounds came his way and hit him painfully in pelvis and thigh. But he's now unarmed. He sees Sidna Edwards with the never-fired .38 Smith and Wesson tucked in his belt.

"I ain't nary a gun," he says. "Let me have yores."

His nephew hands it over. Now, with a loaded weapon and with the steadiness of a veteran gunfighter, he pauses at the foot of the stair, waiting on his enemies. As they emerge on the second-floor landing, he opens fire, slow and deliberate. Floyd knows the old adage, 'Don't shoot fast unless you also shoot well.' Claude has only one round left and no spare ammo. He fires his last shell. The lawmen return fire and duck back inside from the near-fatal volley.

You can go to Hillsville today and still see the bullet holes in the south stair masonry where Floyd's rounds and Claude's final shot impacted. They're the only lasting public memorial to the Allens in the County, you might say. Aside from peoples' memories, that is, which last long in that part of the world. A year later Floyd and son Claude will be dead in the electric chair.

The stunned spectators and witnesses scatter on reaching the courthouse grounds, trembling, disbelieving. Yet the horrified memory of what has happened reverberates in their minds. They flee in all directions as the shooting spills out of the court chamber and onto the grounds.

J. B. Marshall, County Treasurer, finds Betty Ayers doubled over in the yard holding herself about the middle with both arms. He reaches her just as she sinks to the ground, clutching his coat. Marshall cradles her in his arms, and not knowing how badly she's hit, he says the only thing he can say in such a moment. "Miz Ayers, you just hold on now while we git some help. Yore goin' to be all right."

"No, sir," she says with unnerving calm, "they've killed me."

Betty lingered another 24 hours, poor thing, just long enough for me to interview early the next morning. I got to Hillsville the same night as the shootout. She swore that Floyd Allen wasn't the first to shoot, but she couldn't add anything more.

When the shots from the Allens cease momentarily, the law officers again poke out their weapons and fire down on Floyd, whose retreat has brought him into the muddy street in front of the courthouse. Floyd's fighting blood is really up. Enraged, he disdains to take cover and wages battle from the open. Not wise. A bullet fired by one of the three officers hits Floyd in the right knee, passing through the joint and shattering nerve, bone, and cartilage. It has to be an excruciating wound, but somehow Floyd keeps standing and continues to fight.

Floyd's brother Sid has reloaded. Seeing that Floyd is hit again, he covers the clan's retreat. Sons Victor and Claude help their father struggle downhill to their horses. It's amazing that Floyd is able to keep his feet at all. While they escape, Sid Allen leans from behind one of the four huge columns of the front portico and shoots at Dexter Goad and company every time they try to descend the stairs. The lawmen jump back under cover. When they return the fire, Sid ducks behind his column; but a round from the second floor landing nicks him in the left arm and back. They're only flesh wounds — that makes seven wounded, by the way — and Sid keeps them at bay. This lethal cat-and-mouse gun battle goes on until Sid is sure the Allens and Edwards are clear of the zone of fire, and when all the shooters again run out of ammunition.

Sid Allen uses the pause to dash out from behind his protection and join his kin down the street at the Blankenship stable. Dexter Goad, Woodson Quesenberry, and Eliahu Gillaspie return to the clerk's office to reload Goad's two automatics just in case the Allens return, and to see to Dexter's wounds. They count eleven bullet holes in the Clerk's clothing. As I said, Dexter Goad has been an extraordinarily lucky man. But the great Hillsville Shootout has finally ended. Now comes the pursuit -- and where I come back into the story.

Chapter Seven

The Hillsville battle ended five lives, seven if you count the execution of Floyd and Claude Allen, which you must. Eight, if you assume the subsequent murder of their brother Jasper Allen was connected to the event, which is likely. It profoundly changed many other lives forever. It changed mine, too. It may've even saved my life.

On the afternoon the shootout occurred, I was at the Roanoke train station, waiting on the Norfolk and Western to take me to Bluefield, West Virginia and from there to the coal fields in southern West Virginia. A place called Cabin Creek.

Cabin Creek was the scene of growing violence between mine owners and their employees, aided by union organizers from the United Mine Workers. Baldwin-Felts had been hired to police the coal fields for the mine owners, an assignment I'd grown to despise. It wasn't just aimed at suppressing union violence as the Agency liked to claim. It meant doing violence on behalf of the coal companies. The Agency carried out some good policing, true; but we also engaged in strong-arm tactics against the miners and their families, whose only crime was to seek a decent life in exchange for the back-breaking labor and mortal dangers of their calling.

You can understand I wasn't the least bit unhappy when the Agency's messenger arrived breathless at the station and handed me a note from Thomas Felts. It read, "Most urgent! Cancel your train reservation and return at once to headquarters to discuss a new assignment. I will send Cunningham to Cabin Creek in your stead. Thomas Felts."

Most urgent, it said. Wasting no time, I grabbed my kit and handed my Springfield '03 rifle in its leather case to the errand boy. We dashed to a streetcar and headed back to Baldwin-Felts.

Dumping my gear in the first-floor anteroom, I loped upstairs to find William Baldwin and Thomas Felts in Baldwin's office, surrounded by a half dozen of our people, all in dark suits or tweed. He was listening intently on the telephone, one of the old-fashioned kind with a separate earpiece. He motioned me with the handset to take a seat. I looked around quizzically at my colleagues, who all wore unusually grave expressions but kept silent until the boss had finished his conversation.

Finally, he said into the mouthpiece, "Very well, Governor. We'll have our best men up there as soon as possible. You know you can count on us." He placed the earpiece in its cradle, took a deep breath, and scanned the puzzled faces in the room.

"Well, that was Governor Mann, obviously, with an update from the earlier call," he said. Then he looked squarely at me. "Carter, you've spent some time in Carroll County, I believe."

It was a question, not an assertion, and I answered at once, "Yes, sir. I know it well. From my timber scouting days. I've passed through Hillsville many times on Agency business. May I ask — "

He cut me off. "And you know the Allen clan, I believe? Floyd and Sidna Allen in particular?"

"Yes. I wouldn't say we're personal friends, but I do know them."

He looked at his partner while I fidgeted in my chair, and all other eyes turned on me. "What do you think, Tom?"

Felts answered, "I'd say we have no one better. He knows the people; he knows the terrain. He's a proven leader in war and one of our most capable men in every respect."

It was uncomfortable being discussed in this fashion in front of my peers, but I was glad at least of the bosses' good opinion of me.

William Baldwin was a man who made up his mind quickly. He smiled faintly, or grimly, and said, "Carter, do you remember our first meeting at the Hotel Roanoke, when I opined about man-hunting as the greatest sport? And we talked about your man-hunting days in the Philippines?"

"Yes, sir, I do indeed," I said. My curiosity was about to explode.

He said, "You haven't had much opportunity for it, guarding trains and coal mines and catching pickpockets and such. But now the Agency — and the Commonwealth of Virginia — needs our best detective and our best man-hunter rolled into one. I think you're our man."

I could contain myself no longer. "You know I'll do my best, whatever the assignment. If I may say so, my best is pretty good. But please tell me what the hell has happened."

He grimaced and said, "You will scarcely believe what has happened. It's like nothing in the annals of the state. This morning at about 9:00 AM, Floyd Allen, Sidna Allen, and their kin invaded the courthouse in Hillsville and assassinated Judge Thornton Massie right on the bench, along with Bill Foster, the Commonwealth Attorney, Sheriff Lewis Webb, and several other people. They are still armed and at large and terrorizing the town."

Shock and incredulity must have shown on my face, for he nodded and said, "Yes, it's true — straight from the Governor himself. With Sheriff Webb murdered, there's no longer any law in the County, if indeed there ever was with such people free to commit mayhem at will. The Commonwealth has deputized our Agency. We are now in essence the state police in Southwest Virginia. Carter, you're already packed and you're the right man anyway. I want you to get on down to Hillsville and take things in hand. These gentlemen will go with you now. Either Mr. Felts or I will join you soon with more men. But the urgent thing is to get there quickly and restore law and order. Proceed carefully, spare no reasonable expense, and use deadly force if you have to. Above all, uphold public order and protect the innocent citizens of the County from these assassins. The Governor stands behind us fully, and he will not see the laws of the Commonwealth flouted nor anarchy allowed to reign unchecked. And neither will I," he added.

He handed me a leather satchel and said, "These funds will carry you and your people for the next few days. Mounts, saddles, and tack for all of you are being loaded now on a special train that will take you as far as the siding at Dugspur. Nothing else will be available until tomorrow midday, so that's what we've had to arrange. But it means you'll have to ride the train all night, then on horseback the last ten miles to Hillsville. Any questions?"

"Well, yes. Several dozen to be exact," I said, still shocked and bewildered. Maybe it does me no credit, maybe I was a dissembler, but I'd learned to keep my own counsel. I'd never shared my growing concerns about the Agency, especially its violent tactics against

the poor miners in West Virginia. And now I kept to
myself any doubts regarding Floyd Allen. I didn't
believe on its face the report that he and his kin had
attacked the court for the purpose of assassinating its
officials. There had to be more to the story. I figured
the Allens would get better treatment from me than
anyone else in the Agency, that the Allens would know
it, and this might help de-escalate the situation. Any
other detective likely to get the job would take it as a
license to kill without warning.

"There's no time for a dozen questions," said
Baldwin. "But I'll ask Mr. Felts to ride with you to the
spur line. He can put you in the picture on the way.
Quite frankly, confusion and chaos are loose in
Hillsville, so there's not much more we can tell you
anyway that you could depend on. Mr. Felts will
follow as soon as he can with more men. Best of luck,"
he said, extending his hand. "I know you'll do us
proud."

It was one of those moments you look back on
decades later, and with the benefit of hindsight you
realize it was the critical turning point in your life.
Instead of getting typecast as a union-busting specialist
for the coal companies, I went to Hillsville and became
the famous captor of the Allens, the Melvin Purvis of
my day, a national celebrity. That in turn led me to
Emma, my wife, and in time, a career as a criminal
defense lawyer. If I'd remained one of the strong-arm
men at the mines, no doubt I'd have been present eight
years later at the Matewan Massacre in 1920. I'd
probably have died there in the streets of Matewan
along with my erstwhile colleagues Lee and Albert
Felts and five other Agency men, including C. B.
Cunningham, who went to West Virginia in my place
on March 14, 1912.

***

The rhythmic rocking of the train toward Hillsville set free my thoughts, and I pondered the whole affair, or as much as Tom Felts could tell me. Over and over I asked myself the same question countless others have asked since the day: why did such a needless tragedy have to happen? I've wrestled with it for 56 years and still don't have the final answer. I don't think there is one, which is why this story continues to fascinate people half a century later, and will continue to for a long time to come.

In any case, the explosion occurred, and I was called in to pick up the pieces. So there I was, rattling along in an old logging train along the north edge of the Blue Ridge toward Carroll County, congratulating myself for having kept silent in Roanoke. Something about this case drew me in, and I wanted to be here. I knew if I had sounded off to William Baldwin, he'd have pulled me off the case in the same way the Marines had yanked me in the Philippines for being too sympathetic to the natives. Lee Felts and Deck Goad for certain remembered my remarks about Floyd Allen that day we had dinner in the Texas House Hotel. I was beginning to have doubts, too, about my chosen line of work. But I had no doubts at all that I was never going back to West Virginia to terrorize poor coalminers and their women and children. Even taking on the Allen clan was preferable.

We de-trained very early the next morning of the day after. It was, fittingly, a gray chilly dawn, and the lowering skies told me it would likely stay that way. We'd already tacked up our mounts before arriving at the water tower siding in Dugspur. Leading the horses down the boxcar's ramp, we tightened girths and off we went along the muddy highway, heading due west.

In a quarter hour we overtook a one-horse buggy struggling along the same way. A voice clearly not from those parts hailed us out of the gloom. "Say there, friend. Are we going the right way to Hillsville?"

I kneed my mount alongside and studied them, two men in dusters and cloth driving caps, clean-shaven, respectable looking. "Yes," I said. "Straight on, about nine more miles."

The man stared back at my boys who'd caught up with me, our rifles in their scabbards, my leather coat and old Army campaign hat — what folks call a 'Smokey Bear' hat, the kind Marine DI's wear today. I must've presented an imposing spectacle, for he asked warily, "Are you the law?"

"Yes, we are," I told him.

"Thanks goodness. For a moment there I thought we might've fallen afoul of the Allen gang. Such desperadoes you never heard of," said his companion. "You're going to Hillsville to arrest 'em, aren't you?"

I didn't answer. "And who might you be, gentlemen?"

"I'm Chase Buttram, from the *Richmond Times-Dispatch,*" the first man said. The other one identified himself as Oscar Wilentz from the *Washington Herald.*

"Reporters, eh?" I made no effort to conceal my low opinion.

"Yes," the first man said, ignoring the obvious distaste in my voice. "We heard about the massacre yesterday from the Governor's office, that he was calling in the Baldwins. I suppose that's you fellows."

I ignored his query. "It didn't take you long to get here. You're even a step ahead of the law."

The Richmond reporter chuckled. "Well, you know what they say — the early bird catches the worm. I assure you, there'll be plenty more birds flocking in here soon. The story of the 'Hillsville Horror' has gone out over all the wires, all over the country."

"All over the world," the second man added.

"It's the biggest thing since... well, since the Jesse James gang," said the Richmond reporter. "We heard they've killed all the court officers and all the jurors. They've taken over the town and are holding the city fathers hostage. Their associates are arming and streaming in from the countryside. It's an insurrection."

A cold drizzle had begun to fall, which did not improve my temper. With a curt laugh I said, "Before we left Roanoke, my office wired the Elliott House for accommodations. Now, if the Allens were any kind of insurrectionists, they'd have cut the telegraph and telephone wires right off, don't you think?"

"I hadn't thought of that," the second man said.

I said, "When you get to Hillsville I expect you'll find a lot less drama than you've heard. But don't let the facts get in the way of a good story," I called back as I spurred my horse. She cantered forward, her hoofs throwing up a spray of mud on the hapless reporters behind.

***

We arrived in Hillsville about 7:00 AM, soaked around the edges of our mackintoshes. Weary men and horses plodded through muddy streets lined with grim-faced armed men, many of them now unemployed deputies of the late Sheriff Lew Webb. They had built a bonfire at the edge of the street in front of the courthouse, around which they huddled for warmth. Although the County's deputies had lost their formal legal authority with the death of the Sheriff, they still had what you might call 'common law' authority. By that I mean the magistracy that any sovereign citizen may exercise — to defend himself, to intervene and stop a crime if he's sees one in progress, and so on. But we Baldwin agents were now the formally constituted authority by act of the Governor, the chief magistrate of the Commonwealth, under the common law doctrine of *posse comitatus* as well as state law. We had broad powers of pursuit and arrest. What powers we didn't have, we knew we could simply assume, and no one would challenge us.

Dexter Goad and Woodson Quesenberry met us at the courthouse steps in the pale wash of the gas streetlamps against the drizzle. Dexter wore a bloody bandage around his neck like a combat decoration, and was still in his suit from the courthouse, with its incredible eleven bullet holes. As I said, he was a brave man, and as lucky as he was brave. Perhaps I imagined it, but thought I detected an I-told-you-so expression. No doubt he remembered our conversation about the Allens a few months earlier.

But he gave us a gracious welcome. "I sure am glad to see you gentlemen," he said as I dismounted and shook his hand. "All the devils from Hell been unleashed on us yesterday here in Hillsville. There's talk the Allens are planning to come back and finish the job, and rescue Floyd."

"Floyd Allen's still in town?" I asked, surprised.

"Yes, over in Tom Hall's Boarding House. He got shot up kinda bad, and we don't know if he'll live. Doc Nuckolls is with him now. His son Victor stayed with him. I'm sorry to say Floyd's the only one a the Allen Gang that was hit. The rest of 'em lit outta town."

"Who're the rest?" I asked

Dexter said, "Floyd's brother Sid Allen, their nephew Friel Allen, Floyd's son Claude, and the Edwards boys, Wesley and Sid."

***

All the witnesses agreed that the Allens and Edwards had milled around town for an oddly long time after the smoke settled. Here's what happened in the aftermath.

Floyd went to get on his horse but collapsed from his three wounds, especially the shattered knee. He remained in the stable, lying on a pile of hay covered by a couple of horse blankets, his reloaded revolver still in hand. Even after all the mayhem, he still was not a-goin' if the law had come for him then. But he'd lost a fair amount of blood and was convinced he was dying, and the fight went out of him. His son Victor, who'd taken no part in the shootout, remained by his side. His sister Alverta Edwards, mother of the combatants Wesley and Sid, came to comfort him, too. When I saw Victor later, his hands were caked in dried blood from staunching his father's wounds. Floyd's subsequent acts showed that he would have preferred to die then and there and spare himself the ignominy of a state execution.

In fact, still in shock, he said to his son Victor and a small group gathering around him, "I fear I'm goin' to meet my Maker. I think I see him now."

A stable hand snorted, "That ain't yore Maker, that's the devil you see."

Floyd's kinsmen also thought he was dying, and after a while the urgency of self-preservation began to assert itself over clan loyalty. No one wanted to leave Floyd to die alone, but Victor and sister Alverta were there to keep vigil. They all knew Victor had been unarmed and had taken no part in the battle, and he'd be safe staying behind.

Floyd lingered on. Finally they all decided if he was going to die, there was nothing they could do to prevent it. And if the good Lord was going to allow him live — well, that was out of their hands, too. Either way, there was nothing be gained by staying and being captured. After about two hours they casually mounted up and rode out of town with no apparent sense of urgency, Sidna Allen being the last one to leave.

Their erratic behavior tells me they were in shock from the enormity of what had just happened, and still in the physical and emotional lassitude that follows the adrenaline-fueled high of a gunfight, sometimes to the point of actual incapacitation. I saw it many times in the Philippine war. But it was clear to anyone with the semblance of an open mind — which ought to include those with the title of detective — that the Allens had no preconceived escape plan. If they had no plan or apparent idea what they intended to do afterwards, is it likely the shooting itself was premeditated? To me it's not logical to say it was.

***

When it became apparent that Floyd was not going to expire, Tom Hall, innkeeper of the Elliott House Hotel, generously invited Victor and a knot of townsmen to bring Floyd out of the cold and into a spare room at the hotel, and served him a meal. It was there that I went about 9:00 AM to make the arrest, and ran into Doctor Nuckolls on the way out, clutching his medical bag and shaking his head.

I introduced myself and inquired as to Floyd's condition.

Nuckolls told me, "They smote him hip and thigh. He's been shot three times in the midsection and lower extremity, and lost a fair amount of blood. The shock's begun to wear off and he's in a lot of pain. But I don't believe his life is in any danger. Not from his wounds, anyway. I can't vouch for the townspeople, or the law."

"Is he fit enough to move to the jail? Just in case the clan comes back to rescue him, or in case one of the townspeople wants to finish the job?" I asked.

"Yes, he is. Just make sure you keep him plenty warm and give him lots of fluids," said the doc. "Lots of fluids. Might put out the fire in him." Touching his hat brim and shaking his head, he departed.

I was carrying the new Colt .45 Model 1911 automatic that had first seen service with the Army in the Philippines. It's a big gun with a heavy round that'll take down just about anything or anybody. One of John Moses Browning's greatest designs. I loosened the flap on my holster just in case and entered the room where Floyd lay, wan and pale. The stuffing had really been knocked out of him. Victor Allen and Alverta Edwards were still at his bedside, along with a few neighbors and family friends. Interestingly, no deputies or other lawmen had come near him. Guess they figured they'd done enough and weren't going to risk any further encounters, knowing a mountain lion is most dangerous when wounded and cornered.

With a commiserating smile I said, "Floyd, I'm truly sorry to see you here. You look like the hindquarters of bad luck."

"Yessir, Mr. Hayne," he replied, "I been chewed up and spit out."

"From what I hear, it was the law that got chewed up and spit out," I said.

Floyd agreed. "Yes. I'm sure sorry 'bout Judge Massie. He was a fair man. None a us Allens had any call to want to hurt him. But them others... Folks always said of me, there's no better friend, no worse enemy. I guess I lived up to it."

I told him, "You realize this isn't a social call, as much as I wish that neither one of us was here in these circumstances. The Baldwin-Felts Agency has been deputized with full police powers by the Governor. Dr. Nuckolls says you're going to be all right, and that you're fit to be moved. I'm here to arrest you and Victor, and I'm afraid duty requires me to move you to the county jail."

Floyd protested, but weakly. "Victor had nothin' to do with this. He wadn' even armed."

Victor weighed in. "That's right, Mr. Hayne, I had no gun and I didn' shoot anybody."

I said, "Gentlemen, I believe you. But your name is still on the warrant, Victor. This will all get sorted out in good time, but right now it'll be better for all if you come along peaceable. If I were you, Victor, I wouldn't want to be out on the streets now anyway. It ain't safe. We can call it protective custody if it makes you feel any better."

"What's more," said Victor, "the law fired first. The family was just defendin' Pa. They didn't shoot until Pa had already been shot."

Floyd nodded as best he could supine and said, "That's right, that's right."

I neither believed them nor disbelieved them. They had every reason to lie, yet I knew Floyd pretty well, a hothead, a violent man when provoked, yet still a man of rough integrity known for the value of his word.

Without comment, and putting all my trust in a display of trust, I held out my hand. Floyd reluctantly brought out from the blankets a Smith and Wesson .38 and deposited it in my hand. I motioned in my colleagues. After tucking him in warmly against the outside chill, eight of them picked up Floyd's cot and laboriously hauled him to the street and toward the jail, while I escorted Victor. As we exited the boarding house, I noticed a strange motion under the blankets. Telling the men to stop, I stripped back the covers as they set down the cot. Floyd's eyes blazed at me. His neck was covered in blood, as was his right hand, which held a serrated knife evidently purloined from Tom Hall's breakfast tray.

"Floyd, Floyd, this ain't the way!" I shouted, snatching away the knife.

The wound was bloody but didn't look life-threatening. I sent again for Dr. Nuckolls, who came cursing under his breath, and bandaged the wound after Floyd was safely deposited in the county jail. "Wish he'd had a sharper knife," I heard the Nuckolls mutter as he packed up his kit. I was struck by the venom of a supposed healer, 'til I remembered he was also the county coroner and no doubt had friends among the dead officials.

The word took only a millisecond to reach the press, and how they do it I have never understood. Anyway, the attempted suicide led the next day's lurid headlines, further adding to the circus atmosphere in Hillsville. I remember one from the Bluefield paper in particular: FLOYD ALLEN TRIES, FAILS, TO CHEAT HANGMAN BY CUTTING OWN THROAT. Stories like that went out all over the country. In fact, all over the world, just like the man said.

This was also when my name began to appear nationwide, and for all I know, internationally. VIRGINIAN CARTER HAYNE BRINGS LAW TO EMBATTLED HILLSVILLE, and WAR HERO ON THE WARPATH FOR THE ALLEN GANG. I didn't like it at the time; I avoided the press and gave no interviews. Such reporting slighted the work of many others equally active in the restoration of civil order, including my bosses. They frowned on sharing the limelight with a subordinate. But the reporters needed a name, they needed to personify the manhunt, they needed a hero. There was nothing I could do about it. So I focused on the mission, making sure order was re-established and that the Allens weren't coming back to shoot up the town or rescue Floyd, not that I'd ever believed that anyway.

I also started the detailed investigation I mentioned earlier, making the rounds and talking to all those who were there in the courthouse. Then I caught up with Judge Bolen, Floyd's defense counsel, as he was about to leave town. He had just said his goodbyes to Floyd and Victor, whom we were transporting to the jail in Roanoke because it was more secure. As we spoke I was surprised to hear him claim that Claude Allen had fired the first shot, evidently with deliberate aim, at Judge Massie. I didn't know what to make of it, but filed it away in my mind. His account made it clear he was facing Claude, which meant his back was turned to the court officials and deputies. Unless he had eyes in the back of his head, he couldn't possibly have seen what Dexter Goad or the lawmen were doing, or that they might have fired first. Still, a version from a respected attorney, a former judge, and Floyd's own defense counsel had to carry weight. I knew his testimony didn't bode well for the Allens.

This was also my first practical lesson in the limits to the reliability of eyewitnesses, a lesson that served me well in my later years at the defense bar. It's not that eyewitnesses are malicious, though some are. But what they report seeing is not always accurate. They may have been under stress, or in low-light conditions, or lacking a panoramic view, like Judge Bolen. This kind of testimony is certainly relevant and admissible, but it should never be the final word.

***

Then began the greatest criminal pursuit in U.S. history, in terms of numbers and resources, and especially in newspaper hype. Nothing like it was seen again until the late 1920's and early '30's, the days of Bonnie and Clyde and the Ma Barker Gang, and when the FBI came into its own chasing down celebrity criminals like John Dillinger.

I'd always believed that speed and decisiveness were essential, whether in combat or police work. But men and horses were tired and spent from the long sleepless trip from Roanoke. Though I was familiar with the southern County where the Allens had most likely gone to ground, I certainly didn't know it as well as they did. They had nearly a twenty-four hour head start. It made no sense to go after them now and in our reduced condition. Giving orders to rest and recover, I made my rounds of the town and talked to anyone who might shed light on the shootout. I even spoke to Betty Ayers a short time before she expired. The team of agents rubbed down the horses and left them with their fodder in the stable. Then we bedded down in the Elliott House for a needed rest, with plans to strike out toward Fancy Gap and Allen country at first light.

Our first target was Sidna Allen's famous house south of Hillsville on the road to Mt. Airy. As I said earlier, it's still there and has become an historical landmark. It's a large, ornate Late Victorian structure with turrets and spires and wrap-around porches. Quite handsome and quite unusual for the region. I knew we'd find no one there, but as a matter of standard operating procedure we had to check it out.

By this time Tom Felts had joined us with 20 more guns, and he gave our gang the somewhat pretentious name of "The Grand Posse." He and I divided the agents into three teams and we converged on the Allen house, triggers on fingers, to be met only with silence. Entering the home we found no evidence of Sid Allen except the bloodstained garments he'd worn in the gunfight. He'd had ample time to put on some outdoor clothing and gather supplies and equipment.

Felts had sent two men to bring Sidna's wife along from Hillsville where she'd remained since the shooting. Once it was clear there was no danger, he ushered her into the house with the demand that she produce a photo of her husband for our wanted posters. She did so with great dignity, and I enjoyed an immense if surreptitious belly laugh a few weeks later when I learned that the picture she'd given us was authentic, but thanks to the vagaries of 1912 photography it looked very little like Sidna Allen. The true likenesses she hid away. Alverta Edwards played the same trick when forced to provide a photo of her son Wesley. Of course, we had the photos of Sid Allen and Wesley Edwards' plastered on posters every dozen yards across a dozen counties in Virginia and North Carolina. But no one ever reported seeing the two fugitives, partly because they looked nothing like the public images. It took me back to my lumber scouting days, when I learned the native shrewdness of the Blue Ridge mountaineer would trump the so-called sophistication of the flatlander every time.

Next we raided Floyd's house in Fancy Gap and his sister Alverta Edwards' nearby home. The results were the same — evidence that the fugitives had been there to stock up on supplies and warm clothing, but otherwise, nothing but a photo of dubious value. No one was talking, despite all our threats and blandishments.

I soon realized this was not going to be easy, and that we'd capture the gang only with old-fashioned detective work: interviewing neighbors, ferreting out those with grudges. They were sure to exist even in the pro-Allen stronghold of Fancy Gap; offering rewards for information, cultivating informants, and active surveillance.

It was a strong part of my leadership ethos never to ask anything of my men I wasn't willing to do. I lay out in the cold and wet with them watching the trails from the mountain hollows that the Allens' partisans might use to support the fugitives. It was miserable work, and our rest was broken frequently by false alarms, nocturnal animals mostly; yet it was exhilarating all the same, at least for a while. Ernest Hemingway once wrote, 'There is no hunting like the hunting of man, and those who have hunted armed men long enough and liked it, never care for anything else thereafter.' William Baldwin knew this, too, and was what he tried to communicate to me the day we first met in Roanoke years earlier.

The search went on, stretching into a week, and still no results. Every day I expected my patrol or some other team to be ambushed. The Allens could have done it easily. Another reason I began to see 'em in a different light. If they'd been as bloodthirsty as reported, why didn't they knock off some of the hated Baldwins when they had the chance?

One day one of the locals intercepted us on the road and told me that Sid Allen and Wesley Edwards were hiding out in Devil's Den, an unusual geological feature near Fancy Gap well known to the neighborhood. He refused to guide us but gave us good directions. We rode to within a mile or so, then dismounted and crept down the mountain in a wide cordon. But by the time we discovered it, the birds had flown. Devils' Den was a deep fissure in the earth located a half-mile down the mountainside. It was not what we usually mean by the word 'cave,' but was a vast rupture in the very crust of the earth. Mammoth slabs of stone — we're talking the size of a two-storey building — had been thrust upward by some primeval cataclysm into a kind of inverted V, creating a space underneath where a handful of men could hide from pursuers, and shelter in relative comfort from the elements.

The fugitives were moving from place to place, never staying in one location more than one or two nights. Family and friends, using secret paths and deer trails known only to them, brought them food and whiskey and blankets. Their supporters, and there were many, were equally cautious, varying their routes and seldom using the same trail more than once every few days to avoid a discernible pattern. I knew we'd never be able to cover all the possible trails and hideouts. It appeared their plan was simply to wait us out, exhaust our patience until we gave up and went home.

The only possible counter-strategy was to make ourselves so visible, to make the fugitives feel such pressure, that it might eventually wear down their patience and force them to surrender.

In the event, it worked. A little more than a week after the shootout, Jack Allen came to see me in my room at the Elliott House. Dressed in his best dark suit, Stetson hat in hand, he stood at my door and asked politely if he could come in.

Jack was not as handsome as his younger brothers. He was heavier, fleshier, and coarser in features, his face heavily veined in red, evidently from sampling too much of the family product. But moonshine was really a sideline. As energetic and enterprising as the rest of the family, he ran a sawmill and a freight business, and was rumored to be the wealthiest of the brothers, Sidna included.

I offered him a chair while I sat on the bed and he began. "Mr. Hayne, I'm worried 'bout my son Friel. He's a good boy and ain't never been in trouble with the law. He only... " He paused, obviously thinking how not to further incriminate his son, "... uh, got involved in the shootin' 'cause he saw his kinfolk bein' shot at. It was kind of like self-defense. It just sort happened all of itself, you know what I mean?"

I replied, "Mr. Allen, I certainly respect your family's loyalty. But five people are dead, including the most prominent public officials in the county. Surely you understand the Commonwealth is not going to rest until all those who were, uh, involved, are brought to account."

"Yessir, I understand that," he nodded. "But my son ain't no murderer."

"Well, that's for the courts to decide. My job is to bring him and his kinfolks in so the courts can decide. It's a duty I hold under trust, and I aim to carry it out." Already I wasn't feeling as committed as I sounded, but I had to play my role convincingly. "My best advice is for Friel to turn himself in. It'll go a lot easier with him if he does."

"You really think so?" said Jack.

"I'm a policeman, not a judge and jury," I told him. "But when a perpetrator of a crime surrenders voluntarily, it's usually taken into favorable account in their trial."

"That's what I wanted to find out," he said. "And that's why I'm here. I wanta know if you'll give Friel a deal if he'll turn hisself in. I don't want him shot down like a dog in some holler by you Baldwins afore he has a chance to come in on his own."

That phrase later came to haunt me: 'give Friel a deal.'

"Mr. Allen, if it was up to me, I'd certainly be willing. But I'm not high enough up the chain of command to decide that. You need to speak to Mr. Baldwin or Mr. Felts. Unlike me, they're in direct contact with the Governor and the Attorney General. If the Commonwealth is willing, they're the one who can arrange it."

"Can you take me to see 'em? If you go with me, I know they'll listen," he said.

It was late, and Tom Felts was in his room. He looked annoyed when I knocked on his door with Jack Allen in tow, until I explained the purpose of the visit. Then he was all business, firm but respectful.

Felts said, "All right, Mr. Allen. I'll wire the Governor tonight." He gave me a sidelong look to quell my surprise. I knew the telegraph was closed. I thought he meant he was going to telephone the Governor. But that was equally unlikely at 11:00 at night.

He continued, "I'll send Mr. Hayne out to your place tomorrow with his answer. But you'd better be getting Friel ready to come in. Mr. Hayne can tell you; we've got posses scouring the mountains and sooner or later they're going to come across Friel and the rest. When they do, they've got authorization to shoot on sight. Remember, our detectives are not required to issue a warning."

Grim-faced, Jack said, "I'll remember, all right. You jes' git Friel a deal and I'll bring him in by ways yore detectives won't never come across." He put on his hat with a determined frown and stalked out.

I asked Felts, "You're going to call the Governor tonight?"

He gave me a long, pointed stare, the significance of which escaped me until later. Then he told me, "Stop by after breakfast. I'll let you know in the morning what message to take to Jack Allen."

The next morning Felts stopped me on the way into the dining room. He announced without preamble, "Five years."

"I beg your pardon?" I said.

He explained, "The Commonwealth agrees to let Friel Allen plead guilty to second degree murder in exchange for a sentence of five years."

Today we call it a plea bargain, and it's fairly common in criminal law. In fact, more criminal defendants 'plead out' than go to trial. But in 1912 it was unusual, and my skepticism must've been evident.

"It's all right," Felts assured me. "The Governor and the A.G. have signed off. But he's got to come in right away. The deal is good only for 24 hours. And he must... cooperate."

That last critical word was left hanging, and I didn't question it. We'd come up dry in our search for the fugitives, and the demand was growing intense to bring them in. Baldwin and Felts were under tremendous pressure to show progress in such a high-profile case and they didn't shy from using almost any means that were justified by the ends. The credibility and nationwide reputation of the Agency were at stake. So I didn't ask what he meant by 'cooperate,' but I knew Friel Allen would be highly reluctant to betray his kinfolks. Furthermore, I was doubtful any such agreement had occurred between the Agency and the Governor's office. But even though I was a valued employee, I wasn't in a position to challenge my boss — in effect, to question his veracity. I got my rifle and gun belt and gathered up a gang of four men from the Grand Posse. We went to the livery stable to saddle our horses and headed south toward Allen country at Fancy Gap.

Jack Allen met me at the stoop of his home before I could dismount. Hands on hips, he stood on the front steps in his denim overalls with a truculent look on his face as he surveyed my armed patrol. "Well?" he said.

"The state agrees," I told him, hoping I wouldn't have to go too far to take him into custody. "Five years in prison under a plea of second degree murder. The deal is good for 24 hours. Remember. He has to... cooperate," I added quietly.

"What's that mean, cooperate?" Jack asked.

"Quite honestly, Mr. Allen, I don't know," I told him. "I don't think it's been defined. But my belief is that the Commonwealth expects you and Friel to persuade the rest of the clan to surrender. And it'll be far better if they do. I got a lot of men out there with itchy trigger fingers, and I can't be everywhere to rein 'em in. I don't want to see your folks get hurt, and they're goin' to get caught sooner or later anyway. Now why don't ya'll try to get 'em to come on in?"

Jack studied me carefully. I knew the Allens trusted me, at least as much as they could trust any officer of the law. I looked him confidently in the eye and waited. After a few moments he decided.

"All right," he said. "Wait right there."

He stepped inside and re-emerged a moment later with his Winchester rifle. A momentary fright ran through me, but he shook his head as I reflexively reached for my sidearm. He walked out into the yard, raised the rifle in the air and fired three shots in quick succession, waited ten seconds or so and fired two more, then another ten seconds and fired one. A pre-arranged signal, obviously.

He said, "We'll go collect Friel."

"Where is he?" I asked.

"Well, by now he orta be in the barn," said Jack.

We rode 'round back of the house and dismounted. Several of my team pulled their sidearms, but I ordered them to holster the weapons. I stepped inside where several wagons and buggies loomed in the semi-dark. Jack Allen followed.

"Hey, Mr. Hayne," came a voice from the sepulchral darkness.

"That you, Friel?" He was sitting in the front seat of the family carriage. His father opened the doors wide, allowing light to stream in. Friel climbed down and stood abjectly in denim overalls and a weathered wool coat. He was slightly disheveled and with a growth of beard, but looked none the worse from his weeks in the bush. He nodded at his father, then at me. "Hey, Pa," he said. "Hey, Mr. Hayne."

I nodded back. "I'm glad to see you, Friel. For your own sake. Now, do I need to search you? Or you can hand over whatever you're carrying, or I'll take your word you're unarmed."

Actually, I was hoping he would give me the gun he'd used in the shootout. In 1912 the science of ballistics was too primitive for reliable matching of a particular gun with a particular bullet taken from a victim. But if we had his weapon, at least we'd know what caliber he'd used and could match it with the caliber of rounds recovered from the dead. Baldwin-Felts prided itself on being a scientific and up-to-date detective force, so to me this was standard operating procedure. Little did I suspect that it would have been a waste of time, because no forensics was done on the victims and no bullets were saved from their bodies.

That's right, none. I was shocked when I learned of it. But more about that later. I'm gettin' ahead of myself.

Friel snorted. "Even I know better'n to give myself up armed." He opened his coat wide, turned around, held out his arms. "Satisfied?"

Looking back on this episode, I have to laugh at how casual we all were. If this happened today, the cops would've swarmed all over him in force, maybe even those cops who wear combat gear and call themselves SWAT teams. Even though Friel surrendered voluntarily, they'd have him spread-eagled and face down on the ground and with handcuffs on him in a flash. Nowadays it seems the police can't arrest anybody without also humiliating 'em. But once I had his word and that of his father, I felt not the slightest danger. We rode wordlessly for the most part the two hours back to Hillsville. I was inclined to question him alone in his brooding silence. I knew he wouldn't give up his kin in any case. Four of them, to be exact.

***

The pressure of our surveillance and patrolling succeeded in the end, but indirectly, as I'd hoped. While we never actually discovered the fugitives in their hiding places, we did force them to lie low, and that by itself took a toll. These men were accustomed to a free and active life. They were leaders in their small world, engaged in business and other pursuits, part of a vibrant community. Being forced to squat in a covered hole or laurel thicket all day and all night, doing nothing day after day, week after week, proved too much for them.

The next to surrender was Sidna Edwards. According to him it was at the urging of his Uncle Jack Allen, pursuant to 'the deal for Friel.' Sid hadn't fired a shot in the courthouse that day, although he had helped his relatives escape and had given his pistol to his Uncle Floyd in the final stage of the gunfight. He remained separate from his brother Wesley and his other kin while on the lam. Doubtless he reasoned he'd get off with a light sentence.

Weighing that hope against the life of a hunted animal, the decision was easy. He rode up early of a morning to one of my mounted patrols, wearing a sheepish grin as if he'd only been playing truant from school. The agents spurred their horses alongside him as he raised his hands, and one of them snatched him out of the saddle by his collar. Totally unprepared, Sidna hit the ground hard and was lucky not to be injured. Then they dismounted and as roughly as they could, jerked his hands behind his back, lashed them painfully and tied him around the middle, and thrust him back on his horse for the ride into town. They threatened to shoot him 'attempting to escape' is he so much as twitched or opened his mouth. The arrest was witnessed from the shadows, by whom I never learned, but the word spread quickly through the 'mountain telegraph' that the Baldwins meant business, serious business. I suppose that helped us some, but it also left bad feelings toward Baldwin-Felts in the hearts of the locals that exist even today. Any good will I might've gained for the Agency from the humane handling of Friel Allen was instantly lost.

There were some fine men in the Baldwin-Felts ranks, some of the finest I ever knew, just as there are many fine men in police work today. But then as now, I'm sorry to say, some of them were pure thugs, the sort that get swollen up with a little bit of authority and

141

take sadistic pleasure in using it to torment their fellows. Problem was, we'd had to expand our force considerably and in a hurry, and that left our screening of people hasty and haphazard. There simply wasn't time to do an exhaustive background check, and there was only a limited pool of applicants to start with. We still had to maintain our other commitments to the railroads, the mines, and so forth. We couldn't draw down those assignments in any big numbers. By the time the Allen pursuit ended, the Agency had added nearly a hundred new men in Southwest Virginia. That may not sound like a lot, but it represented almost a hundred percent increase in our strength, and all in about two months' time. It was inevitable, though regrettable, that the quality of our agents would suffer.

Anyway, we now had Sidna Edwards and Friel Allen. That made two down and three to go.

A week later, when the need for results to justify our efforts — and the expense — was becoming intolerable, Claude Allen gave us a break. Somehow he had eluded all our patrols, but the constant pressure got to him and he gave himself up. He never claimed it was because of Uncle Jack's influence. Somehow that never came up in the interrogation. But Jack and Friel Allen claimed him as proof of their promise to cooperate. Too bad our side didn't keep its promise.

A routine agency sweep came across a forlorn Claude Allen standing by the roadside in his overalls and a mud-stained Navy pea jacket. He had a burlap bag containing some food and spare socks, two wet and filthy quilts under his arm, and $84.00 in his pocket — his life savings, he said. He also had his father's compact five-shot revolver. The Agency men trussed him up and hustled him off to jail, and he soon followed his father to Roanoke. That made three down and two left.

Even now, after all the years, I still wonder about Claude and marvel how he came in of his own accord when he might have eluded us indefinitely. If he'd foreseen what lay at the end of the road a year later, he would never have surrendered; nor would I if I'd been him.

The final two outlaws, Sidna Allen and his nephew Wesley Edwards, proved to be more resourceful and elusive than the others; and I guess, more determined to remain free. They escaped our net, avoiding detection despite all the wanted posters and news headlines. They not only made it out of the state, but also out of the South. I'll tell you shortly how they did it. Their escape provided the greatest challenge to the Agency, and certainly the greatest in my career as a detective. But we got 'em in the end, although by then I'd left the Agency. Baldwin himself garnered the laudatory headlines.

But while I was the lead pursuer, I was also colorful, you might say. I carried a Springfield '03 rifle instead of the more common Winchester lever-action, and I wore an Army campaign hat instead of the preferred Baldwin-Felts bowler. I'm ashamed to admit I began to enjoy the attention — secretly — although I never wavered in my refusal to talk to the press. Yet that seemed to whet their appetites for a story. True or not, it made no difference, as long as it sold papers.

The capture of Sid Allen and Wesley Edwards is one of the most fascinating chapters in the whole story; fascinating and sad, because it's a story of love and love betrayed. I was the architect of that betrayal.

Chapter Eight

After a month scouring the hills and hollows in three counties, we had to acknowledge that Sid Allen and Wesley Edwards had indeed given us the slip. The Agency was billing the state an enormous amount to keep a hundred men in the field hunting the fugitives, and Bill Baldwin finally decided to economize and scale back. I took advantage of the drawdown and respite to go home for some R&R, although we didn't use that term in 1912. I was totally exhausted — physically from the exertions of the hunt, from the cold and wet nights laying in futile ambush in the hills, and emotionally from gnawing doubts about my role in bringing the Allens to justice. It was beginning to dawn on me as I read the hysterical accounts in the papers, even if I was the hero in many of them, that these accounts were fed by hatred, not by any desire to tell the truth. That meant I was more likely helping bring the Allens to injustice. Sure, they'd committed a serious crime. But I had strong doubts about the charges of conspiracy or a pre-meditated attack on the court. I began to question whether the Allens could get a fair trial. The state wanted their blood, but I wanted no part in a judicial lynching.

My parents were delighted to have me home, obviously relieved that I'd avoided the fate of many sons of prominent old families; namely, becoming a wastrel. Since I was now a local celebrity, they took some pride, especially my father, in showing me off. In spite of myself, I found it pleasant that fame opened many doors. After being allowed to get some needed rest, the folks launched me on a round of neighborhood parties and balls and hunts, which quickly began to pall — until Emma. Emma Romilly.

It was at a meet of the Rappahannock Hunt, of which Mother was Master of Foxhounds; one of the first, if not the first woman MFH in this very conservative state. I'd spent so much time on horseback hunting the Allens that I wasn't too excited about a fox hunt, but I went along to humor my parents. It was nice for a change to dress up in hunting pinks and stock tie and partake of this ancient rite.

We assembled at Owings Meadow near Sperryville after a sumptuous breakfast and the traditional stirrup cup. The pack was milling about with yelps of excitement and anticipation, and that spirit began to communicate itself to me. I was atop one of the Hayne's legendary Arabians bred by Mother. Mandrake was a chestnut gelding that pranced and tossed eagerly. I collected the horse and rode him around to warm up and settle him down. Circling the gathering riders, I almost collided with a young woman who'd quietly ridden up on a dark bay Thoroughbred mare. She flashed me a dazzling smile as I reined in.

"Too much horse for you?" She taunted, though with a friendly laugh.

I'm seldom at a loss for words, but I was stricken speechless by the image of this girl. The first thing I noticed, beside her musical voice and beatific smile, was that she was riding astride and dressed in — well, I guess you'd say the female version of a man's traditional riding habit — hard cap, high boots and breeches, and form-fitting black hunt coat. I'd never seen a female so attired and was duly shocked down to my old-fashioned Virginia roots.

This may come as a surprise even to those who know anything about horses and equestrian culture. For most of the modern period — say, the 16th Century through the beginning of our own 20th — women riders in the European world rode sidesaddle, and that included the U.S.A. The typical female riding attire was full skirts, perhaps a matching, fitted jacket, and often a top hat or female bonnet of some kind. My mother was a great equestrienne who rode to the hounds at every opportunity, and this is almost always how I saw her dressed, and riding sidesaddle.

Nothing is more becoming to a woman than modern riding habit if she has the figure for it, which Emma certainly had. She was tall and slim, yet shapely in all the right places. She peered at me with a searching look, and I feared she's construed my tongue-tied state as discourtesy, a failing no Virginia gentlemen should ever be guilty of. I cleared my throat awkwardly, searching for something clever to say, when she leaned over her horse's withers and extended her hand. I tried valiantly to keep my eyes elevated and not glued to the front of her hunt coat.

"I'm Emma," she said. "Emma Romilly."

It was another one of those moments I recognized as life-changing even as it was unfolding, a moment heavy with expectancy, when time and motion were frozen, and all I saw and heard was… her. But finally I found my voice. "Pleased to meet you," I said, somehow managing to avoid a stammer. "I'm Carter Hayne."

"Oh," she laughed, a ripple that delighted the ear. "The Carter Hayne? Intrepid tracker-down of desperadoes? Wily catcher-in-chief of outlaws?"

"The very same." I laughed, too, at her irreverence of my exalted status. I was taken with her obvious sense of fun.

"Then Eleanor Hayne is your mother," she said.

"The very same," I said again, and we both laughed.

The Good Book says that a soft voice is an excellent thing in a woman. Hers was throaty, soft, and excellent, unlike the tinny, reedy voices of so many modern women, who sound like perpetual adolescents. It was much like my mother's, whose speech retained an echo of Tidewater Virginia. Mother pronounced my name something like 'Cyahtah.' And she said – almost -- 'hoose' and 'oot;' instead of 'house' and 'out,' 'gyahden' instead of 'garden.' Emma's accent was similar.

I asked, "Where are you from?"

"Aiken, by way of Charleston," she answered. That accounted for the accent.

"Aiken, South Carolina?" I repeated. "The self-anointed horse capital of the South?" I was deliberately sarcastic, seeing if I could bait her. But she kept complete control.

"The very same," she grinned.

"Well," I said, gesturing at her attire. "If you Aikenite ladies are wearing pants and riding astride, I suppose it won't be long before the contagion hits us here in Virginia."

"Can't be soon enough," she smiled that smile again that melted my heart. "You may not care to know it; but after all, you Virginians didn't invent the equestrian arts all by yourselves."

The hunt began and away we trotted, she on her swift-footed mare, and I… Well, my attention was on Emma, not on keeping my seat. Fortunately I'd been riding since boyhood; taking fences and ditches was more or less automatic and unconscious. I was

147

conscious only of her seamless fluidity, of her complete oneness with her mount. She rode divinely at the trot, canter, and gallop — easily, with a grace equal to her appearance and her speech. I tried to keep pace with her but felt leaden and earthbound, while she was lithe and free.

***

That evening the Hunt hosted a formal supper and ball at Windy Hill, a sprawling 18th Century manor house between Madison and Sperryville. I felt stiff and awkward in the unaccustomed scarlet tails and white tie, but hoped my discomfort would pass itself off as the steely reserve of an intrepid tracker-down of desperadoes. Scores of people came up to congratulate me and, I suppose, bask in my fame. But I scarcely saw any of them and remember none of them. I only had eyes for Emma Romilly. I scanned the crowd in growing despair that she wasn't there.

After the morning hunt, I had interrogated Mother to within an inch of her life about this mysterious beauty. I learned that she came of an old South Carolina family and was one of the country's noted horsewomen, a pioneer in riding as an international competitive sport. Emma had been picked for the American equestrian team to compete at the 1912 World Equestrian Games in Paris and had come to Virginia horse country with its long, open meadows to practice for the cross-county event. To help pay her way she was also conducting a riding school for the local belles in 'Little' Washington, the county seat of Rappahannock County. She was staying with the Marshalls, old friends of our family.

I was taken aback at the concept of a riding school. I'd always thought horsemanship was something young Southern boys and girls grew up with and learned naturally. Formal instruction in riding was as new an idea to me as women riding astride. But, as my mother explained, "It's a new day dawning, Carter." At any rate, I was delighted to learn Emma would be in the area for a couple of months. Suddenly I had something fresh and marvelous to look forward to besides wrestling with my doubts and troubles. But where was she? Mother had said she was invited to the ball and was certain to attend.

At the last minute, just as the guests were being called in to supper, she tripped through the wide double door, holding her skirts and trailed by a hapless fat man whom I'd never seen. The chandeliers picked out the highlights in her thick honey-auburn hair. Suddenly there was a strange tightness in my chest I'd never experienced.

My training at VMI and the Marine Corps was not in vain. Earlier I'd conducted a reconnaissance of the dining room, then staged a bold raid upon the place cards, switching mine — easy enough to do as a single male — to the seat next to hers at the long glittering table. As the butler sounded the chimes, I sidled innocently in to the banquet amid a gay hubbub of voices and laughter. Then I noticed she was scanning the room as diligently as I'd done earlier. Could she possibly be searching for me? My heart began to thump as I intercepted her at her place. Glad of the opportunity to cut a dash, I pulled out her chair before her cumbrous escort could perform the duty.

"Carter Hayne," I said. "Wily catcher-in-chief of outlaws. At your service."

She laughed her silvery, sparkling laugh again, and by this time I was enchanted. No, I was helplessly ensnared. She was a swirl of silk and taffeta in a white ball gown cut just low enough to tempt my gaze again.

I stole a glance at her décolletage as I seated her and took my place. She wore a tight little smile that made me suspect she knew exactly what I was doing but didn't mind. Her dark eyes, somehow both grave and merry, danced as she looked up at me boldly.

The soul of politeness, Emma introduced me to her date, a visitor of her hosts in Little Washington whose name I immediately forgot. While she gave most of her time and attention to me, she always tried to include him in the conversation and was careful not to snub him in any way. I was as impressed by her kindness as by her beauty, wit, and charm.

Frankly, I know there are — were — more beautiful women, at least in a technical sense. But Emma wore her loveliness unconsciously, like an afterthought. It was all the more attractive because it was unstudied, because it was utterly authentic and without artifice. There was something ineffably graceful about the way she held and carried herself that transcended beauty. And her hands. Ah, what hands. It's often said of a skilled rider that he or she 'has good hands.' She had good hands. Strong hands, elegant hands, exquisite hands, hands to match her voice. Yet her voice and sparkling laugh contained a touch of sadness or wistfulness, as if she knew how fleeting beauty was, and life itself.

It's still hard for me to believe after 56 years since it seemed so unlikely at the time — you might say impossible — but it turned out that Emma was as attracted to me as I to her. We 'were surprised by Joy,' as the poet said, although we were blessed to drink of Joy for woefully too short a time.

After supper she turned to me with a sly smile. Then she stared pointedly across the table with a subtle nod to Leyla Marshall, a daughter of her host family, whereupon that young lady went into a classic

Southern swoon. Emma had orchestrated an episode straight out of a 19th Century romance novel, but it worked. Naturally Miss Marshall had to be taken home at once, and naturally Mr. Ponderous, the Marshall family's other out-of-town visitor, was obliged as a gentleman to do the honors.

"But what about Emma?" he asked plaintively. All the dowagers nodded in agreement like a tree full of owls.

I stepped forward gallantly. It took an effort to keep the triumph out of my voice. "I'll see that Miss Romilly gets home," I said.

From that moment Emma and I were together until the summer of 1917, when I shipped out to France with the AEF, the American Expeditionary Force, our contribution to World War I. And even then she tried to wrangle a posting as a Red Cross volunteer and follow me to France, although that attempt failed. There was also the interlude soon after we met. In the summer of 1912 she went to Paris for the world riding competition and came back with a bronze medal for team eventing. It was the first-ever such medal for a U.S. equestrian team. By that time my glory had begun to fade as mention of me in the papers subsided, while she became the heroine of the horse set.

But, oh, that first night at Windy Hill, a night of discovery when all things seemed possible, when the world stretched before us like a land of dreams. After supper on that magical, memorable evening, we went out on the terrace and looked at the stars and the dark shadow of the Blue Ridge in the distance where my destiny had taken such a strange turn.

Staring up at the sparkling night sky, she said to my utter surprise, "'I have loved the stars too fondly to be fearful of the night.'"

I was surprised and thrilled as she quoted one of my favorite passages, and I quoted the companion line back to her: " 'Though my soul may set in darkness, it will rise in perfect light.'"

Now it was her turn to be surprised. "Why, Mr. Hayne, you amaze me. I didn't expect such a hard-bitten lawman to be a lover of poetry as well."

I stammered, "I, ah... I'm afraid you've discovered my guilty secret. I do love poetry. But I've always kept it concealed. As you observed, it doesn't fit well with my chosen line of work."

"Well, your secret is safe with me," she said. "But I don't know why you should hide it so. Think of the Cavalier Poets, great poets and great men-at-arms. Frankly, I believe a man without some poetry in his soul is little more than a brute."

She was not just a shallow socialite, not just another pretty face. Her intelligence surpassed her beauty. She was widely read and spoke French and Italian. She could recite Dante and Shakespeare by the bushel. And she had a seriousness of purpose, a deep reservoir of common sense, and compassion for her fellow man that you might not expect in a daughter of privilege. I felt at once this was someone I could confide in, someone who'd understand the inner struggle I was waging with myself.

I also knew I'd fallen in love. It seems foolish, perhaps, to have decided so profound a matter on such short acquaintance. But it was less a decision than a recognition. And for those who scoff at such a love, scoffers who've never known a Great Love, whose hearts are closed up like a miser's fist, I can only offer this old wisdom of Marlowe's: "Where both deliberate, the love is slight: who ever loved who loved not at first sight?"

Like most people in that place and time, Emma was fascinated by the 'Hillsville Horror' and hung raptly upon the tale, and especially the story of my pivotal role in the aftermath. As my confidence grew, I began to share the reservations about the conduct of Baldwin-Felts, and especially my worry that the Allens were going to be railroaded to their deaths.

"The state doesn't want justice, it wants blood," I told her. "The politicians in the Commonwealth are already calling for the death penalty for all the Allens. The state has seized all their property in Carroll County, even before they've been tried. Now they have no assets with which to mount a defense."

"So it's 'Sentence first, verdict afterward,' is it?"

"Yes, you might say that."

"'Stuff and nonsense, said Alice.'" She quoted Lewis Carroll with some asperity.

"Except this nonsense is deadly serious," I replied. "The state seems to regard the shooting of public officials as the most heinous of crimes, and that fact more than the mere fact of murder itself is what justifies capital punishment. Yet these same officials were trying to kill Floyd Allen and his kin. Are the lives of public officials more sacred than the lives of private citizens?"

I guess I got kind of worked up. She was the first person with whom I'd ever felt able to unburden myself. "I'm truly sorry about Judge Massie, the Sheriff, Bill Foster, and the others. The Allens will have to pay for their deaths. But if the dead had just been regular folks, they'd be facing prison time, not execution. Are public officials really our servants, as they like to claim, or our masters? Is killing one of them worse than killing one of us peasants?"

"So it would seem, as a practical matter," she said.

"Well, I hold the quaint idea that public servants are just that. They take the job knowing it carries risks, especially police work, and they accept those risks as part of the privilege of serving us, their employers, who pay them with our taxes."

"Maybe you're too much of an idealist," she said.

"That's what Tom Felts tells me all the time."

"Well, if you can't be true to yourself and serve Baldwin-Felts, then it's time to look for another line of work," she said.

I was taken aback, even though I knew intuitively she was right. From the very beginning we had that kind of communication, the ability to verbalize what the other was thinking. When I remained silent, musing, doubting, she pressed on.

"Carter, like all men, you desire justice," she said in her rich, inimitable voice that alone would have held me captive to every word. "But man is a fallen creature, and the societies he creates are flawed. Perfect justice in this life is impossible. History is full of men and women falsely accused for state expediency or to satisfy the passions of the mob. But we can't hide behind our human fallibility as an excuse. We have to strive for better justice, even if perfect justice is beyond our reach. And if we want to be treated justly, we must act justly. That means you must act justly. I don't mean to presume with unsolicited advice, but after what you've told me, I don't see how you can continue on with Baldwin-Felts."

"Miss Romilly, I'm sure you're right. But... but except for riding and shooting and catching bad men, I don't seem to have a lot of skills. I'm ashamed to reveal this dark side of my nature, but after the Philippine War and then the years as a hired gun for Baldwin-Felts, I've developed a taste for... for what,

I'm not sure. The danger and excitement, I suppose. Now I don't know what else I'd do; what else I'd be good for. Poetry won't get me far in this mad world," I said, surprising myself at confiding so intimately to a virtual stranger. But then, she didn't feel like a stranger.

She took my hand and held it in both of hers, sending a bolt of joy right down to my toes. "Call me Emma." Then she said, "I know this is hard for you. But the soul's duty to itself is to find its purpose. You must be willing to get rid of the life you've planned so as to have the life that's waiting for you. You must create who you want to be instead of re-enacting who you were."

No one had ever spoken to me like this before, man or woman. It plunged me into a kind of astonished ecstasy — her remarkable insights, and the evidence that she cared about me.

"I hear you, and I think you must be right, but... but..."

"But you don't know how to turn it into concrete action, is that what you're trying to say?"

"Yes, precisely."

She said, "The best advice about life I ever had, advice from my riding teacher when jumping fences is, 'head up, heels down, heart in the right place.'"

"But what does that mean, in terms of real life, in terms of making such an important life choice?" I was almost beside myself trying to decipher the wisdom she was sharing.

"Oh, you poor man," she laughed, and the music of it relieved my anxiety in an instant. "It's obvious. You've been on the enforcement side of the law. Now the time has come to be on the other side, to jump the fence, as it were. You should become a lawyer and defend people. People like the Allens, people like your coalminers who've been denied justice."

***

At Tom Felts' request, I stopped in Roanoke on the way back from Rappahannock County, where I could hardly tear myself away from Emma. But she'd promised to come down to Roanoke the following weekend, and I couldn't keep my mind on anything else. However, as long as I was in Baldwin-Felts' employ, duty called. Tom Felts and I met for breakfast at the Hotel Roanoke before I caught the train for Galax, where one of the Agency men would meet me — in a new Ford automobile of all things, and take me on to Hillsville to wrap up the manhunt.

We went over the plans for scaling back the search, since Felts agreed with my conclusion that Sidna Allen and Wesley Edwards, the only remaining fugitives, had flown and were no doubt far from the Blue Ridge by now.

Felts was a great admirer of the Royal Canadian Mounted Police, considered by many the premier police force in the world. Of course, they were a government agency and we were private. But Baldwin and Felts wanted to be able to claim the Mounties' motto for their Agency: 'We always get our man.' To achieve that success, both men believed in 'turning' family and friends, paying informants, and running a network of spies. Tom Felts especially believed anyone could be induced to betray a wanted man with the liberal application of cash. Carter Hayne the idealist was less certain, although I have to admit Felts proved right more often than not.

To locate Wesley Edwards, Tom's idea was to tighten up surveillance on the Iroller family. The

daughter Maude Iroller was known to be Wesley's girl.
And since he and his Uncle Sid Allen were presumed
to have stuck together, the trail to Wesley would also
lead us to Sid, who was the bigger game. With some
hesitation, I acknowledged the directive and promised
to put it into effect.

Then, amid the hum of voices and the clatter of
dishes, Felts pursed his lips and asked, "Have you seen
this report in the paper?"

"No," I said modestly, thinking he was talking
about another Carter Hayne article.

"It's incredible. That fantastic new passenger liner
Titanic sank two days ago in the North Atlantic. Over
1500 souls were lost. They're saying it's the greatest
maritime disaster in modern times."

"Let me see," I said. He handed over the newspaper.
I skimmed the article on the front page and was about
to turn to the inside continuation page when I noticed
another headline below the fold: FLOYD ALLEN'S
NEPHEW FRIEL ARRAIGNED ON MURDER
CHARGES; FACES LIFE IN PRISON.

The blood drained from my face and I felt a surge
of lava rising in my chest. I glared at Tom who sipped
his coffee and eyed me impassively until he noticed
my expression.

"What's wrong, Carter? Did you know someone on
the Titanic?"

I had to fight down the surge of anger. "This is
what's wrong," I snarled, jabbing a finger at the Friel
Allen story. Normally the epitome of aplomb and self-
control, Tom seemed momentarily agitated.

"Well, what did you expect?" he said defensively.
"Friel Allen is a murderer. Just like all his kin."

"That's for a jury to decide, not you or me. I've
been the one huntin' 'em, these so-called crazed
murderers who invaded the Hillsville courthouse to

perpetuate a massacre and who were going to come back and shoot up the town, remember? They could have killed half of us from ambush in the hills and hollers they know like the insides of their pockets. But not one ever took a shot at us. Doesn't that make you wonder at all about the official version?"

"No, but I am beginning to wonder about you. Whose side are you on?" asked Felts.

"I'm on the side of keeping our word. We made a promise to Friel and his father if he'd surrender voluntarily. Have you forgotten so soon?"

"I didn't regard it as a promise. Anyway, an offer made to a felon to bring about his capture is hardly binding."

"We didn't capture him," I exclaimed. "Matter of fact, we didn't capture any of them. They all gave themselves up — Sid Edwards, Claude Allen, and then Friel. Sid Allen and Wesley Edwards have flown. But they never fought us." My voice had risen, and several nearby diners turned and stared in surprise. "Maybe you think a deal with a fugitive isn't binding, but you assured me that Mr. Baldwin had contacted the Governor and that Friel was promised a lesser charge and a light sentence. Five years, remember?"

Felts said nothing, only glared at me.

I went on. "And I gave Jack Allen my word, based on what you told me. But there was never any deal for Friel, was there? No one got any agreement from the Governor."

Felts said finally, "Of course not. How can you be so naïve?"

"You used me and the trust I'd established to deceive Jack Allen in order to snare his son."

I was furious beyond words, but had to tread carefully. He was still my boss, after all. Yet Emma's image and words hovered in my mind, infusing me with a new kind of courage — moral courage, you might say. I wanted to be worthy of her.

Felts said, "I did what was necessary to fulfill our commission."

"I don't presume to tell you how to run the Agency," I answered. "But in this case it's my honor on the line. You exploited it without any regard for my good name. You thought only that you could use such a low trick because you've already tried and convicted 'em."

"I don't understand why you're making a personal matter of this, Carter," said Felts. "Bill and I did only what was right and necessary to bring these assassins to justice. I can only conclude the stress of the case has affected your judgment. Maybe you ought to take a long sabbatical." There was a heavy emphasis on the word sabbatical that implied more than a temporary separation. "That seems to be the only option, since you've declined to help us police the mines in West Virginia."

"Yes, maybe that's just the ticket," I said, staring him down and calling his bluff, but hoping it was a bluff.

Felts's eyes opened in alarm and he began to back-paddle at once. "But let's not be hasty," he said. "Or angry without cause. It never occurred to me that you believed we were making a sincere deal with Friel. Had I understood your feelings, I would have handled it differently." I knew that was as close to an apology as I was likely to get. He continued, "I do think you need some time off. We've all been pushed to the limit by this Allen case. But you're our best man and we need you now more than ever. Help us get close to the Irollers. Bring in Sid Allen and Wesley Edwards, then take a month off. With pay," he added.

159

I sighed in acquiescence. Why I didn't resign outright then and there, I honestly can't say. I had the ability to see all sides of a question, which can be a blessing and a curse. I understood Felts' view of justice, even while mine was starting to diverge significantly. The Allen clan had committed serious crimes, after all, and shouldn't be expected to escape punishment. I just wanted to see the punishment commensurate with the deed. I wanted no part of official vengeance, especially when official persecution had goaded Floyd into the fatal deed in the first place.

Also, I suppose I thought by staying on I could somehow make restitution, repair the damage from the Agency's cynical deception of Friel Allen and his father Jack. And I really didn't expect the Irollers to betray Wesley Edwards. But though I couldn't know it at the time, this was a rare case when my instincts failed me. In any case, I hoped to buy some time by going along with Felts' plan. Time to do what I couldn't have said, so with hindsight, I see I was just temporizing. I knew Emma was right. I had to jump the fence. But knowing and doing are two different things, and I couldn't yet muster the full courage to make the jump. I could only proceed in small steps. From then on I worked persistently, if not openly, to satisfy my own sense of justice, including the gathering of evidence that might mitigate the charges against the Allens.

From then on, my days with the Agency were numbered. It only took one more outrage to push me over the edge.

***

On the train ride to Galax, I mentally reviewed the remaining agents to decide who might be suitable to approach the Iroller family, win their confidence, and try to suborn Maude. By the end of the ride, and despite my increasingly unsettled mind, I'd hit upon a solution. At the same time I rationalized that while Sid Allen and Wesley Edwards shouldn't be allowed to escape unpunished, I'd do what I could to ensure their punishment was just, once we had them in custody. For a short spell Emma's urging me into a different branch of the law subsided into the background of renewed activity, although my thoughts of her beauty and soothing presence did not.

I picked Philo Hylton, a ruggedly handsome Carroll County man of winning smile and disposition — a born womanizer according to some of his colleagues — to pay court to Maude and try to get a lead on Wesley Edwards' whereabouts. With her black hair and sloe eyes, Maude was a mountain beauty. Inspired by the chance to get close to her, Philo came up with a clever solution: first get close to Pa Iroller.

Philo rode up one afternoon leading Mr. Iroller's prize gelding quarter horse. An Agency 'detective' had borrowed it earlier — let's put the right word on it and say confiscated — when his mount was worn out in the strenuous search for the Allens through the rugged terrain. To be sure, he'd left his foundered horse in exchange, but then it had promptly expired. Pa Iroller was naturally irate, as were scores of residents of the lower County who suffered similar outrages in the name of the Baldwin-Felts brand of justice. So when Philo reined in with the animal in tow, sleekly fed, groomed, and re-shod, and with $20 in Yankee gold for its use, the delighted Irollers invited him in for supper. With his legendary charm, it was all he needed to make his play for Maude, while winning the confidence of her pa at the same time. Moreover, Felts had authorized him to pay Iroller Senior up to $500 'for information leading to the capture of Wesley Edwards and Sidna Allen.' In practical terms, that meant a $500 bribe to the pater familias to coerce his daughter into turning in her boyfriend. In retrospect, and in light of the Irollers' minimal loyalty to poor Wesley Edwards, half that figure would have sufficed.

Chapter Nine

Here I am, an old man in a dry month. After all I've seen and done in my long life, I ought to be a storehouse of wisdom. But in my waning days all I can affirm for certain is that life is inscrutable, unpredictable, and perplexing. This is true now, and it was true when I was young. The Hillsville tragedy made me aware of this fact of life more than anything else could have.

It was the spring of 1912 that in the midst of my greatest happiness I experienced my greatest crisis. As Floyd and Claude Allen went on trial for their lives, I reached a critical turning point. I was 32 years old and just on the threshold of finding myself at last. I wasn't at all sure what I'd find. Yet I had found Emma and a Great Love. Without her support and encouragement, I might not have taken the right turn when put to the test. To pass the test required a radical departure, no doubt about it. There I was with an exemplary career, the darling of the press and my contemporaries, and suddenly my sterling reputation exploded in controversy that dogged me for years. My father all but disowned me. I made the right decision. But since life is messy and complicated, doing the right thing still brought painful consequences in its wake.

First I need to tell about the hunt for Sid Allen and Wesley Edwards, which was still my responsibility while I remained on good terms with the Agency. Everyone in the lower County knew Wesley was hopelessly in love with Maude Iroller. But it was rumored that Maude didn't necessarily return the sentiment, and especially now that her fellow was one of the most wanted fugitives in U.S. history. Consequently, I believed she was the key to finding them. My agent Philo Hylton engaged room and board with Maude's family and gained their confidence. And though he never said anything — too much the gentlemen — I suspected that he gained more from Maude than just her confidence.

He dutifully turned in detailed reports. Since there were money payments to the Irollers, and I wanted to make sure all was accounted for scrupulously. This is what saved me in the end, when the crisis with the Agency reached its boiling point. With a twinge of conscience about engineering a betrayal, I urged Philo to use all his tricks, within the law, to induce Maude to reveal where the two fugitives were hiding. I was suddenly in love and felt somehow I wasn't just suborning the betrayal of Wesley and his beloved, but of love itself. I guess it's true that love is the wisdom of the fool and the folly of the wise.

To avoid public attention, Philo and I arranged our meetings in the hayloft above a livery stable in Hillsville. We settled on some bales of hay, and I offered him a pull from my pocket flask, which contained not the moonshine he was used to but fine Kentucky bourbon. Smiling, he examined the monogrammed sterling container with interest, grabbed it and took a long happy swig.

I said, "Now that you're properly lubricated, Philo, let's have your report."

He produced a sheaf of papers from his side pocket, covered in a surprisingly neat hand. In fact, I never ceased to be surprised by the citizens of the Blue Ridge. His archaic Elizabethan speech may have conveyed the impression that he was barely educated, but his written language was quite literate.

"It's all in there."

"Thanks," I said. "Just give me the short version."

"Wahl, I done like you ordered and got close to the Irollers. I tell you, that Maude, she's a beauty. She's got me wound up like an eight day clock." Reaching for the flask, he took another pull. The sterling gleamed softly in the half-light, and he shook his head slowly, whether from wonder or disdain, I couldn't tell.

"The question is, have you got her wound up?" I said.

"Oh, yes, she's a hot-blooded 'un. And a talker. Her tongue wags at both ends."

"And Wesley Edwards?"

"He's been a-writin' her ever couple of days. But he should of stayed closer to home. With Maude, it's out of sight, out of mind, even with his love letters. I swear they would melt the horns off a swayback bull."

"Have you seen any of the letters? Have you learned where he and Sid Allen are hiding?"

Philo smiled triumphantly. "Yes, sir, I finally got a peek at 'em. No return address, but I seen the postmark. And then I put it hard to Pa Iroller, who finally talked. Mr. Hayne, you jest ain't goin' to believe it." He scuffed a wad of hay with the heel of his boot and looked at me intently.

"Try me," I said.

"Them two is hidin' out in Des Moines, Iowa," Philo said triumphantly. I smiled at his pronouncing the city Dees Moines. "That's as far as they got when they run plumb out of money. So they holed up there an' got theirselves jobs."

Des Moines! I'd never been to Des Moines. In fact, like many people of my place and time, I'd never been west of the Appalachians, except for my tour of duty in the far Pacific. But I had an image in my mind's eye of Iowa, whether accurate or not I couldn't say, of endless flat and featureless plains. Des Moines. I could hardly conceive of a more unlikely place for two Virginia mountaineers.

Six months later Bill Baldwin himself led the team that with Maude's help located Sid Allen and Wesley Edwards and brought them back to Virginia in irons. I'll tell about it in the proper order. By that time I'd broken with the Agency during the capital trial of Floyd Allen, the next episode in the saga. Suddenly, though temporarily, I was as much a villain in the headlines as I'd been a hero before.

***

The Sixth Amendment of the Bill of Rights to the Constitution guarantees a criminal defendant the right to a speedy trial, although 'speedy' isn't actually defined. The Framers clearly had in mind the corrupt judicial system of England which they had escaped, and in which an accused person might languish in jail for years at the whim of the Crown without ever being charged, much less tried. But I wonder if the Framers considered the potential injustice of a trial that was too speedy, when the defendant was hustled into court before passions had time to cool and reason to re-assert itself. This is precisely what happened to Floyd Allen, his son Claude, and his nephew Friel near the end of April 1912. Victor, too. He was tried with the rest of the clan on capital charges, although his only crimes were to be the son of Floyd Allen and to remain with his wounded father after the gun battle to tend his wounds. Victor was tried for murder and acquitted within 30 minutes. The state clearly realized they'd never get a conviction, so all the other charges were dropped and Victor went free. In relating his story now, I'm not following the actual sequence of events, but I dispose of his part in the tale since he was no longer a defendant in the main trials that followed.

The defense had petitioned for a change of venue, and the Allen trials were to be held in Wytheville, the County Seat of Wythe County, about 30 miles north of Hillsville. The state spared no expense. There was a bottomless well of state funds to pay for five attorneys for the prosecution and a seemingly endless parade of witnesses to testify against the Allens. I was one of them, or so they thought.

Floyd Landreth headed the prosecution team. He'd been Assistant Commonwealth Attorney under the slain Bill Foster, was in the Hillsville Courthouse that day, and had survived the gun battle. Needless to say, he was out for blood.

Floyd's case was to be the trial of the century in Virginia — literally a show trial — intended to erase the international shame of the Hillsville Horror. The state was out to prove to the rest of the world that the Best People still ruled in Virginia and had the will and the means to keep the bootleggin', gun-totin' highlanders in their place.

Wythe County was more urban than its neighbor Carroll County. Its people were mostly townsmen, valley dwellers and not mountaineers. The state was glad to move the trials from Carroll County, evidently in the belief the citizens of Wytheville would be inclined to see things different from the rough-and-tumble denizens of the Blue Ridge. Why defense counsel didn't understand this, too, eludes me. Perhaps it was fear that feelings were running too high against the Allens in Hillsville to ensure a fair trial. But in retrospect, I believe the defense erred, the first of many fatal errors — literally fatal for Floyd and his son Claude.

Popular sentiment in Carroll County was evenly divided or even ran slightly in support of the Allens, as subsequent events showed. In neighboring Wythe County, there was little sympathy for the plight of the mountain people, little grasp of the fierce pride they needed to cope with a modern world they scarcely understood. The irony is that the defense might have been able to call a more sympathetic jury in Hillsville than anywhere else. But sadly, that's a matter of hindsight.

As if to accentuate the difference in local sensibilities, the Wytheville courthouse was positively ornate in contrast to the stark simplicity of its sister edifice in Hillsville. It boasted a Rococo cupola with an actual working clock surmounting the Greek Revival portico and four splendid Corinthian columns.

Below the lofty pillars hundreds thronged the courthouse square, spawning a circus-like atmosphere. In fact, on the Saturday before I arrived in Wytheville, an actual circus came to town to take advantage of the ready-made crowd. Its calliope hooted and tooted, and bands played in the square, barely heard above the cacophony of voices — vendors hawking lemonade and flavored ices, bookmakers mobbed by scores of people shouting their bets on the outcome of Floyd's trail. Would it be acquittal, conviction on a lesser charge, or death? Win, place, or show? It was unreal, a kind of barely controlled madness.

As in Hillsville in March, reporters streamed into Wytheville from all over the globe. The massacre had faded from the front pages in mid-April, when the sinking of the Titanic supplanted Hillsville in drama and pathos. But now that the Allens faced the death penalty, their story was once again an international sensation. An indescribable feeling of expectancy, of intense anticipation, hovered over the town.

Everybody wanted to cash in on the publicity. Along with the gaggle of reporters was a mob of 'penny dreadful' and dime novel authors seeking to exploit the richest mother lode since Wyatt Earp, Doc Holliday, and the Gunfight at the OK Corral. Detective E. C. 'Ed' Payne, a Baldwin colleague who'd taken part in the manhunt, wrote a highly colored account of the desperate capture of Claude Allen, Friel Allen, and Sid Edwards, conveniently ignoring the fact that all the fugitives were captured peacefully. A Wytheville jail guard rushed into print with a lurid insider's exposé, hardly a word of which was accurate. I was offered a considerable sum if I would tell my part of the story, which I refused to do then and many times over the years thereafter — until now.

In that atmosphere of spectacle, and hype, and noise, and teeming streets — and by the way, the main streets and town square were paved, unlike muddy Hillsville — I arrived for my brief turn upon the stage, still saddened at having to leave my beloved only hours, it seemed, since we declared our love for one another.

Emma had wanted to stay with me for the trials of Floyd and the rest, and naturally I hungered for her presence and moral support. But she had to rendezvous with the U.S. equestrian team in New York. From there they took a steamer to Paris, where the competition was to begin in mid-May. She wouldn't return until July. By then Floyd and son Claude would be on Death Row at the state penitentiary in Richmond.

I saw her off at the station in Roanoke. Forlorn, we stood on the platform looking on each other with barely concealed passion. She was dressed in a bottle green suit that set off her rich coloring, looking like ...well, like the famous Gibson Girl of the early 1900's, the era's personification of feminine beauty. Her skirt was long and flared, worn with a tailored high-necked jacket and close-fitting sleeves. It accentuated her shapeliness, deep-breasted, with the generous hips of the habitual horsewoman, set off by a tiny waist.

"I do hate to leave you, my love," she sighed. "Just when you need me most."

"Yes, I wish you could stay, I agreed. "But, it's a matter of honor. You've made a commitment, an important one. Besides, I want bragging rights when it's all over, that my Emma was the first woman rider to win an international medal for horsemanship."

She did, by the way. But more about that later.

"Yes," she said. "I must honor my commitments. That's who we are, you and I."

Unable to resist, I murmured, "'I could not love thee, Dear, so much, loved I not honor more.'"

"Ah, yes. I said you were a Cavalier poet, didn't I?"

"A Virginia cavalier, perhaps; but no poet," I smiled.

Grasping my hand, she looked at me with a question suddenly serious in her deep grey eyes. "You're sure you want to go through with it?"

"Yes," I said.

"There will be a price to pay," she replied.

"I know."

"But you don't know in advance how high the price will be. They'll try to destroy you. Have you really considered that?" she asked.

"Love, if I don't go through with it, the personal price in lost self-respect will be greater," I said.

A current ran through us, a perfect communication in which all was understood without being uttered. Then the conductor called, "All aboar-r-r-d!" and the spell was broken. She smiled wistfully, took off her gloves and laid smooth hands on my cheek, those strong but elegant hands full of grace, the good hands of a champion horsewoman. Looking into my eyes as if to imprint the memory of the scene, she kissed me deeply, un-self-consciously, despite the public place. My heart melted as she mounted the steps to her car. With a look of infinite longing, she blew me a final kiss with her red bow of a mouth, and disappeared inside. And left me desolate.

***

The state stinted not in paying Baldwin-Felts to lay on plenty of armed guards to protect the courtroom from another gun battle, to patrol the streets, and to keep tight control of the prisoners. The reputation of the Allens had grown so fearsome under the onslaughts of the press that rumors sprang up overnight like mushrooms — the Allens' kin under command of Floyd's brother Jack Allen, even more irascible than Floyd, were armed and on the way to spring them free; that Floyd had seized a Baldwin's weapon and escaped, and the like. None of it was remotely true, but it created an atmosphere that justified lots of paid Baldwin men. At times I even wondered if the Agency itself wasn't stoking the wild rumors.

Our agents liked the Wytheville duty because when not on a guard shift, they could slip off to nearby Hiwassee in the New River Valley and its notable house of ill fame. Puritanical Baldwin and Felts tried but couldn't discourage these excursions. Most of our men behaved properly, but there were still plenty who sampled the wares of the area's women of easy virtue or swaggered about town full of self-importance, basking in the glare of the world's press and ostentatiously checking their weapons. And why shouldn't they? They had the power, and there was no one to call them to account. The spectacle reinforced the decision I'd made and the manner in which I intended to carry it out.

Laughing ruefully to myself, I reviewed my coming testimony as one of the prosecution's star witnesses. In fact, I was to be the first to testify, to set the stage and give the court an overall picture of the gun battle and its aftermath, the manhunt, the arrests, and my investigation of the tragedy. But I'd managed to let it be known in the right quarter, and without breaking any laws or my oath, that the prosecution might be in for a surprise when the defense cross-examined me.

Because I was a witness, Baldwin-Felts had assigned a colleague the task of escorting the prisoners from Roanoke to the trial venue. Elmo Brim was a slender, dapper man who typically favored the dark suit and the bowler hat worn by many Baldwin men almost as a uniform. More educated than most of our detectives, he was decent, not a thug, at least no more than required by Agency policy. But he was a Company man. Shrewdly he sensed the growing tension between me and the big bosses, and evidently hoped to profit from my coming fall. In the event, he didn't have long to wait. But until then he remained cordial, obviously hedging his bet.

I asked for a report on the movement of the prisoners from Roanoke to Wytheville, a task Elmo had performed with credit. We met in the hallway outside the courtroom after he'd delivered the defendants to the holding cell.

"Now, then, Elmo," I said. "Tell me about it. Well done, by the way. You got 'em all here without losing any."

He smiled grimly. "Not that they wouldn't have tried, given the chance. Floyd had a sharp look in his eye the whole trip. Kept studying my Winchester. Gave me the feeling he was always looking to escape."

"He wouldn't have gotten far, with three bullet holes in his leg and a busted knee," I noted.

"Well, wounded or not, we stuck to him like a duck on a June bug. Same with Claude and the others. Poor Floyd, we had to take away his readin' glasses lest he use a broken lens to slit his throat, like he tried in Hillsville the day after the shootout. And we had to watch him eat every mouthful, then take away his knife and fork when he was done."

"How'd the rest of them behave?" I asked.

"Fine. They were right biddable, as the mountaineers say. I was impressed with Claude especially. Polite, friendly, composed. The perfect gentleman. Sat for hours readin' the Bible to Floyd in their cell. Which they are goin' to need, if you ask me. You'd never think he was a murderer about to go on trial for his life and him only 21. And his girl. She would've him made a fine wife. I almost find myself feelin' sorry for that young man."

Elmo went on to describe the trip by rail from Roanoke to Galax, where they were all treated to a sumptuous breakfast in Thomas Felts' own home. Then they proceeded to Hillsville by horse and wagon, making sure Floyd, still hobbled by his wounds, was bedded down comfortably in a nest of quilts in the cargo bay. They had to travel first to Hillsville for the arraignment, since by law that procedure had to occur in the county where the crime was committed. Learning through the 'mountain telegraph' that the prisoners were en route, scores of locals lined the roads, standing silently as they passed, many with hats off in respect or as gesture of final farewell.

The prisoners spent the night in the Hillsville jail, and then Elmo and his team brought them by horse and buggy the 30 miles to Wytheville the next morning, April 29. Once again, hundreds of silent spectators stood along the route as they passed by.

Floyd's case was first on the docket. Now he was about to be tried for the highest possible stakes, a scant seven weeks since his first trial and the ensuing shootout.

***

I said the defense committed a number of fatal errors, but in all fairness, I'm not sure it would have made much difference had their case been error-free. The deck was stacked against the Allens from the outset.

First, as I mentioned, their lawyers were severely hampered by the lack of time to prepare a solid defense. How much time does it take? It depends on the circumstances of each case. But in this case, certainly far more time than was allowed. It takes weeks and weeks to travel all over the countryside to interview witnesses and evaluate their potential testimony, weeks and weeks to review the relevant case law and precedents. An effective defense is in essence a convincing story, and it takes time to construct the narrative, just as it takes time for an author to write a book. Six weeks was insufficient for such a complicated case. It certainly wasn't enough lapsed time for the mass hysteria to subside.

Next, the defense was hampered by lack of resources. Even though the Allens were not yet convicted of anything and should have enjoyed the presumption of innocence, the Carroll County court had attached all their property — homes, land, businesses, livestock — to compensate the victims of the shooting. The result was the Allens had virtually nothing with which to pay their lawyers or travel expenses for their witnesses, many of whom were deterred by the time and distance and cost of making the trip. Also, I'm sorry to add that many potential defense witnesses reported acts of intimidation by some of the Baldwin agents, which added to the difficulty of assembling friendly testimony.

But the greatest obstacle, one which the defense never overcame, was the lack of accurate ballistic data or autopsy reports. I had already concluded — reluctantly, I might add — that the state deliberately failed to perform any forensic tests because they didn't want to know the whole truth. Consciously or unconsciously, they feared the autopsies and ballistic examination would show that Judge Massie and William Foster, and possibly the juror Augustus Fowler and the spectator Betty Ayers, were hit by bullets from the lawmen as well as from the Allens. Ballistics was an infant science in 1912, and it might not have been possible to say with certainty which bullets came from which guns. But proper autopsies could have at least identified the caliber of each fatal bullet and raised the unavoidable possibility that the Courthouse Ring hit as many victims of the crossfire as Floyd and his people did. And that would have seriously undermined trying the Allens for a capital crime.

Carroll County Coroner C.W. Nuckolls, whom I'd encountered the day of the shoot-out, was responsible for the autopsies and ballistic examinations. Why he failed to carry them out thoroughly I never learned. But I knew from my first encounter with him that he hated the Allens and blamed them for the deaths of his colleagues in county government. Like many officials with the same bias, one that had hardened into a conviction, he was unaware of it. That's the insidious nature of bias. No doubt he'd have stoutly denied it if he'd been so accused. Yet this underlying attitude influenced the performance of his official duties in ways that served the state's capital case, with which his own biases were congruent.

Nevertheless, despite all the disadvantages and to their great credit, five local attorneys agreed to defend the family. I suppose they did the best they could under difficulties that no one could have surmounted. Since the Allens had no way to pay for their defense, the Court appointed two lawyers from Roanoke. They were joined soon afterwards by retired Judge K. H. Hairston, Judge N. P. Oglesby, and Mr. R. H. Willis, a noted criminal defense expert. These latter three led the team, working for a fraction of what they normally earned. If the title 'Judge' seems confusing, remember that many of the lawyers on both sides were former judges, and they kept the honorific after service on the bench. But they are not to be confused with Judge Staples, the presiding trial judge.

Hairston, Willis, and colleagues opted for self-defense as the foundation of their case. It was a risky strategy; yet in the circumstances, the only possible defense against the charges of conspiracy and pre-meditated murder; that is, murder in the first degree, which in 1912 carried a mandatory death penalty upon conviction. If a lesser charge had been offered, perhaps the defense might have accepted it and the tragedy would have had a different outcome. But they had no such option. Moreover, self-defense was simply a matter of the facts as they saw them. The law had fired first. Floyd was the first one hit. He and his relatives had only returned fire when they came under lethal attack. Defense counsel had to make the jury believe this narrative while discrediting the state's charge of conspiracy; a charge that buttressed premeditated murder. If they could succeed in showing there was no conspiracy or premeditation, they might get off with second degree murder, possibly even manslaughter or negligent homicide.

In fact, if they were tried today, and whether I was defending them or not, it's highly unlikely the state could make a successful case for murder in the first degree. Floyd and Claude would not have gotten the death penalty. Today the most likely outcome would be a mistrial or even an acquittal on grounds of reasonable doubt because of the lack of authoritative forensic and ballistic evidence. It was a miscarriage of justice, though perhaps not a knowing, deliberate one. It was simply how the System operated. 'No villain need be! Passions spin the plot. We are betray'd by what is false within.'

***

The prosecution called me first. Commonwealth Attorney Floyd Landreth had coached me to paint as awful a picture as possible, what we defense lawyers call 'waving the bloody shirt.' It's a form of inflaming the jury that would not be permitted under today's criminal procedure. But this was 1912, not 1968. I said nothing during the pre-trial conference; and full of righteous anger, Landreth took my silence as assent. But I saw my role not as opposing the state's angry passions with my own, but as trying to cool the passions by introducing the voice of reason. Knowing I'd pay the price, but with Emma's encouragement holding me firm, I was determined to make sure all the facts were laid on the table, hoping they would speak for themselves.

On the morning of April 30, the players began to assemble. The grim-faced prosecution arrived and arrayed their files in order on their table. Shortly thereafter, flanked by two Wythe County deputies armed with shotguns and pistols, Floyd Allen hobbled in behind his lawyers on crutches, his right leg in a full-length cast. Armed Baldwin men stationed themselves at watchful intervals around the courtroom as the spectators and reporters filed in, clutching their tickets to the few precious seats at 'the trial of the century.' Of course, this time only the lawmen were armed.

Floyd had aged considerably since I'd seen him last on the streets of Hillsville. And no wonder. He'd been shot three times, including a round that shattered his right knee and must have still hurt badly. He'd survived a crude attempt at suicide. He'd been in jail for seven weeks. Though treated humanely, the experience had to have been debilitating to such a free and independent spirit. But above all, what I think burdened him the most was the uncertain fate of his sons, brother, and nephews — and especially his ailing wife. He was stouthearted enough to face the death penalty without flinching. But the knowledge that he'd dragged his loved ones into such jeopardy by his unruly passions left him bent under an insupportable woe.

Floyd's wife entered with him, shuffling along and clutching his arm. She'd become a pitiable creature since my encounter with her years ago. Frail and stooped and all in black, she wore a look of sorrow on her lined face, as if she already knew the outcome and had gone into mourning. Shifting his crutches awkwardly, Floyd helped her to her seat behind the railing. He gave her a solicitous pat on the shoulder, smiled wanly, and limped forward to sit at the defense table. His shattered right leg in its rigid cast extended straight into the open space before the table. During the course of the trial, his attorneys had to step around it carefully when approaching the bench, making their arguments, and questioning witnesses.

Floyd wore a dignified black suit. A toothbrush and comb protruded incongruously from his breast pocket. Unperturbed, he seemed to follow the proceedings dispassionately but with interest, smiling or nodding occasionally at something a witness said, but otherwise displaying little reaction.

Following traditions reaching back to Medieval England, the trial began. Presiding Judge Walter Staples issued the standard guidance about courtroom dignity and decorum, then recognized the state for its opening remarks and explanation of the indictments.

I was called to begin the state's case. After explaining the commission given Baldwin-Felts by Governor Mann and my role in the Agency, I outlined for the court my post-Hillsville report, including an account of the six-week manhunt in the hills of Carroll County. I made sure the court knew that Sid Edwards, Friel Allen, and Claude Allen had surrendered peaceably. The prosecution tried to drag more damaging testimony out of me, but I stuck to the bare facts. Finally, puzzled, defeated, Landreth sat down and awaited cross-examination by the defense.

Defense attorney Willis, wearing a deceptively worried expression, stood slowly and began his cross. Studying the floor at his feet for a moment, he said, "Mr. Hayne, let's understand this: you've testified that you conducted a painstaking investigation for the Commonwealth after the shootout, interviewed all the witnesses, and so forth."

"Yes, that's right."

"Makes you something of an authority on what happened last March in Hillsville, which is why you're the lead-off witness for the state, am I right?" he said.

"You could say that. As much of an authority as anyone, I suppose."

Floyd Landreth looked puzzled, but so far I'd said nothing to give him concern.

"Well, then, Mr. Hayne," said Willis in a tone as if hostile to a prosecution witness, which intensified the surprise of his next few questions and my reply, "as the state's principal expert on the event, what is your informed opinion about who fired the first shot?"

Prosecutor Landreth let this go without objecting because he assumed I would put the blame on Floyd Allen. But he rose from his chair wide-eyed and mouth agape when I said, "On the basis of all the evidence I could gather afterwards, I believe the first shot was fired by the Deputy Clerk of Court, Woodson Quesenberry. At about the same instant, only a second apart, the Clerk of Court, Dexter Goad opened fire. At almost the same moment Sheriff Webb was in the act of drawing his sidearm, but it got hung up in the fabric of his coat," I added.

Instant pandemonium ruled the courtroom. The prosecution team came to their feet as one man, gesticulating and shouting incomprehensibly. Whatever they were saying was drowned out in a chorus of exclamations from the spectators. Judge Staples pounded his gavel 'til the block leaped off the bench, but his shouts for order were also lost amid the hubbub. I sat impassively. Lawyer Willis and I simply looked at each other calmly until the bedlam subsided.

Judge Staples barked out, "Any more such outbursts and I'll clear the court. I mean it, now. Go ahead, Mr. Willis, if you please."

Until then, there had been a complacent feeling in the court. But now the atmosphere was charged, expectant. The process had begun routinely, and everyone just knew Floyd was guilty as charged and would be condemned. The planets would follow their orbits, the firmament would remain fixed, and the world would continue as it had from Creation. But suddenly all comfortable assumptions were swept into the dustbin. Even Judge Staples, who was impartial, in theory anyway, looked down at me in consternation.

Willis led me through a series of questions laying the foundation for self-defense. He asked, "Mr. Hayne, you don't seem to share in the state's zeal to condemn Floyd Allen, even though you've been called as a witness for the prosecution. Yet you were the first of Baldwin-Felts' detectives on the scene in Hillsville back in March. You arrested Floyd Allen, and you led the manhunt for the other members of his family. What brought about this change of heart?"

"Well, sir," said I, "I'm an officer of the law and I believe the state does have the responsibility to deter and punish lawbreakers. We all acknowledge that. And to carry out that responsibility, the state asserts the right to use deadly force. However, that assertion sometimes runs squarely up against another right, the right of self-preservation and self-defense."

"In other words," said Willis, "what do you do when the state's use of deadly force threatens your life, and you see that in another instant you're going to be killed?"

I nodded. "That was exactly the dilemma facing Floyd Allen and his kin. But they had no time to weigh the consequences. They had only a split second to react. I think it was an instinctive reaction not to submit to being shot and killed like sheep just because the guns being aimed at 'em were those of public officials. I mean, does the citizen's obligation to obey law officers mean you have to just stand there submissively as a target, under any and all circumstances?"

"You're saying the shooting in the Carroll County court was a natural and spontaneous reaction to the sudden threat?"

"Yes," I replied.

"Not the planned, premeditated act of a conspiracy?"

Ex-county judge Wysor rose for the prosecution and said in a loud voice, "Objection, your honor. Calls for a speculative conclusion on the part of the witness."

Judge Staples said, "Sustained." But the thought and my presumed answer still hovered over the courtroom.

Willis said, "Then I'll put it another way. If street thugs break in, you have a right to defend yourself. On that we'd all agree. But if the state behaves like a street thug, don't you still have the same right? "

Judge Wysor, still standing as if in anticipation, shouted, "Objection, your honor! Prejudicial and inflammatory!"

"Yes," I answered, managing to make myself heard above the objection and the outbreak of another storm of angry voices. In the eyes of the jurymen I could see the argument had hit home. They knew their kin might have done the same thing in the circumstances.

Willis turned to the bench, spreading his arms. "Your Honor, I'm trying to establish the frame of mind of the defendant when suddenly thrust into an unexpected situation of mortal danger."

Floyd Landreth leaped up from the prosecution's table. "Your Honor, it hasn't yet been established that there was any mortal danger to the occupants of the Carroll County court except that posed by the defendants themselves. The question is prejudicial, inflammatory, and argumentative."

Judge Staples pondered for a moment, then said, "I'll allow it. But counselor, I won't allow you unlimited scope along this line of inquiry."

"Yes, Your Honor," said Willis. "But may it please the court, I must remind the court that Mr. Hayne is their witness, not mine." He gestured toward the prosecution.

"Now, Mr. Hayne," he continued, "are you familiar with Blackstone's *Commentaries on the Laws of England?*"

"Yes, sir. I'm not a lawyer, but I've certainly read Blackstone."

"You'll agree that his *Commentaries* are part of the foundation of our common law?"

"Yes, sir, especially in the Commonwealth of Virginia, as I understand it," I said.

Willis went to his table and picked up a large volume, turning to a marked page. "This is what Blackstone says: 'Self-defense is a part of the law of nature; nor can it be denied the community, even against the king himself.' Now, you're the state's leading expert on what happened that tragic March day in Hillsville. That's why the state has put you on the stand first, to paint us a picture of that sorrowful event. Am I right?"

"Evidently," I said.

"Now, then, Mr. Hayne. We've heard from you about the gun battle and we've heard from Blackstone. Having heard this passage from the *Commentaries,* would you not agree that Floyd Allen acted in self-defense, in peril of his life; and that he had a right to do so, 'even against the king himself.' In other words, he was acting within the scope of the laws of the Commonwealth of Virginia?"

Landreth and Wysor both leaped up, but Judge Staples quieted them with an upraised hand.

"Yes, I do agree," I said. "As I've testified, his only other choice was to stand there and be slaughtered." Another tornado of voices swept the courtroom. Judge Staples let it vent for a moment, then gaveled the court back to order. As soon as it was quiet, I added, "And the same goes for Claude Allen and his kin. They saw Floyd under attack and — "

"That's enough of that, Mr. Hayne," interjected the Judge. "We're concerned in this trial only with the acts of Floyd Allen." He glared at Judge Hairston and R. H. Willis. "Counselors, are you finished with your cross-examination of this witness?"

"Yes, sir, we are," they answered in unison.

Staples looked at the prosecution and asked, "Is there redirect from the prosecution?"

"Yes, Your Honor," Floyd Landreth replied, standing, his voice thick with disgust. "Just to make sure the court has the complete picture. Mr. Hayne, you testified that on March 14, 1912, when the Carroll County jury came in with a guilty verdict on the original assault charge, the defendant stood and announced for all to hear, 'Gentlemen, I ain't a-goin'.' Is that right?"

"Yes," I said. I knew what his next question would be, but there was nothing I could do except answer truthfully. But in his zeal, Landreth made a misstep in the way he formulated the question, giving me the opening I'd hoped for.

"Whereupon he reached into his coat for his revolver, right?" he said.

"No, that is not quite right," I replied, touching off another buzz of angry voices. Floyd Allen leaned forward eagerly at the defense table, a gleam of surprised triumph in his eyes.

When the noise subsided, Landreth sneered, "Your Honor, may I remind the witness he's under oath." The irony was not lost on the jury that I'd been called as his witness. Landreth stalked forward to within a foot of my face, glaring. "How is it 'not quite right'? Did Floyd stand threatening the court and reach for his gun or not?"

I told the court, "He did stand and say he wasn't going. But he reached into his inside coat pocket for a list of witnesses he hoped to call in support of the motion for a new trial. To be sure, it was out of order at that particular moment, but Floyd Allen's not a lawyer and he couldn't have known that. He wore his revolver under his coat at the back, near his right hip. If he'd been going for his sidearm, that's where he would have reached. That's where he did reach after he came under deadly fire from the court officials."

Angry voices followed that answer, but not as irate as before.

"His right hip. But the court officials couldn't have known that, could they?" growled Landreth.

"Possibly not," I said. "Floyd had pointed out where he carried in earlier testimony during the March 1912 trial. Possibly the court officials forgot that piece of testimony."

"Then it was reasonable for the court and law officers to believe that Floyd Allen was going for his gun, especially given his violent reputation and the threat he'd just uttered in the court?"

"It was not altogether unreasonable," I said.

Landreth spun on his heel, smiled and nodded at the jury as if he'd demolished my testimony. But I knew he hadn't — not completely, anyway. I had knocked the props from under the first degree murder charge, and you could feel the changed atmosphere in the court. "That's all I have, Your Honor," he said.

"Then the witness may stand down," Judge Staples announced. "And we'll recess two hours for dinner. Court will resume at two o'clock."

Amid a beehive's hum of murmurs, I made my way back to the gallery, as all eyes followed me, some accusing, some approving.

***

I waited in my seat for the spectators and participants to clear the courtroom, uncomfortable under the stares of the audience as they filed by. Then I slowly exited at the tail end of the crowd and went downstairs, satisfied that I'd done what truth and honor required. Baldwin and Felts had been waiting, not to my surprise. They pursued me down the stairway to the first-floor landing, where I turned at bay.

Baldwin shouted, "What do you mean, sir!" His normally pale countenance was beet red and his bushy mustache quivered. Tom Felts, standing at his side, was equally afire with indignation.

"What do you mean?" I answered.

"You have utterly wrecked the state's case by your folly," he shouted. "And you have embarrassed this Agency, rendered moot all the work and sacrifice of the past few months. Whose side are you on?"

This wasn't the first time I'd been asked that in connection to the Allens. I'd had plenty of time to consider my answer, knowing it would be thrown at me again. "I'm on the side of justice," I replied. "Justice is truth free of passion. I only told the truth."

Tom Felts interjected, "The truth! The truth is because of you, these murderers may well go free."

"That's up to a jury of their peers, not us," I said.

Perhaps it was the years of screaming upperclassmen at VMI; perhaps it was my year of combat in the Philippines. Whatever the reason, I found that when the stress and decibel levels were at their highest, I was at my calmest. Though I'm passionate by nature, I kept myself under control during their joint verbal assault.

Baldwin got right in my face. Hands on hips, he demanded, "Have the Allens paid you to go over to their side? Or have you simply gone mad? I can't fathom what has gotten into you. You were once our best man. Now you've endangered the reputation of the finest police force in the land."

Backing up slightly, I said, "No, sir. You — we — have done that to ourselves."

"Explain yourself!" Felts barked.

"Gentlemen," said I, "Floyd and Claude Allen do not deserve to die just to preserve the reputation of this Agency or to satisfy the bloodlust of the state. The Allens did wrong and they must be held accountable. But they didn't act with premeditation. There was no conspiracy to murder Judge Massie or anyone else. Nor did they act without severe provocation from the law. When our men went down to Carroll County to hunt 'em down, our so-called detectives ran amok. The Agency acted like the people of the lower county were all criminals. Treated 'em like an occupying army treats insurrectionists. Which is to say, atrociously."

Felts tried to interrupt but I held up a restraining hand and said in a low voice, "Yes, I know what you're going to say, you tried to prevent the outrages. But you — we, I fault myself, too — didn't try hard enough and you failed. You gentlemen believe that any

187

means is justified against criminals, even if it means committing crimes yourselves, under the color of law, of course. The time came when I could no longer tell the difference between us and the criminals we're supposed to suppress. We have the greater responsibility because we're supposed to uphold the dignity and majesty of the law. So let me ask you gentlemen, whose side are you on? The side of law, or the side of raw power?"

Baldwin ran his hand across his face with its helpless expression. He said, "Carter Hayne, you are dismissed, as of this instant."

"Yes, I should think so," I laughed, surprising myself with my *sang froid.*

Felts jumped in again. "Don't take it so calm, my friend. I believe you are guilty of misprision of a felony."

'Misprision' was a new word to me then, but it added to my eagerness to begin studying the law. It means guilty knowledge of a crime, or covering one up, I soon learned. "Oh, and what's that?" I said with an innocent air.

"Aiding and abetting," said Felts — incorrectly. Aiding and abetting is a different thing altogether and a more serious crime, but somehow to him 'misprision' sounded worse.

I said, "You may know the letter of the law, but not the spirit."

That made him even more belligerent. "I believe you contrived to allow Sid Allen and Wesley Edwards to escape, a gross breach of your sworn oath and a dereliction of duty. You wait 'til — "

Baldwin elbowed him sharply, but the rat was out of the bag. They were masters of controlling all around them, and instantly I saw the line of attack they'd use to discredit me from here on and limit the damage I might do to their version of events.

Baldwin said, "Turn in your badge and gun."

I pulled the Agency badge from my inside coat pocket and flipped it high in the air with my thumb, like a coin. Their eyes followed it as it spun high in the air, the light glinting off the gilt edges. Baldwin caught it deftly and thrust it in his side coat pocket.

"Heads or tails?" I said.

"Both," snarled Felts. "Your head and your tail."

I laughed heartily. It was a good comeback. "Well," I said, "I'm guilty of no such crime, so do your worst."

"You can depend on it," said Baldwin.

Yet I wasn't feeling as bold as I let on. For over four years I'd enjoyed adventure, excitement, good pay, and a sense of purpose in my job. Nothing had changed except the last item. How was I to know in 1908 when I joined the Agency that the sense of purpose would turn out to be an illusion? Moreover, I still retained a degree of respect for Baldwin. He was basically a good man, caught up in a bad system. But in such situations, the bad system usually prevails over the good man and not the reverse.

"And now your sidearm, if you please," Baldwin ordered.

Detectives Estil Meadows and Hugh Lucas had come down the stairs and joined Baldwin and Felts, standing just behind them on either side at their shoulders, with eyes narrowed and a hard set to the jaw. Seeing the four of them from the other side, arrayed in their dark suits like so many beetles and with grim, menacing stares, for the first time I understood what it was like for the poor miners in West Virginia or the small farmers in Fancy Gap to face a phalanx of armed Baldwins. For the first time I knew in my soul what it meant to be powerless before naked, pitiless, unaccountable Power.

I shrugged off the sudden fear. "Bill, Bill," I laughed. In five years of his employ I'd never called him that. "My sidearm is my own, not the Agency's. And in any case, look where we are. Surely you don't think I'd be carrying a firearm inside a courthouse, do you?"

***

Although I'd struck a blow for justice in my testimony, the disadvantage in being the lead witness was that the prosecution still had plenty of other witnesses to call. They had ample opportunity to undo whatever damage I might have done to the state's case and whatever good I might have done to Floyd.

Former judge David Bolen had been Floyd's defense counsel in his first trial in Hillsville, the one that resulted in the gun battle. Now he was a witness for the prosecution. His testimony inflicted fatal damage to Floyd's defense — in large part because all present knew he'd defended Floyd and couldn't be considered a tainted witness.

He told the court, "When Judge Massie ordered Floyd into custody, Mr. Allen hesitated a moment and then he arose. He looked to me like a man who badly wanted to say something but hadn't quite made up his mind what he was going to say. But as he straightened up and moved off to my left a few feet, he seemed to decide, and he said something like this, 'Gentlemen, I tell you, I ain't a-goin'.'"

Bolen's version of events was damaging enough, but the prosecution inflamed the jury with raw appeals to emotion. If I sound angry even after so many years... well, I'm not altogether. I understand how they felt. The state cared only that five people had been shot dead, including a respected circuit judge and Bill Foster, one of their own fraternity. Such an attack on the state to them was especially heinous, because to them the state was the only thing that stood between the citizen and chaos. To them, the Allens were obviously guilty of a grievous crime and deserved the full weight of the System. The prosecutors felt they were the embodiment of civilization against the rule of terror. They were avenging angels, justified in using any means to ensure justice was carried out against the Allens. Seen from their perspective, they weren't villains. But neither were they heroes.

You might say I was underwhelmed by the quality of the defense. I suppose Floyd's lawyers did the best they could in the circumstances, for as I already indicated, the deck was stacked against them. But all along I had the impression they were just going through the motions. Attention to procedure is of course important. The law is in part a set of procedures, after all. But their arguments seemed to lack... well, passion. They did a poor job of challenging and cross-examining hostile witnesses. They let opportunities slip by that seemed obvious even to me, a layman, intensifying my desire to become a defense lawyer. They failed to exploit the lack of conclusive forensic and ballistic evidence.

The defense's somewhat casual approach was no match for the fiery indignation of the prosecution, which ended its case with a parade of inflammatory appeals to the jury the likes of which I never heard, before or since. But then, this was an unprecedented case.

Prosecutor Poage characterized Floyd and his kin as cold-blooded murderers who had terrorized their section of Carroll County for a generation and had to be suppressed.

Escalating the rhetoric, Prosecutor Campbell said, "If you do not find Floyd Allen guilty as charged, then all the courthouses in the Commonwealth might as well be closed. Remember, the eyes of all Virginians are upon you to see that justice is done."

Judge Wysor was not to be outdone. Like an old-time evangelist, he paraded up and down before the jury box and preached at them in a trained orator's voice. "Gentlemen of the jury, this crime is worse than the assassinations of Julius Caesar and Presidents Lincoln, Garfield, and McKinley. These murders must be avenged! Virginia not only demands it, but also all of America and the world. Long live the law! Down with anarchy! Long live the Commonwealth!"

I could see poor Floyd wilt by degrees under these avalanches of condemnation. He must have seen then he'd never really had a chance. After the defense's summation and closing arguments, Judge Staples charged the jury, including a detailed explanation of the law as it pertained to conspiracy and premeditation. Then the jury retired at 2:30 in the afternoon. The defendant sat twirling the ends of his walrus mustache and in low conversation with his wife Cordelia. As the day wore on, Floyd seemed to grow increasingly tense, rubbing his temples as if plagued by a headache. His brother, the formidable Jack Allen, sat in the gallery reading a newspaper, and I smiled grimly to myself to see that the spectators gave him a wide berth. The seats on either side of him were empty.

Finally, at 9:00 PM it appeared the jury was unable to reach a verdict. The rumor spread that they were evenly split between first and second degree murder. Judge Staples adjourned for the evening, the jury returned to their hotel, and Floyd went back to the

Wytheville jail under heavy guard, no doubt encouraged by what appeared to be an impasse among the jurors.

At 9:00 AM the next morning, the session resumed. Judge Staples gave additional instructions to the jury and urged them to reach a verdict, going way over the line of impartiality, in my opinion. The jurors filed into the jury chamber and began to deliberate again. To the surprise of all, about half an hour later there were five sharp raps on the door of the jury room, and the jurors emerged to their places in the box.

The Sheriff called the room to order and Judge Staples asked, "Have you reached a verdict?"

Foreman Frank Nelson stood up and cleared his throat nervously. He glanced at Floyd as he held up the legal form, and I noticed the paper trembled in his hand. Looking now at Judge Staples he read, "We the jury find the defendant Floyd Allen guilty of murder in the first degree, as charged in the indictment." Handing the form to the clerk of court, he sat down.

Floyd's wife burst into tears and slumped over, holding her face in both hands. Floyd sat impassively, expressionless, even though '…small justice was shown, and still less pity…'

Floyd's attorney Judge Hairston immediately stood and moved to set aside the verdict and demanded a new trial on the grounds that the defense had been denied the opportunity to offer exculpatory evidence. It seemed pro forma, and to no one's surprise, Judge Staples denied the motion. The Judge then announced, "Mr. Allen, you are remanded into custody until such time as sentence will be passed, but sentencing is deferred pending the completion of your testimony as a witness in the trials of the other defendants in this case. Court is hereby adjourned."

THOMAS MOORE

It was not much of a respite, for everyone knew the first degree murder conviction carried a mandatory sentence of death. The only question that did seem to remain unanswered was this: would it be death by hanging, or in the new electric chair the state had just installed at the penitentiary in Richmond?

Chapter Ten

I was now under a cloud as Baldwin and Felts spread accounts of my alleged misconduct and dismissal from the Agency. I was never called again to testify for or against any of the accused. This brings us to the worst travesty of all, the trial of Claude Allen — or I should say, trials. Reasonable men can — and did — disagree about the culpability of Floyd Allen. I concluded that a charge of first degree murder was unjust, but I don't fault those who honestly believe otherwise. But in my view the case of his son Claude doesn't offer room for such differences of opinion. Nevertheless, the Commonwealth pursued Claude like the hounds of hell. The prosecution was as determined to put him to death as they were his father. It makes me ashamed to relate the state's relentless campaign even after all these years. In fact, I think it was Claude's fate more than that of the others that impelled me to go into the law. Having brought Claude in to face trial, I then had to watch helplessly as he was subjected to little more than a judicial lynching, something I vowed I'd never do again if I could in any way prevent it.

Claude's first capital trial began on May 20, 1912 in the courthouse in Wytheville. A venire of one hundred Wythe County men was called, and after two days of jury examination, twelve were chosen to try Claude for his life for the premeditated murder of Judge Thornton

Massie. As in Floyd's trial, a heavily armed team of
Baldwins escorted the handcuffed Allens and cousins
Friel Allen and Sid Edwards from the Roanoke jail
each day for the proceedings. Claude's ailing mother
and his girlfriend Nellie Wisler sat behind the defense
table and whispered encouragement. The family
members who were also charged would speak out
valiantly on Claude's behalf, and until his third and
final trial I would say their testimony helped. It was
consistent with the physical evidence, such as it was.
They came across as sincere and honest even though
obviously biased in favor of the defendant. I attended
as well, but this time only as a spectator.

The prosecution's star witness was again the
perplexing Judge Bolen, who'd defended Floyd Allen
in his assault trial in Hillsville in March, and whose
testimony seven weeks later would send Floyd to the
electric chair, even though Bolen's vantage point to the
shooting was cowering on his vast paunch face-down
under the table.

Bolen now testified against Claude. In answer to
prosecutor Wysor's opening question he said, "I've
tried to persuade myself that I might be wrong, but I
can't escape the conclusion that it was Claude Allen
who fired the first shot that struck Judge Massie."

The defense went after him hammer and tongs, but
the words of Judge Bolen, who the jury assumed was
on the Allen's side, after all, carried considerable
weight. Still, the case for premeditated murder wilted
under defense counsel Willis' questioning of Carroll
County Coroner C. B. Nuckolls, who was clearly
hostile to the defense. When put to the question,
Nuckolls said with obvious reluctance but truthfully, "I
reached Judge Massie as he lay dying on the dais and
tried to render assistance, hoping to save his life. He

told me before he expired that it was Sidna Allen who shot him."

Other testimony showed that the Judge's chair was in the direct line of fire between Dexter Goad's desk and where Floyd Allen had stood at bay by the defense table. And other witnesses swore credibly that Dexter Goad had fired the first shot. His bullet could have killed Judge Massie in the confusion as easily as one of the Allens'. With no ballistic evidence in hand, it was all a matter of conjecture. Yet the state treated the matter as settled: Claude Allen had wantonly killed Judge Massie with premeditation.

In fact — and here I digress somewhat from the actual sequence of events, but out of necessity — many months later when Floyd's brother Sid Allen was captured in Des Moines and went on trial, someone finally — finally! — probed for actual physical evidence. Sid Allen's defense lawyer had Judge Massie's chair disassembled. And what do you think they found embedded in the horsehair stuffing? A steel-jacketed .32 round. The type used by the court officers, and which could not have come from the Allens since their guns fired all-lead .38's. But by that time it was too late to help Floyd or Claude.

On the second day Claude took the stand and conducted himself superbly. He was the best witness of all who appeared on his behalf — sober, unassuming, sincere, and displaying none of the vaunted Allen passion despite a severe grilling by the prosecution. He kept his head under the barrage from prosecutor Wysor and said, "Sir, I had no bad feelins' toward Judge Massie whatever, and surely no reason to want to kill him. In fact, he'd been right decent to the family when the Edwards boys were arrested. We thought him a fair-minded man, unlike some of the others in the Courthouse." He stared at Dexter Goad in the gallery.

"Last thing any of us would want to do is shoot down the one fair-minded man of law in the County."

"Then who were you aiming to kill?" Wysor asked sharply.

"Well, Sir, I wasn't aimin' to kill nobody," Claude said with equal sharpness. "I only drew my gun when I saw the law all shootin' at my pa. I felt duty-bound to try and pertect him."

The next morning all the testimony was at an end, and the prosecution and defense consumed seven hours in summation. We spectators and participants sat in various postures of anticipation, awaiting the jury. The high-stakes wait had to be excruciating for Claude and his family, yet he never lost his aplomb. He sat chatting quietly with his mother and Nellie Wisler under the steady scrutiny of a dozen Baldwin guards.

Finally, about nine o'clock that evening, the jury filed in after deliberating less than three hours. Judge Staples called for the verdict and the foreman stood.

Without looking at Claude he announced, "Your honor, we find the defendant guilty of murder in the second degree and recommend a sentence of fifteen years of penal servitude."

An audible sigh of relief swept the courtroom, but the prosecution team snorted in disgust and glared angrily at the jury as Judge Staples dismissed them. It was clear the state wasn't going to rest until Claude was condemned to death. The prosecution had more dead victims for whom they could keep trying him until they got the verdict they wanted.

Sure enough, they put him on trial a few weeks later, this time for the premeditated murder of Commonwealth Attorney William Foster. At least in this instance Claude couldn't claim he regarded Foster a fair-minded man. Everyone knew the Allens feared him as a leader of the official vendetta against the clan.

Nonetheless, despite much of the same testimony as
before, the jury reported it was deadlocked and could
not reach a verdict after deliberating for several hours.
Judge Staples released them and declared a mistrial, to
the further disgust of the prosecutors.

The vengefulness of the prosecution came to a
rolling boil after this second repudiation. They might
have remained content with the first trial's verdict of
second degree murder. While that was still too harsh in
my opinion, at least it fell within the bounds of reason.
But they wanted his blood, and they moved to try
Claude a third time for the murder of Sheriff Lew
Webb. Claude had given them the opening in his prior
testimony when he admitted he'd fired at Sheriff Webb
and Dexter Goad, but only after his father came under
fire from the court officials.

Now occurred one of the most disgraceful episodes
in the whole legal process, the sleaziest trick I ever saw
from rogue prosecutors in all my years at the bar.
Before Claude was to be tried again, it had been agreed
that Friel Allen would go next, and the defense team
duly prepared to defend cousin Friel. Claude Allen's
sentencing was deferred so he could appear as a
witness for the defense. On the morning of July 17, the
defense team and the Allens duly reported to the
Wytheville courthouse prepared to try Friel. But, to the
anger and astonishment of defense counsel Hairston
and Willis, the Commonwealth moved to re-try Claude
Allen for the murder of William Foster in the first
degree, in view of the mistrial. I mean, try Claude right
then and there. Moreover, the prosecution had called a
venire of 96 men from distant Washington County —
at what enormous expense I can't imagine — from
which to empanel the jury. It was clear they expected
men from more urban Washington County, where the

local anti-Allen newspaper had been especially vicious, to get the job done.

The defense objected strenuously, but to no avail. Judge Staples sternly gaveled Holiman Willis to order when he expressed his contempt for the prosecution in pointed terms. Then he ruled against the defense motions to set aside the trial and quash the clearly prejudiced jury.

The last act of the travesty — that is, the last act of the travesty preceding Claude's execution — was set to proceed. It was a virtual replay of Claude's second trial, in which he again credibly denied any desire or attempt to take the life of Bill Foster. Judge Bolen and Dexter Goad added nothing new to their accounts from the second trial. Then the summations began. Prosecutor Wysor demanded a guilty verdict and death sentence for the "... perpetrator of the most dastardly crime in the annals of the Commonwealth. Only a guilty verdict and the forfeit of Claude Allen's life can balance the scales of justice and restore Virginia to its formerly good name among our sister states."

Defense counsel Willis launched an hour-long summation, emphasizing Claude's youth, his sterling character, his high repute in the community where he'd never before been charged with any crime, and his filial devotion to defend his father, who he saw was about to be killed. The jury sat stone-faced, then retired. Only an hour and a half elapsed when they returned to the courtroom. I wondered why they'd bothered to retire at all when Judge Staples queried them and the foreman stood and replied, "Your Honor, we the jury find the defendant Claude Swanson Allen guilty of murder in the first degree, as charged in the indictment."

The court erupted in cries of dismay, since Claude had acquired a substantial following of local women drawn by his movie-star good looks and his appealing manner. Claude's mother fell weeping on one shoulder and Nellie Wisler on the other as he was handcuffed and taken out by three Baldwin men bearing Winchesters and sidearms. He was moved more by pity for their anguish, I believe, than by his own dire prospects. As he exited, I saw him raise his chained hands awkwardly and wipe the tears from his own eyes.

***

Then came Friel Allen's turn to be tried. And now I paid for my disdain of the press and my refusal to cultivate reporters, even while basking in their attention. I hadn't reckoned on how quickly and totally that worm could turn. Baldwin and Felts had no trouble planting all the stories they wanted about my 'treachery.'

I had hoped to testify on Friel's behalf, thinking I might redeem my promise to him and his father, at least in part. But the stories generated by Baldwin-Felts made me out a criminal in league with the Allens. They hinted that I'd deliberately allowed Sidna Allen and Wesley Edwards to escape, or that I was guilty of financially defrauding the Agency — and by implication, the state of Virginia. The worst offender was the ever-acrimonious Washington County Ledger, the same paper that had inflamed its readers toward Claude — readers of it had condemned him to die. Typical of the headlines were, DID FORMER DETECTIVE LINE POCKETS WITH ALLEN REWARD MONEY?, and MISSING FUNDS BUY SAFETY FOR REMAING ALLEN FUGITIVES — FOR A WHILE. The Allen defense team concluded my appearance in court would hurt rather than help, so

I followed the unfolding of Friel's case from a distance.

There's an old saying that a lie will be halfway 'round the world before truth can lace up its boots. These lurid slanders ate at me something fierce. I can't tell you how despondent I was to have my good name so foully besmirched and to feel so helpless to do anything about it. Taking refuge but little comfort in my pride, I remained aloof and refused to engage in a battle of headlines.

Emma came to my rescue. By this time, late July 1912, she'd returned from Europe a front-page heroine in her own right and the toast of the horse set. She brought back vivid tales of her adventures and was in great demand by the press. The first female rider of the first U.S. equestrian team to win an international medal; beautiful, poised, confident, clever, and articulate, she found it easy to beguile the Fourth Estate.

She selected Chase Buttram, the reporter from the influential *Richmond Times Dispatch*, and poured on the charm. With her it seemed utterly natural and not feigned — because it was natural. Chase Buttram was the reporter I'd met on the road to Hillsville the morning of the mad rush there after the shoot-out. I'd been enormously condescending to him at the time. It's a wonder he hadn't joined in the gang mauling by the press. But Emma won him over completely.

Buttram visited us at my parents' home in Little Washington where I was living until I could start law school and find quarters in Charlottesville. Emma was still staying with her friends in the same town. Ostensibly, he planned a human-interest story on Emma's riding triumph, with a sidebar on her relationship with the once celebrated and now tarnished Carter Hayne.

You've heard of ambush interviews, where the reporter catches the subject by surprise? Well, this was an ambush in reverse, where the subject caught the reporter by surprise. Playing along for a while, she gave him just what he wanted, a series of fascinating vignettes of the Paris games, full of drama and color. He was practically panting as he lapped it up. She awaited her moment shrewdly. I sat next to her in silence, admiring her aplomb.

Then the journalist remarked, "You must have been aware of the Allen trials. They were worldwide news. Did it affect your concentration in the riding ring to know your fiancée was suddenly a villain and not a hero?" He looked at me pointedly, expecting a reaction. "After all, Miss Romilly, you're known as one of the best show jumpers in the country, yet you took a few faults over the fences on the second day's event. Our readers wonder if you might have done better without the distraction of the corruption rumors aimed at Mr. Hayne. Why, the U.S. team might even have brought home gold."

She smiled her serene smile. "No, Mr. Buttram, it didn't affect me at all, because I knew the rumors were totally false. When you really know someone as well as I know Carter Hayne, and I don't mean in the Biblical sense" — her gray eyes danced merrily, Buttram turned red, and I suppressed a laugh — "then you know he's totally incapable of such things. It doesn't pass the common-sense test. Why would Carter betray his employers and the state of Virginia he loves for what amounts to pocket change, when he doesn't need the money in the first place?"

She gestured with a sweep of her hand at the fine furnishing and appointments in the family drawing room, the portraits on the walls, the damask curtains and silver candelabra. All bespoke dignity and propriety. "His family may not be millionaires," she went on, "but they're people of ample means, not to mention one of the most respected families in the Commonwealth."

Buttram said, "Well, the Baldwin-Felts Agency is equally respected, and when they claim — "

"Ah, that's just it, Mr. Buttram," she interjected. "My question to you is, why is the most respected newsman in the Commonwealth taking the Agency's word for things without checking more deeply? Is it possible Virginia's best reporter is missing the real news, the story behind the story?"

"I'm not sure I understand what you mean," he said warily.

"Just this," she said, producing a brown folder with all my notes, Philo Hylton's reports, and an accounting of all the money I'd handled in chasing down the Allens from the first day on March 15, 1912.

While I continued to sit in admiring silence, she continued, "Carter Hayne can account for every penny given him by Baldwin-Felts, which also means given by the taxpayers of Virginia, for the pursuit of the Allens and Edwards. I dare you to challenge Baldwin-Felts to do the same. Frankly, I don't believe they can. Not only is every penny accounted for, but also you'll find some interesting expenditures, including $500 to the Iroller family to suborn their daughter Maude to betray her lover Wesley Edwards."

She told Buttram about Philo Hylton and his role in the Wesley Edwards-Maude Iroller affair, and how to find him for an interview. "Go see Philo Hylton. He'll confirm every word I've said. He'll prove it's a lie to suggest Carter allowed Sid Allen and Wesley Edwards to escape."

She pressed on. "But Carter did find this purchase of an act of a woman's treachery most objectionable, as I think most of your readers might, too. Yet he followed the orders of his chief William Baldwin, as he did all his lawful orders, effectively and to the letter. In the circumstances, why is Baldwin-Felts now trying to destroy the reputation of Carter Hayne? If he's such a villain, why was he placed in charge of the Allen investigation in the first place? I think a little probing on your part will reveal it was only when he insisted the state honor its promise to Friel Allen that the Agency began to turn against him."

Her voice rose, passionate yet controlled. Buttram was totally under her spell, as was I. She said, "I ask you, is it likely that Carter would have jeopardized such a stellar career and reputation unless a promise was made to Friel and Jasper Allen, in which Carter's good name and honor were the bait? Does it seem reasonable to you? And then, to try to impute selfish financial motives to him... I ask you, is it reasonable?"

"No, ma'am, when you put it that way, it isn't," Buttram agreed.

"So, Mr. Buttram, this is the real story behind the Allen story," she said. "To what lengths are Baldwin-Felts and the Commonwealth of Virginia prepared to go in their insane lust to destroy the Allens? Destroy this good man as well, because he insisted on honoring the law while enforcing the law? Is it acceptable to lie, steal, and cheat in the name of justice?"

"It does seem like a case of the ends justifying any means," the reporter mused.

"Yes," said Emma. "Which raises questions about the state's fundamental approach to the Allen case from the outset."

"Meaning?" said Buttram.

"Meaning this," she said. "If you can't get justice in the courts, where do you go? If the courts dispense injustice rather than justice, isn't what happened in

Hillsville last year inevitable, a deeply disordered society, with violence and anarchy?"

"Perhaps you're right," he said after a long silence. "Perhaps I have been failing to see the forest for the trees."

Emma knew just when to close. She stood, bathed the man with her warming smile, and extended her strong lithe hand. I almost expected to see him bend and kiss it in Continental fashion, but he merely shook it and thanked us for our time. I'd hardly said a word during the whole interview — or needed to.

Within days Buttram's articles began to appear, and it was evident he'd done his homework. The prestigious Richmond Times-Dispatch simply sank the competition. His interviews with Philo Hylton and the Iroller family confirmed Emma's claims in print. He sought interviews with Agency men, none of whom would talk to him besides Philo, who'd left the Agency; and he managed to portray their collective silence as a nefarious cover-up of major abuse of due process. Interviews with Friel Allen and his father Jack, while admittedly based on self-interest, had the ring of truth, causing the controversy about the 'deal for Friel' to erupt anew all across the state. Suddenly I found the wheel turning again, and I was no longer quite the pariah I'd been for the few weeks after the close of Floyd Allen's trial.

Unfortunately, none of this behind-the-scenes effort helped Friel. Despite the growing belief that he'd been double-crossed by Baldwin-Felts and Governor Mann, he was convicted of murder and received a sentence of 18 years instead of the hoped-for five. What hurt him badly was his own testimony earlier on behalf of his cousin Claude Allen. Seeking to save Claude from death, Friel had admitted on the stand to firing three shots at prosecutor William Foster. It was simply too damaging an admission to overcome. But at least he escaped the death penalty.

***

And now, to my own turn of fate – embarking on a career as a criminal defense lawyer.

In July 1913 I returned from a joyous cross-country ride with Emma to find a letter in buff-colored vellum waiting for me on the silver salver in the hallway. The return address was University of Virginia Law School. With some trepidation I walked back to the kitchen, found a paring knife, and slit it open. Mother and Emma sat 'round the kitchen table as I scanned the contents, and their eyes widened as my face fell. I stared at it in silence for some time.

"Might as well read it to us," Mother said. "Bad news doesn't improve with age."

I read, "To Mr. Carter Hayne, et cetera, et cetera, greetings. The Dean of the University of Virginia Law School regrets to inform you that the Faculty Council has decided not to accept your application to enter the school for the term of study commencing in the fall of 1913. We wish you success in your law studies elsewhere or in any other endeavors you may undertake. Yours truly, Dorsey Pender, Dean, et cetera, et cetera."

I tossed it with contempt on the table, and Emma snatched it up, her eyes blazing with fury.

"It doesn't even say why," she snarled.

"Do they need to say why?" I replied. "Ain't it obvious? I'm a renegade. Friend of assassins and coddler of outlaws."

"Short, sharp, and brutal," Mother said, agreeing with me as she read it again. "But there's more than one way to skin a polecat. I'll just call your Uncle

Randolph. He was on the law faculty for years. He'll not only find out why, but also tell us what — what to do, that is."

Randolph Burwell was mother's older brother, partner of a prestigious law firm in Charlottesville and professor emeritus at the Law School. He no longer taught but still had lots of friends on the faculty and enjoyed lots of influence. Of course, that's how things are done in the South, through family influence and informal personal connections. It's generally why the first question a Southerner asks on meeting someone new is not 'What do you do?' but 'Where are you from, and who are your people?'

A few days later I came in tired, hot, and sweaty from another cross-country trek, this time by myself, and fast and furious, trying to purge the toxins — anger and bitterness — from my soul. As I untacked the horse and brushed him down, Mother came out to the stables and stood waiting expectantly.

"Well?" I said, seeing in her expression that she had news struggling to burst free.

"I've heard from your Uncle Randolph," she informed me. "You're to report to the offices of Professor Boyd Brockington at the law school tomorrow at 3:00 PM, shaved, pressed, and shined as if on parade at VMI. And with a little deference in your soul, something I regret your father and I were never able to beat into you."

"Mother," I said softly, "I can't remember a time when you ever beat me. About anything." And I embraced her. I didn't say, Father was another matter.

"More's the pity then. May it be on my head," she sighed, then relented with a smile. "Professor Brockington is the faculty member who vetoed your application. And I needn't elaborate on why. He teaches criminal law and holds great sway over the rest of the faculty. Thanks to Uncle Randolph's intervention, you have this one chance to win him over. I urge you to make the most of it if you're determined to become a lawyer. If you plan to practice in this state as you've said, then a Virginia Law School diploma will prove invaluable. Not to mention affordable. If you have to go out of state, say to Harvard or Yale, and that's even assuming you could get in, which is doubtful, the cost would be prohibitive."

I said, "Thanks, Mother. I'll do my best. It's all I can do."

She gave me a rueful smile and said, "It will be the first test of your aptitude in which you'll be the advocate for yourself. It may reveal not just whether you can become a lawyer, but whether you ought to."

"Any advice?" I asked.

"Yes," she said. "'To thine own self be true.'"

***

In Charlottesville, one of my favorite Virginia towns, I had a light lunch on High Street late in the afternoon, too nervous to eat much, then walked down the street the half-mile to the law school, rehearsing in my mind what I needed to say. The school secretary, a surprisingly young and pretty woman, was evidently expecting me. She showed me to the faculty conference room with a deferential smile and a cup of tea. Professor Boyd Brockington entered five minutes later, and I was grateful not to have been left stewing long in my own apprehensions.

The professor was a big man, not stout, but tall and massive, with an authoritative air, yet not deliberately intimidating. In different circumstances I might have even found him affable. He had been Commonwealth's

Attorney for Albemarle County for years before joining the faculty at UVA. It was said he looked upon criminal defense attorneys as his natural prey. In any case, he was a notorious conservator of the law-and-order mindset. One wag suggested his motto was, 'Hang 'em all and let God sort 'em out.'

He sat at the head of the broad oak conference table, while I sat a few places down from him. He took up my file, gave me a polite smile, and said, "I suppose you've heard that I blocked your acceptance to the entering law school class. Well, it's true. You have the floor, Mr. Hayne."

I replied, "I'm grateful, Professor Brockington. I realize this is not a judicial proceeding governed by any statute or code of laws, except the universal law of decency and fair play. But it seems to me the law school ought to practice what it preaches. It ought to set a good example."

He asked, "What exactly does that mean in practical terms?"

In his dark three-piece suit, with thick black hair, a beard flecked with gray, and a broad square face, he bore a curious resemblance to Ulysses S. Grant. And when he smiled, which was seldom, he revealed a mouthful of large white teeth, and then he looked a bit like Teddy Roosevelt.

I answered, "That I ought to be given a chance to present my case, defend myself from the scurrilous attacks that — presumably — are the basis of the Faculty Council's rejecting my application."

He said, "Are they scurrilous? I'm too wise an old bird to believe everything I read in the papers. But even if one discounts the sensationalism common to such news outlets, it does seem that you went over, that you inexplicably took the side of the Allens, and at the most critical moment in their prosecution."

"Sir, it's odd," I replied. "Everyone uses the word 'inexplicable' to describe my actions, yet no one ever gives me a chance to explain. There are perfectly good and justifiable reasons for what I did."

He smiled. "Well, now's your chance."

I replied, "I was closer to the Allen case than anyone. I sincerely believe Floyd Allen and his son Claude are not guilty of conspiracy and pre-meditated murder. In fact, the evidence suggests otherwise. They may well deserve time in prison, but not death. The court dispensed neither justice nor mercy. I felt conscience-bound to speak out."

"Ah, yes," he sighed heavily. "The ancient conundrum: justice versus mercy. But how much mercy is enough? How much is too much? Only God knows for certain. We fallible humans must struggle with the question the best we can, while trying to protect civilization from the chaos that hammers constantly at its gates."

He interjected suddenly, "How old are you, Mr. Hayne? A little older than the normal law student, I believe."

"Yes, sir," I answered. "I'm 34."

He nodded and said, "And a war veteran and experienced lawman. 34 is old enough, I would think, for youthful idealism to have given way to an appreciation of things as they are. Or do you believe you've solved the equation of justice versus mercy that has eluded the best minds down the centuries?"

"No, sir," I said. "I haven't solved it, not by a long sight. But I'm still young enough to be willing to try, at least in my own day and circumstances."

He laughed, and seemed more humane at that instant than I expected of him.

He said, now more seriously, "Yet Floyd Allen didn't seek mercy, didn't throw himself on the mercy of the court in Wythe County. Instead he tried to justify what happened and excuse the deaths of five innocent people. How does that fit in to your justice versus mercy conundrum?"

I reflected on that for a while and then recalled Emma's words to Chase Buttram, which proved to me she understood the essence of the matter better than anyone, perhaps including me.

Finally I said, "Professor Brockington, Floyd had already learned the hard way not to expect fairness from the courts. He knew the deck was stacked against him. What else could he do? He had to defend himself aggressively, on the best grounds he had. Grounds that I believe were valid, by the way. We ought to be greatly troubled by the outcome, lest tens of thousands of Virginians like the Allens become convinced that the courts are only for the wealthy and powerful and politically-favored, that the courts dispense injustice rather than justice. If such an impression ever takes hold, then believe me, you will see chaos not just hammering at the gates but breaking them down. You will see revolution. And all the laws and all the policemen in the world won't be able to stop it."

Brockington frowned and said, "This is troubling talk, Mr. Hayne. I hope mass revolution is not something you're advocating, but only warning against. Otherwise I would have to agree with those who call you a renegade."

"I'm not advocating it at all," I said, "only trying to prevent it, as you suggest. And to be sure, I have been called a renegade. But, Sir, I'm a Southern conservative. I'm an old-fashioned product of Virginia and its traditions as much as you or anyone at this law school. We're the ones who should be champions of civil liberty. We're the ones who claim the centuries-old heritage of the struggle for liberty and its hard-won fruits — habeas corpus, due process, the right not to incriminate oneself, the right to cross-examine witnesses. If we forfeit this calling, then the so-called Progressives will highjack the cause of civil liberty, to the detriment of us all and of true civil liberty. It's because I'm an old-fashioned conservative that I believe what our founders believed, men like Jefferson and Madison, and Patrick Henry and George Mason; the law should be a shield for the people, not a weapon for the wealthy and powerful, nor for the aggrandizement of the state."

He mused on that for a while and said, "There's much in what you say. I can see you've given these matters a lot of thought."

"Yes, Sir," I agreed. "I've given it a lot of thought while I was strong-arming people in the name of law and order. I couldn't help but come to believe that in a healthy society, authority is not coercive. In a healthy society people obey the law willingly, not out of fear of force, but because it has moral authority, because it's written on their hearts and it flows out of their own consent to be governed justly."

As you can see, I lacked Emma's knack of knowing when to shut up. But at last I did shut up. Sitting there with a heavy heart, I knew I'd just talked myself right out of law school. I could just hear Mother scoffing on my return, 'Lost your first and last case, did you?'

Brockington appeared sunk deep in thought as he thumbed through my file absently. I assumed he was searching for the right words to soften the blow. Finally he looked up, stared hard at me with his prosecutor's penetrating eyes and announced, "All right then, Mr. Hayne. I hope I'm not making a huge mistake, but I'm going to take back your *ostrakon.*"

I was stunned, but only for an instant. I grinned gratefully and reached over to shake his hand. "I can't thank you enough, Sir. I'll do my best to see you don't regret it."

"You know what an *ostrakon* is?" he asked.

"Certainly," I said, thanking the Lord for my brief immersion in the classics so many years ago.

"Then tell me." His eyes narrowed. Obviously he wondered if he'd caught me in a trap, and a lie.

I replied, "It was the practice in the ancient Athenian democracy that the demos could exile anyone they thought a danger to the state by writing his name on a shard of broken pottery — an *ostrakon* — and placing it in a common receptacle. Anyone receiving enough *ostrakoi* — " I prayed I was using the correct form of the plural — "was sent into exile. It's where we get our word ostracize."

Brockington smiled again, nodded, and ... well, I was no longer ostracized. I entered Virginia Law School in the fall of 1913. Boyd Brockington became my favorite professor, taught me most of what I learned about criminal law during law school, even though we argued constantly about justice versus mercy, naturally without ever resolving the issue. He even became a good friend when I began my practice, until he died in an airplane crash on fogbound South Mountain in 1923.

***

Life has it triumphs and defeats. The wise man treats both the same and keeps his head, something I had yet to learn. In the end, I couldn't save Floyd and Claude from the electric chair, and I couldn't save poor Friel Allen from a long sentence. I had succeeded in only one thing, discrediting myself for trying. All my deeds and aspirations were a pile of smoking wreckage. No job, and my reputation in tatters despite a reprieve of sorts, thanks to Chase Buttram. Even my family looked at me askance as a quixotic and self-destructive fool. And though I'd been accepted at law school, it was a consummation accepted grudgingly. But it really pleased no one in the family. I remain tarnished in everyone's eyes except perhaps Mother's and... Emma Romilly's.

Only Emma understood with a perfect understanding what I'd done and why. Only she stood by me without questions or doubts. Her understanding was a shining jewel of the many-splendored love that had grown up between us.

We sat on my parents' porch one evening sipping wine, and suddenly the spirit moved me to announce, "Well, Love, I'm fired and evidently unemployable. Law school doesn't start for several months. We're months from foxhunting season. I've ridden every trail and hollow between Madison and Flint Hill. It's the first time since I went off to VMI that I've been so much at loose ends. Frankly, I don't know what to do with myself."

As on so many other occasions, Emma had the solution. She smiled and said, "That's easy to remedy. We'll get married and take a wedding trip. You'll love Pawleys Island. I'm sure you can think of something to occupy your time."

Chapter Eleven

Now we come to the saddest part of the tale, and strangest.

In all its 300 years of struggle and strife — Indian wars, the Revolution, the Civil War, and Reconstruction — the Commonwealth of Virginia had never witnessed anything like the Hillsville incident and its aftermath. The verdicts were announced with as much noise and as much reach as the news media were capable of in those days before electronic broadcasting. Immediately the people of the state and much of the Southeast were deeply divided, mostly along lines of class and region. Thousands of letters and petitions bearing thousands of signatures poured in to the Governor, William Hodges Mann, demanding clemency for Floyd and Claude; at a minimum, commutation of sentence to life in prison. The state's newspapers were inundated with letters, some irate about the outcome of the trials, some expressing satisfaction that the murderers were going to get what they deserved. Even some of the jurors who'd voted to condemn Floyd and Claude joined in the appeals for clemency.

The formal appeals process finally ground to an end, and the original verdict was upheld. Generally in law an appeal only considers procedural questions, not the merits of the case itself. The Virginia Supreme

Court considered whether due process was followed and decided in the affirmative. The executions of Floyd and Claude were set for March 28, 1913.

Oddly, many journalists, having earlier stoked the fires of civic rage against the outlaw Allen clan, now turned about face. Suddenly they discovered the young man they'd hounded to his death made even better copy now that he was condemned to die. Some wrote out of genuine sympathy, and some because stoking the controversy in a new way sold papers. Claude Allen was attractive, had never been in trouble with the law, and was now about to lose his life only because of loyalty to his father, leaving a lovely young lady heartbroken.

He became a nationwide *cause célèbre.* His movie-star looks graced scores of front pages, while the accompanying articles stressed his unassuming good nature and filial piety. An astonished Claude began to receive countless letters, too, including proposals of marriage and even some half-baked schemes to break him out of jail. His mail was screened and the latter turned over to Baldwin-Felts, although what they did with them is anybody's guess.

Of course, by this time I'd left the Agency and was fighting my own media battle for public rehabilitation. I'd gone from being the Agency's most trusted and effective 'field commander' to its most persistent antagonist. And now, after burning my bridges with Baldwin-Felts, I figured I might as well go the distance on behalf of the Allens — or more precisely, on behalf of justice. I resolved to go see the Governor.

William Mann was a Southern Democrat and Confederate veteran. Ostensibly of the old school, he had 'New South' aspirations, which meant he believed the Old Confederacy had to renounce its past and join in the parade of America's progress. Still, he might

have been expected to show more sympathy for the
Allens but for two key factors. He was from the
Tidewater and carried the usual prejudice of his region
toward the Blue Ridge mountaineers. A former judge,
he took an extremely dim view of gun battles in
courtrooms that resulted in the deaths of sitting judges.
He seldom granted clemency in death penalty cases.

For weeks there was no response to my wire asking
for an audience, whereupon I wired my friend Chase
Buttram. It seemed eons since that day I'd overtaken
the journalist on the muddy road to Hillsville the
March morning after the shoot-out. His sources
assured him Governor Mann would be in Richmond
for several days with no major public events or
ceremonies on the schedule. I'd be taking a chance but
could conceive of no better plan than to just show up,
hoping to catch him on the fly.

The Norfolk and Western ride from Roanoke to
Richmond took four hours, and out of habit I remained
watchful for pickpockets as I had in my Baldwin-Felts
heyday. But after an uneventful trip I arrived at
Richmond and took a hansom cab up Broad Street to
the Executive Mansion, a handsome Federal-style
structure on Capitol Square. As the sleek Cleveland
Bay trotted up the hill, I found myself sweating and
realized I was as nervous as on the eve of my first
battle against the Philippine *Insurrectos.* But now, as
then, my jitters subsided the moment I went into
action. I gave all my attention to the task at hand.
There was too much at stake, the life of Claude Allen,
for me to miss the target from sheer funk.

Several armed guards hovered at the entrance, a
new feature at the Mansion, thanks to hundreds of
death threats from Virginians outraged at the pending
fate of the Allens — threats which only hurt their
cause, by the way. A dignified Negro usher in a

tailcoat and white gloves showed me to the office anteroom, where I paced and rehearsed mentally until a stout woman in grey tweed came in and announced, "Mr. Hayne, I'm Mrs. Campbell, Governor Mann's Executive Secretary. I understand you're seeking an audience. But his calendar is full, and it's doubtful he'll have the time to work you in. Since you have no appointment," she added, with narrowed eyes.

It was essential to establish my clout, and I told her the things I knew would carry weight. "Mrs. Campbell, I do not exaggerate to tell you it's literally a matter of life and death. But perhaps it will be of more interest to His Excellency that my father is Caldwell Hayne, of the Rappahannock County Haynes. He rode with Colonel Mosby. My mother is Eleanor Burwell Hayne, of the Orange County Burwells. And Joint Master of the Rappahannock Hounds." I'd heard the Governor was a foxhunter, too.

The formidable woman stared at me long and hard, obviously worried by my tarnished reputation. Then I saw the moment of decision flicker across her eyes. "I'm probably going to regret this," she sighed. "But come along."

She showed me into the Governor's ornate office. Fine oil portraits of Virginia's famous sons like Washington and Jefferson, Lee and Jackson commanded the chamber, frowning down on a massive cherry wood desk, which was empty. Not even a single paper or file.

Governor Mann entered, lightly gripping the arm of his secretary who whispered in his ear while he cast glances in my direction. He was the epitome of the Southern politician and former Confederate officer, tall and commanding, now running slightly to corpulence. His wavy white hair topped a luxuriant mustache, and

219

he was dressed impeccably in gray morning coat and dark striped trousers. I stood respectfully as he entered.

His florid features darkened as Mrs. Campbell finished her briefing and departed, leaving me alone to face a towering — and scowling — chief executive with the power of life and death over the young man I was determined to save. I had to tread lightly, yet authoritatively; had to reach him somehow behind his armor of social prejudice and false rectitude. It was a bitter foretaste of what it was like in later years to plead for a client in a capital trial.

I extended my hand. He hesitated, then shook it diffidently. He didn't offer me a seat, and we remained standing.

"Mr. Hayne," he began, "I didn't want to see you, and I confess I don't understand your recent actions in the least. I've met with Miss Wisler, Claude Allen's fiancée, with Reverend McDaniel, and with a slew of others. Frankly, there's nothing more to be said. But I have a high regard for your fine parents. I daresay they are as distressed by your inexplicable conduct as I am. It's for their sake and that reason alone that I consented to speak with you."

I said, "Governor, I'm grateful you did, and for your high opinion of my folks. It's well deserved. Please believe me when I say I'm their true son and a true son of Virginia. I learned my principles from both. As for the others you've met with; well, they came to plead on behalf of their personal interests. I have no personal interests. I'm here to plead on behalf of justice."

"Justice!" he exclaimed. "You seem to have a peculiar definition of justice. I simply can't believe you've taken the side of ... of those assassins."

"Sir," I said, "knowing my background, won't you at least try to understand why I acted as I did? You'll remember that I was the first to arrive in Hillsville when you commissioned Baldwin-Felts to intervene. I conducted the most thorough investigation of the tragedy of anyone. Governor, I was your man on the scene. I'm here not because I've turned renegade, as some are claiming, but because of a debt of honor."

"There is no honor among those Allen brigands," he growled. "I can't see why someone of your breeding would ally himself with them, especially under the pretext of honor."

There was no point in arguing the deep error of this view. I was there not to debate but to persuade. I told him quietly, "Sir, I grieve for the death of the innocents in Hillsville. No one understands better than I the terrible blow to the community. But then, neither does anyone understand the complexities of the entire matter better than I."

He seemed to soften a fraction. "If that is true, then you have no business siding with... those people. Especially considering your background," he said.

I said, "Sir, you seem to think I'm a traitor to my class. But Governor, I'm trying to remain loyal to the principles that class represents. Without a spirit of noblesse oblige, are we any better than the predatory British robber barons we escaped from in 1781? What role does our class serve if not to uphold truth and honor?"

"It serves law and order first," he said. "We have to prevent mob rule, which is what has happened in Carroll County."

"Yes, we do need law and order, but just law and a just order, Governor," I said. "And I've seen it from the inside. Law enforcement is not infallible. Yet law agencies can't seem to admit making an error. When caught in a miscarriage of justice, to prove they were right in the first place they hound the innocent without mercy, compounding the original injustice a hundred-fold. I wouldn't call Floyd Allen innocent; but still, this is close to what happened in Carroll County. There was no conspiracy to fire on the court in Hillsville, no premeditation. It was the spontaneous eruption of accumulated anger and ill will — on both sides, Sir. I speak as one who led the investigation and the chase. Claude Allen especially does not deserve to die. I beg you to commute his sentence."

The Governor circled behind the desk and sat heavily, leaving me standing on the other side, the proper place and distance for a supplicant.

He said wearily. "Even if I could accept your version of events, and I don't, mind you; the court has spoken. A duly sworn jury of Virginians has adjudged Claude Allen guilty of premeditated murder along with his father."

"Sir, this is the worst example of what I mean. The first two juries rejected the charge of first degree murder. But the state was determined to pursue Claude to the gates of hell. His final trial was a travesty of justice. The bias in the law is evident in the case of his brother Victor. Victor Allen had no part at all in the shooting. He wasn't even armed, yet the state sought his life simply because he was one of the clan. A jury acquitted him outright in a matter of minutes. Had the court system been truly just, he would never have been charged in the first place."

The Governor paused a long time. "The appeals judges obviously thought otherwise regarding Floyd and Claude. It would be a hard thing for the chief magistrate of the Commonwealth to overturn a verdict of this notoriety on the strength of your argument, sincere though it may be. Or because of … this." He opened the top drawer in his desk. It bulged with correspondence.

"This," he said, "is what I mean by mob rule — angry letters demanding the release or commutation of all the Allens. Threats to my life and family if I don't. To submit to such outrage... Well, we might as well have no courts, no law in Virginia. This case has gained international notoriety. Do you want me to announce to the whole world that the lawless mob rules in this great Commonwealth?"

"No, Sir," I said. "I'm here only to plead for Claude Allen's life, and on the basis of reason, not angry passion. I'm not answerable for those letters, for their intemperate language or threats. But clearly many thousands of our fellow Virginians believe the death penalty for Claude is excessive. I've come to know the people of our mountains. They're not cultivated in the same way as you or I, but they have character and integrity. Most of them have no access to lawyers and politicians and newspapers. They're expressing their feelings the only way they know how."

"Precisely," he snorted. "With violence. And that is what must end, the rule of violence."

"It's an act of violence when the state takes a life. Yet if the state does so unjustly, how is it any different?" I asked. The shot went home — finally.

He sighed deeply, tugged at the end of his mustache, and said, "No one wants to see a young man die who has barely crossed the threshold of life. I make no promises, but I'll consider your request. It may interest you to know that I've already asked the Chief Justice to review the transcripts of the case — again, and informally, of course; to advise me regarding clemency, since the Allens' appeals were denied by the state Supreme Court."

My heart thudded amid the palpable tension. Mann swiveled in his chair, pulled at his chin, and looked at me directly. "I'll look at the files again, but I make no promise of clemency," he repeated. He stood up abruptly. "Now I really must declare this meeting at an end." He did not extend his hand.

I drew a deep breath. I'd done all I could for Floyd and Claude, but there was still Friel Allen. On behalf of Baldwin-Felts, and indirectly on behalf of the Governor, I'd given my word to Jack Allen and his son Friel. They had trusted in me and the implicit word of the Governor. After the encounter with Bill Baldwin in the Pulaski Courthouse, I was no longer certain who had pledged what to whom. But it was a simple matter of keeping faith, and not just with the Allens, but also with myself and with my own honor. Still, I was torn. Perhaps I ought to pocket Mann's concession regarding possible clemency for Claude, vague as it was. Or should I grasp this one and only opportunity to plead for Friel as well? I might jeopardize what good I had done by asking too much.

I had only seconds to decide, and realized I really couldn't read the man. Was he a paragon of old-fashioned righteousness, or simply a politician with a wetted finger in the wind? Earlier in the month he'd ridden in Woodrow Wilson's inaugural parade and received more applause than the President as a staunch defender of law and order. I feared all that praise gone to his head and given him higher political aspirations.

We'll never know. But I prefer to think he was sincere and following the course he believed was right. The encounter encapsulated all the moral ambiguities of the Allen case. The Governor was no villain; neither was he a hero. He displayed a kind of smug assurance he was right simply because the ruling elite enjoyed some sort of infallibility. I was of the same social class myself, yet full of doubts. On the most practical human level our clash was also an encounter with the fundamental, age-old question: how do you know what

know, or what you think you know? Ultimately you
can't know anything for certain. In the circumstances,
you have to observe conscientiously, hoping your
observations aren't deceiving you. You have to listen
to both head and heart and then... then you have to
choose. So in the end, what we call 'knowledge' is
really a kind of faith. But when a man's life sinks or
floats on such uncertainty, you have to give him the
benefit of the doubt.

All these thoughts swirled through my head in an
instant, and I had only an instant more to decide. There
was no sure way to know what to do, and in the end I
could only follow the promptings of my heart.

"Governor," I began, clearing my throat nervously.
"I beg your indulgence a moment longer. You've been
good enough to see me when it went against the grain,
and I don't wish to abuse your good will. But this
additional matter touches on your own promise as well
as fate of another of the Allens. I have no choice but to
raise it."

His eyes opened in surprise. "What promise? I can't
imagine how any promise of mine touches on any of
this, other than my promise to uphold the laws of the
Commonwealth. But one minute more and one minute
only," he said wearily, "for you do abuse my good
will."

"Sir," I replied, "it's the matter of Friel Allen,
Floyd's nephew. I induced him to surrender peaceably
based on your promise to his father Jack that the state
would accept his plea and seek only a five-year term in
prison. Jack and Friel honored their part of the bargain.
I ask that the Commonwealth honor its part."

His face turned another shade darker and he said, "I
never made any such bargain."

I paused, groping for the right words, yet fearing
there weren't any that would penetrate his armor of

righteous indignation. "Frankly, Sir, I don't know what to say to that. Bill Baldwin conveyed to me your promise in no uncertain terms that Friel Allen would receive a sentence of five years if he'd turn himself in. On that basis I gave my word to Friel and his father Jack — "

"I repeat," he interjected sternly. "I never made any such promise."

"Then Bill Baldwin lied?" My inflection unavoidably left the question hanging in air: was the Governor lying?

"I didn't say that. I only tell you I have no knowledge of the matter."

"Then how — " I began.

"Mr. Hayne." He stood up and cast his eyes at the door. "I've heard you out. In fact, far longer than I'd intended. Now this interview really is at an end." He inclined his head toward the exit.

There was nothing more I could do. I said, "Very well, the interview is at an end, and I thank you for your time. But I have to tell you, Sir; someone caused me to forswear myself, and until I'm able to redeem my pledged word, the matter of Friel Allen is not at an end. Good day, Governor." I nodded a slight bow, turned and left, head held high.

***

While the legal process was grinding forward, the search for Floyd's brother Sid Allen and the other Edwards nephew continued, though no longer under my command, of course. Detective Hugh Lucas had replaced me as the principal Baldwin-Felts team leader in the field. Though I was gone, my resourceful informant Philo Hylton remained on the job, in the bosom of Maude Iroller's family. Wesley Edwards was madly in love with Maude, although she didn't feel as warmly about him, especially since the whole mess had started with his stealing a kiss from another girl at the shuckin' bee. That thoughtless act was the foundation of the tragedy. It also sewed the seeds of jealousy in Maude Iroller, which brought about Wesley's downfall. Philo and I believed Wesley would eventually contact Maude and that might lead us to Wesley. If we located Wesley, we'd find his uncle Sid Allen. This is exactly how the capture of the two unfolded.

Homesick and lovesick, Wesley couldn't stay away for long. In Des Moines he and Uncle Sid ran out of money. Sid Allen was a talented carpenter and had no trouble finding work with a building contractor. Less skilled, Wesley got hired as a day laborer. They lodged together in the boarding house of a Mrs. Cameron, under the names of Tom Sayers and Joe Jackson. All Iowa had read the news of the Hillsville Horror and subsequent manhunt, yet no one connected the two polite, hard-working strangers with those faraway events, despite their mountain speech. Sid and Wesley were well situated and could have avoided capture for years, but for Wesley's unrequited longings.

As soon as he'd saved enough cash to make the trip back home, Wesley took the train to Winston-Salem, North Carolina — the stations were no longer under tight surveillance — and trekked into Fancy Gap under cover of night. Once again, superior knowledge of the terrain enabled him to elude the one patrol we still had watching the trails. He met with Maude and begged her to join him in Des Moines. To prove his sincerity, he gave her enough money for train fare, about $50, and she promised to come. Wesley stayed a few days, then slipped out of the hills to travel back to Iowa. Maude promptly reported the plan to her father, who sold the information to Baldwin-Felts; with full payment of $500 contingent on Maude's agreement to accompany the agents to make the arrest.

By this time it was mid-September. The appeals for Floyd and Claude Allen had run their course, and since the Allen case was still a huge national story, you have to assume the news had reached Des Moines about their impending deaths in the electric chair. In which case, it's inexplicable to me why Sid Allen and Wesley Edwards weren't more vigilant. Sid Allen especially. He'd traveled widely and knew the ways of the world, unlike poor simple Wesley, who until the crisis had never stirred farther from home than Mount Airy.

In the March 14 gun battle, Sid Allen had fought a longer and more determined fight than any of the others. He was just as liable to the death penalty as his brother. He also reported later in his memoir that he was certain Wesley's trip back to see Maude Iroller would be their undoing; the Baldwins were sure to follow. Yet he didn't attempt to leave Des Moines or even re-locate to different lodgings. You have to wonder. It seems the well-known tie of the hillsman to his mountains was stronger than the survival instinct. Perhaps Sidna somehow wanted to be caught, ending the suspenseful and rootless existence of a fugitive. His memoir skirts the issue and actually raises more questions than it answers. In any case, his foreboding about Maude Iroller proved to be accurate.

Bill Baldwin took personal charge of the detail, which included detectives Hugh Lucas and Oscar Monday. Whatever his other faults, Baldwin was a brave and resolute man. He'd personally captured more dangerous criminals than the other two agents combined. This was the highest profile chase the Agency had ever handled, and Baldwin wanted to be in at the kill.

With Maude Iroller in their care, the agents boarded a Pullman coach in Roanoke and set out on the three-day journey to Des Moines. Maude had never been more than a few miles from Fancy Gap, and her bewilderment soon turned to excitement as the train ate up the miles crossing the heartland of America. I can only wonder at her thoughts. Did it trouble her to play the pawn in the betrayal of the young man who adored her and whom she'd professed to love? Clearly her father's patriarchal hand stayed on her shoulder all the way. He'd warned her sternly that there was no future with an accused and soon-to-be convicted murderer, so the family might as well enjoy the $500 bounty. That was a lot of money in 1912.

Arriving in Des Moines, the party registered at a local hotel while Hugh Lucas went to Mrs. Cameron's boarding house to scout, posing as a traveling salesman in need of lodging. Knowing the layout would better enable them to avoid hurting bystanders, and the Agency's reputation, in case the two fugitives resisted, which is what Baldwin expected. Sid Allen later reported actually hearing Lucas negotiate the renting of space with the landlady from the upstairs where he roomed near the landing, but it didn't trigger his suspicions.

After a day of meticulous planning and preparation, the whole team, including Maude and a Des Moines policeman in plain clothes, arrived at the boarding house late in the afternoon. They wanted to give the targets time enough to get home from work and settle unsuspecting in their rooms. Even so, they almost missed Wesley.

On Baldwin's signal, Oscar Monday swept in with Maude, announcing loudly to Mrs. Cameron that Mr. Joe Jackson's fiancée had arrived and would she please ask him to come down. Armed and tense, Baldwin and

Lucas remained hidden below the staircase poised to spring forth. Much of what I'm relating I learned years later from Hughie Lucas, with whom I resumed a friendship of sorts when I practiced law.

Mrs. Cameron told them, "I'm sorry, gentlemen. Mr. Jackson hasn't returned, although I expect him any time now for the evening meal. But his friend Mr. Sayers is in. Shall I ask him down?"

"Yes, please," said Monday, positioning himself and Maude in an unthreatening manner where they could be seen at the foot of the stairs.

"Oh, Mr. Sayers," the landlady sang out. "Mr. Sayers, you have callers."

Sid Allen was in his room writing a letter. He reported later he was somewhat surprised at the call, though still not suspicious — as I certainly would've been in the circumstances. Coatless, in stocking feet, and holding a pen in his right hand, he stepped out of his room at the head of the landing and beheld Maude and a stranger in a dark suit. The man held Maude's arm with his left hand and a bowler hat in his right. The bowler alone should have given the game away.

He peered at the girl and then said, "Maude Iroller. I declare, is that really you?"

Whereupon Bill Baldwin and Hugh Lucas sprang from hiding behind the staircase and bounded up to the landing, two steps at a time, revolvers extended. Sid received the onslaught calmly, without moving, without expression.

Baldwin thrust his Smith and Wesson in Sid's face and shouted, "J. Sidna Allen, you're under arrest in the name of the Commonwealth of Virginia! You move a muscle and I'll shoot you dead right here!"

Sid nodded wordlessly. As he was about to raise his hands in submission, he noticed he was still holding his ink pen. Bemused, he passed it over to Baldwin as if surrendering a lethal weapon. Baldwin took it, looked at it puzzled, then thrust it into his breast pocket. He took out the handcuffs, and a ghost of an ironic smile played about Sidna's lips as he extended his arms for the irons.

That left only one more desperado to bag, and Baldwin correctly surmised Wesley might be on the way home. He resolved to go out and intercept him, leaving Lucas guarding Sid Allen out of sight, and Detective Monday and Maude in the sitting room. In case Wesley eluded Baldwin, Monday would nab him when he came in and was surprised at finding Maude. Mrs. Cameron, totally flustered by the invasion and by the awareness she'd been harboring the nation's most wanted fugitives, told Baldwin where he could meet the streetcar.

The policeman had remained downstairs and out of the action, but now he joined Baldwin, and the two men waited on the curb. A few minutes later the electric trolley approached. Looking at each other and by mutual but unspoken agreement, the two lawmen leaped aboard at opposite ends before the vehicle stopped. Tall, commanding, and strikingly handsome, Baldwin surveyed the passengers, suddenly spotting a young man who obviously recognized him. With eyes and mouth wide open in shock, the fellow immediately left his seat and headed for the rear platform, only to see it guarded by another lawman, his sidearm easily visible. In consternation, young Wesley spun back and forth in the aisle like a trapped animal, then submitted quietly as Baldwin collared him. Brandishing his pistol, Baldwin announced dramatically in front of the astonished passengers, "Wesley Edwards, I arrest you in the name of the Commonwealth of Virginia!"

Bill Baldwin had a Virginia arrest warrant but no approved extradition order from either Virginia or

Iowa. It hearkens back to Floyd Allen's violent encounter in 1911 with the Carroll County deputies on the road from Cana to Fancy Gap. Those deputies had no proper extradition order for the Edwards boys either.

Word spread quickly, and a huge crowd gathered at the Des Moines station to glimpse the 'mass murderers' who'd been living in their midst. Baldwin hustled his prisoners onto the earliest train and got out of town quickly, before anyone in authority could raise the legal niceties. Later, when the legality of the arrests was challenged, Baldwin claimed he'd been operating under the 'bounty hunter' principle in common law. But was it truly lawful? The hearer must make of this what he will.

***

Baldwin got his prisoners back from Des Moines without incident. The two men more or less accepted their lot and made no attempt to escape; and in fact became quite friendly with their guards. Sid Allen was an intelligent and well-traveled man, and had the gift of winning friends. Perhaps that helped spare his life when his turn came to be tried. But the main factor was that passions had cooled, and there was this tremendous revulsion against the death sentences handed down to Floyd Allen, and especially Claude. Also, as I explained, forensic evidence finally began to emerge that suggested if there was any conspiracy to start a gun battle, it had been on the part of the Carroll County court officials.

Sid Allen and Wesley Edwards were arraigned in Hillsville in late September 1912. Again, by law, arraignment had to take place where the crime occurred. The venue for trial was again in Wythe

232

County, although the jury pool was drawn from Giles County, where the residents seemed to be more in sympathy with the Allens. Sid Allen received a combined sentence for the deaths of Judge Massie and Sheriff Lew Webb of 35 years. Wesley received a combined sentence of 27 years' imprisonment.

On December 14, 1912 they arrived at the state penitentiary in Richmond to begin serving their time. As it turned out, they didn't have to complete the full terms, although both spent many years in jail, and as model prisoners, by all accounts. In 1926 they received pardons from legendary Virginia politician Harry F. Byrd, which meant they served only fourteen years of their respective sentences.

***

Now that the hunt had accounted for all its foxes, we come to the most bizarre episode in this most bizarre chapter in the annals of Virginia that already defies belief.

In my audience with Governor Mann I'd emphasized that tens of thousands of our fellow Virginians objected vehemently to the death penalty for Floyd Allen, and especially to executing his son Claude. At the time, little did Mann or I realize that one of thousands was his own lieutenant governor, James Taylor Ellyson.

Like Governor Mann, Ellyson was a Confederate veteran, though far more in harmony with the older consciousness of the Commonwealth and with the 'plain folk' of the South than the Governor. Ellyson was not a particularly distinguished man, and except for the unprecedented act he was about to undertake, he would scarcely have been more than a footnote to history.

When Sidna Allen and Wesley Edwards went on trial in and were duly convicted, and although they received prison sentences and not the death penalty, mass sentiment about the case had shifted, even in parts of the state that had been hostile to the Allens. People now asked, why were the crimes of Sid Allen and Wesley Edwards any less than those of Floyd and Claude, who were about to suffer death? Also, critical new testimony came to light, things that Floyd's and Claude's counsel ought to have brought out in their trials. The most damaging allegation was that the day before Floyd's trial back in March 1912, Dexter Goad and prosecutor Foster had armed themselves and made threats about shooting Floyd at the slightest provocation. If this testimony was true — and to be fair, it was never proven — then the charges of premeditation and conspiracy must be laid at the feet of the Courthouse Ring, not the Allens.

These arguments appealed to Lieutenant Governor Ellyson and he quietly decided to do something about it. Since no reprieve had come from Governor Mann and all possible delays had been exhausted, Floyd and Claude were scheduled to die on Friday March 28, 1913, 'between sunrise and sunset,' according to state law. On Thursday, the day before the executions, Governor Mann traveled to New Jersey to give a speech at Princeton University. No doubt he was glad of an excuse to remove himself from the scene of any last-minute appeals from tearful Allen supporters. But he overlooked one key item: when he was out of the state, the Lieutenant Governor became the Acting Governor.

Thursday evening Ellyson huddled with the Allens' attorneys and a number of leading supporters and agreed to seek a formal opinion from the Attorney General whether he could legally and irrevocably commute the death sentences. Late that evening he called and issued an order to the astonished superintendent of the penitentiary in Richmond to delay the morrow's executions, pending the final word from the Attorney General. I can only imagine what this glimmer of eleventh-hour hope did to Floyd and Claude, who'd already written their last statements and had prepared themselves to make the long walk to the end of the death house corridor.

Governor and Mrs. Mann got wind of the so-called coup d'état when their twenty-three year old son William, Jr. called and woke them at 2:00 AM. He happened to be home from college for the weekend and was the only resident in the Mansion when prison superintendent Wood called late Thursday evening to confirm Ellyson's order. The Governor told William, Jr. to call Mr. Wood back and order the by-now confused official to ignore any directives from Lieutenant Governor Ellyson, and that he — the Governor — would catch the first train back to Virginia Friday morning.

Superintendent Wood cleverly skirted between the two opposing directives, playing for time for the impasse to resolve itself. He informed the Lieutenant Governor he would comply and delay the executions, but only as long as he remained within the law and carried them out before sunset Friday.

Governor Mann did catch an early train. By 10:00 AM Friday he arrived in Alexandria, the first stop in the state on the South Atlantic line. From there he telegraphed Ellyson, the Attorney General, and Superintendent Wood that he was back on Virginia soil, resuming the reins of government, and that no stay of execution was granted. Ellyson had done all he could. He bowed to the law and superior force. Superintendent Wood began calling the invited witnesses, which included the two convicting juries, who by state law were required to witness the executions. I was invited, too, and I showed up at the prison death house just after noon, when Floyd and Claude had taken a light meal to fortify them for the ordeal to come.

***

I had deeply mixed feelings about attending. But Floyd had heard of my efforts on his behalf and especially wanted to see me. And I was awhirl with questions I had to answer — you might say for existential reasons, and because I had to know what my own personal sacrifice had been for. Had I fallen on my sword for a man worthy of it, or not?

For months I'd been struggling to understand what in Floyd's life had led to 'Gentlemen, I ain't a-goin'. Was he a violent criminal who needed to be removed from civilized society, as Governor Mann believed? Or was he a tragic hero, a lone fighter against the creeping modernity that reduces a man to a mere number and deprives him of his human dignity. Obviously he was a man out of joint with the times and unwilling to accept it, yet willing to lay down his life. But why? I wanted to believe he was willing to fight to keep his values alive in the greater world, not just his private inner world; and because he had a sense of transcendent values. Yet tragically, he'd ended up causing the death of his own son and long prison terms for his other kin. I had to know if he felt it was worth it. If he did, then I could better accept the sacrifice of my career and good name; it would make some kind of sense. The only way I could know would be to see Floyd one last time in prison.

***

March 28, 1913 dawned wet, grey, and windy, typical of the transitional season and very much like the March day a year before when the dramatis personae had converged on the Hillsville courthouse, unaware of the tragedy about to unfold. I went through the security check and pat-down and followed a guard into the gloomy bowels of the building to death row.

Floyd lay on his cot in a drab prison suit, but sat up with a wan smile as I entered. The guard pulled up a chair and we conversed through the bars. His seemed as gray as his uniform.

He said, "Thanks for comin', Mr. Hayne. I heard what you done for me an' Claude..." He motioned with his head down the corridor to his son's cell. "... and I wanted to thank you."

"It was the least I could do, Floyd," I answered. "I just regret I couldn't persuade the Governor. I thought if anybody could, it would've been me."

He nodded wordlessly, and stared off in space for an instant, as if imagining the success of my visit to the Governor.

I've related earlier some of the things that passed between us. Toward the end of our visit I told him, "If I'd known how this was going to end up, I don't know... I might have been, well, less diligent in pursuing the boys. I just don't know. But I do know I regret my part in bringing you to this... well..."

"No, Mr. Hayne," he said. "You done yore duty as you saw it. Yore a good man, and there's no need for regrets."

"Do you honestly have none?" I asked. I knew I ought to respect his privacy, but I had to make sense of things. I had to understand.

"For myself, no," he said. "For Claude and the others, yes. It grieves me sore that they got sucked into my fight. It lays on me heavily that Claude — no man ever had a better son, Mr. Hayne — is goin' to pay the ultimate penalty for comin' to his father's defense. That gnaws at me hard. If I'd of known that Claude was goin' to get mixed up in this mess; well, I'd of swallowed my pride and served that year in jail. But all I saw was Dexter Goad winkin' at the Sheriff, like he was sayin', 'Whooee, we got 'em now, boys.' It just boiled my blood, and I'd ruther have died than go with 'em. If you take away a man's dignity and pride, you might as well take away his life itself. So for myself, no, I don't have no regrets. They'll think long and hard in Carroll County 'fore they try to railroad somebody into jail just for standin' on his rights."

Over the years I've relived this last conversation many times, trying to learn from it, to extract all its possible significance. I remain convinced that his defiance was more than bravado. It sprang from the depths of the man's character. This is why I say the story is like a Greek tragedy. Floyd Allen was like some throwback to the Homeric Age, when men spoke their minds to power, refused to grovel before anyone, heedless of the consequences, and like some Achilles or Hector, died faithful to their honor. Yet for his pride Floyd sacrificed not only himself but also his son Claude; just as Achilles sacrificed his friend Patroclos before the walls of Troy for his pride.

"I ain't got much time left now," said Floyd, "but I had me a good life." He paused in thought for a while, then said with macabre humor, "This way is better than a hangin', I guess. I never did like the idea of bein' hung."

I looked at him, searching for the appropriate words, and he added with a grim smile, "It ain't the fall that kills you, it's the sudden stop."

"Yes, this way is better," I said, glum and helpless. I didn't know what else to say, though I wanted to comfort him from across the unbridgeable gulf of knowing that I wasn't about the take the long walk down the corridor. I could only hope the executioner knew the business of electrocution and would make a clean job of it. Electrocution was a new science, not yet mastered by the penal system. Reports were frequent about super-heated subjects bursting into flame where the leads connected and passed the thousand volts of current into the body. One could only hope the subject was dead by then.

Floyd was right, there wasn't much time, and I didn't want to waste it sitting in silence. I said, "Floyd, there's nothing more I can do for you in this life, but I give you my word: I'm going to continue working to clear your names. And I'm going into the law, to make sure this doesn't happen to anyone else if I can help it."

Oddly, that mattered a lot to Floyd. You'd think he wouldn't care after... well, after he was gone. He smiled and nodded.

"I always said this wadn' the end of the story," he said.

"No," I agreed. "This is not the end of the story. I'm going to work to set the record straight on what really happened in Hillsville. And I'll not rest until the state honors the bargain it made with Friel and your brother Jack."

"Thanks, Mr. Hayne. Please do what you can for all my nephews. They're young fellers with their whole lives ahead of 'em. I cain't hardly stand the thought of them spendin' the rest of their days in prison."

In his words and demeanor I saw what I'd hoped and expected to see — the mountaineer's fatalism that allowed them to roll with the blows of an inscrutable fate, to accept what they couldn't change. I felt a kinship with this attitude, and saw now that his tragedy was no more than the normal calamity of being born into a world populated with his fellow humans.

There was nothing more to be said. I extended my hand through the bars and Floyd took it in both of his with a bone-grinding grip. Too moved to speak further, I stood up and departed, almost crushed by the pathos of witnessing father and son sharing the same space on death row. Would it have been more merciful to separate them, or let them spend their last hours together? I don't know and can't possibly say. But I thought of my own father and our often-difficult relationship, my awkward search for his blessing and approval, his halting attempts to confer it. It's been said that the story of every son is contained in part in the history of his father.

Sons eventually have to break free of their fathers, sometimes even challenge them, to come into their own manhood. Yet it seems Floyd's sons never did, at least not openly, as I did with my father. They stood by him unflinching and uncomplaining to the very end. Yet, were they any less manly for it? Claude was never heard to utter a syllable of complaint that his father's rash, headlong act had brought him to a premature death. Perhaps it's a mark of true manhood how one handles injustice.

The senior death row guard was a thin, sallow man whose ill-fitting blue uniform hung on his frame loosely, giving him an authority he could have possessed nowhere else but such a place as this. His face was thin and hard as an axe blade. In fact, he had the same lean hardness common among Virginia mountaineers. Maybe he was one, and that was why he relented and showed some compassion at the end, allowing father and son a few last moments together in Floyd's cell.

I had left the cellblock and was waiting to be let out through the security station at the T-junction in the middle of the corridor. From there I was supposed to be taken the long way 'round to the execution room. After a few minutes another uniformed guard had come to fetch me into the witness area in the execution room. But something held me back. I balked. I simply couldn't go in and join a crowd watching these men put to death, men whom I'd grown to appreciate if not admire. Instead of entering the death chamber I remained in the security area and observed what I could from that odd vantage point. From there I heard Floyd and Claude chatting as insouciantly as if they were having dinner at home in Fancy Gap. Then to my astonishment I heard them laughing. I wish I knew what had made them laugh. It might've served me when jests were few.

The sallow guard returned to Floyd's cell to escort Claude back to his. There were muffled farewells, and it was somehow all the more heart-wrenching because I heard only murmurs and not the words themselves.

As Claude padded back down the corridor, the guard looked vexed. With the complacency of one who would continue to live addressing one about to die, he said to Claude, "You should be prayin' instead of laughin'."

Like his father, Claude was a man who could stare death in the face unblinking. He barely gave the guard a glance. "They're the same thing," he said quietly.

***

Not long after — and I can't say how long, it seemed an age — the door at the T-junction between death row and the main prison creaked open. Mr. Wood entered, flanked by four uniformed guards, and followed by Reverend Scherer in a black suit, holding his Book. They looked at me in surprise, then left me standing and passed on to the holding cells.

It's too painful to remember, yet impossible to forget. The warden read the death warrant and announced with evident sadness and announced, "Floyd, it's time."

In the end, I'm glad I didn't witness the execution. Perhaps it was cowardly on my part. It might have eased their exit to see a friendly face among the witnesses. Yet I have a hard time believing it would have made any difference. The electric chair was supposed to be a humane method of execution, modern technology at the service of enlightened penology. Maybe so. No one has ever survived the experience to say otherwise. But it still seemed shockingly brutal and barbaric to me, although certainly no worse than hanging, I had to admit. Perhaps this is when the seeds were sewn of my opposition to capital punishment that is imposed so… well, so cavalierly in Virginia.

The procedure was less solemn than businesslike. The state's dispatching someone from this world to the next must be done calmly, dispassionately, like any other routine government task. There is an appointed time, and appointments have to be kept. And suddenly time itself was without substance in the face of eternity. Time seemed merely an artifice of man. Did Floyd sense that, too; or were the last fleeting moments of man's artifice precious to him? For at the end of the process, Floyd would no longer be in the land of the living. And only minutes later his 22-year old son, who ought to have a full life before him, would follow into that undiscovered country.

I felt as though I was out of my body, looking down, outside of reality. Knowing the son would immediately follow the father turned the normal dynamic of fathers and sons on its head. If the father lives long enough to reach his dotage, the child becomes father to the man. But this...

Floyd passed me by without acknowledgement. Still limping from his wounds of a year ago, he wore a grim expression and his eyes seemed fastened already on the next world. The steel door closed behind him with a muffled clank. A few minutes later the lights dimmed and flickered for a short spell as the current was drawn away to power the engine of death inside. I bowed my head.

Claude stopped and smiled at me as he passed. We shook hands. It seemed like such an odd, empty gesture in the circumstances, yet we are all creatures of habit.

He said formally, "Tell them I did not shame my kin."

"I will, Claude," I replied. "But they will know that without my telling them."

Preceded by the pastor and flanked by four guards, he walked lightly down the corridor toward his death as if on a Sunday afternoon stroll, head held high. At the threshold of the chamber he turned and gave me another slight smile, then entered, unhesitating and unafraid.

On an impulse, perhaps because I suddenly realized how precious time is, I took out my watch. Exactly eleven minutes elapsed. The lights dimmed and flickered again.

Only then, crushed by a sense of my own futility in redressing the cruelty of the world, did I slip unobserved into the night. Hardly aware, I passed through checkpoints and barred doors, making my way outside, where I leaned heavily against the rough stone of the prison wall. I wanted to weep, but the desolation was too great and my heart was blocked up. The welcome release of tears was denied.

Chapter Twelve

Well, I'm coming to the end soon now, and glad of it. The telling has taken more out of me than I expected. Getting old for some people means they need more rest; for others it means less. I'm one of the former. But I've only got a short time left and I hate to sleep it away. Still, we're all prisoners of the flesh, and the body makes demands that can't be denied.

I've told what became of Floyd Allen and son Claude, of Sid Allen and the Edwards nephews. But I'm not quite done, for the story is about more than just what befell the Allen clan. It's also about how violence reverberates far beyond the scene of the act, for the Carroll County tragedy rippled outward across distance and down the generations far from obscure Hillsville, a place few people had ever heard of or cared about. It changed the lives of those who were connected to the Allens and their fate; namely, the Baldwin-Felts Detective Agency. Also, Floyd's brother Jasper 'Jack' Allen. Then me. And even my beloved Emma.

As I related, the tragedy led me to reverse the pattern of my life altogether. Instead of bringing outlaws to justice – sometimes a dubious form of justice, I became a criminal defense lawyer. But in all modesty, not just a run-of-the-mill lawyer but one of the South's best – 'legendary' in the words of a 1963 article in Practicing Lawyer.

If you ask why I became legendary, I would say it wasn't because of any great scholarship of the law. It was a simple passion for justice – and for freedom, a passion born that night in the Virginia penitentiary, when Claude Allen smiled as he entered the death chamber. I believe justice is the handmaiden of freedom. You can't have one without the other. Politicians are always extolling freedom. But I've discovered that many people don't really want freedom. It demands too much self-responsibility. Yet everyone does want justice, at least for themselves.

But first I had to learn the law and get admitted to the bar. In those days, formal legal education hadn't quite matured, if that's the right word. You could go to law school or you could read law, which meant basically apprenticing yourself to an attorney and learning the trade under him. I did both. Went to Virginia Law School for a year and then worked in my Uncle Randolph Burwell's law practice.

My father despised lawyers. He wasn't happy with my new career choice and refused any financial help or an advance on my inheritance. We'd always been at cross purposes, a condition not unusual between fathers and sons. But the real issue was that the arc of Dad's life had crested when he was still a young man riding with Colonel Mosby, the 'Gray Ghost.' Dad was 70 when I left Baldwin-Felts. Nothing in his long life since had come close to matching those Civil War days for excitement, drama, and a sense of high purpose. I knew, although he didn't know I knew, that he'd come to re-live his war experience vicariously through my exploits and my fame catching the Allens, temporary though it was.

Yet my father was unreasonably bitter about my becoming a criminal lawyer. His reaction showed me the strange and demanding terrain traversed between sons and fathers. We all know the son wants and needs the approval of the father. Do I measure up? Are you proud of me? Am I a man? It's the role of the father to rear his son so that the answer is yes to all these vital questions. It's what empowers the son to enter into responsible manhood. But what sons don't know, and perhaps neither do many fathers, is that the father also wants and needs the approval of the son. It's like a hall of mirrors. The father equally wants to be a hero to his son. Did I do a good job? Was I a good dad? Did I let you down? At least a worthy father feels this way.

My father didn't seem to feel that way, for all the reasons I stated. He was too wounded a creature from his own war, as I was from mine. I never got the validation I needed from him, the Biblical blessing of Isaac, the steady guide into manhood. I was left to do it for myself. And oddly, for a while, William Baldwin gave me the validation as a man I had needed. But after Hillsville and the Allen trials, I no longer felt that way about Baldwin. It was the hardest thing I'd ever had to do, but I made the break with him as I did eventually with Dad.

However, I didn't just quit Baldwin-Felts. I decided to defend the kind of people I'd previously been chasing. To Dad the about-face wasn't merely abhorrent; it was incomprehensible. Happily Mother had ample means of her own. In her own quiet, determined way, she approved of my decision. Without making a fuss, she put at my disposal enough money to attend the University of Virginia for the two-year law program. I had some of my own, but had never been able to save enough of my Baldwin pay to finance two or three years of education.

Yet even Mother didn't fully grasp what lurked in the recesses of my mind. She thought I'd finally settled down to a safer existence than chasing armed outlaws in the hinterlands. I'd marry the beautiful horsewoman Emma Romilly, and we'd become sleek and plump and connubial and have sleek, plump babies; and the most dangerous thing we'd do would be to ride to the hounds. No, even Mother, the wise and far-sighted Eleanor Burwell Hayne who understood me far better than Dad, couldn't foresee that I'd become a guerrilla lawyer, a renegade; and to the Best People of Virginia, little more than an outlaw myself. I couldn't explain it to those closest to me. Even now it's hard to explain. But I felt like the balance of my life was a debt I owed to Floyd and Claude Allen. I repaid it by going to work at the defense bar.

I spent the end of 1913 and first half of 1914 at Virginia Law, accelerating the two-year program. Then I read law under Uncle Randolph in Charlottesville. I wanted to go into criminal defense, and the Burwell firm was one of the most active such firms. They'd defended Samuel McCue, the former mayor of Charlottesville, one of Virginia's most celebrated cases. McCue was convicted and hanged in 1905 for the murder of his wife Fannie, the last legal hanging in Albemarle County. But questions about his guilt remain even today. It was the kind of thing for a defense lawyer to cut one's teeth on, and I got the training I was looking for.

During the Allen trials, I'd observed with growing dismay that their lawyers were entirely process-oriented. They seemed to believe as long as they followed the protocols, procedures, and processes of the law, then they'd mounted an effective defense. But something was missing — something vital, what I call 'telling the right narrative.' Now, law is a process. Due process we call it, and we should be glad for it. Due process represents centuries of struggle and sacrifice, with milestones along the way like Magna

Carta, the Oxford Provisions of Simon de Montfort, the 1628 Petition of Right, and so forth. But I believed there had to be something more than just crossing the t's and dotting the i's when defending a man whose life was at stake. The attitude of the Allen defense team reminded me of the complacency of Medieval doctors: 'They answered as they took their fees, / There is no cure for this disease.'

I was approved by the Virginia Bar in 1915 and began practicing what I call 'street law,' criminal defense, domestic and juvenile, small plaintiffs' work. Before the Federal Rules of Procedure in the 1960's, 'trial by ambush' was common because there was no right of discovery. Prosecutors weren't required to disclose exculpatory information; there was no Miranda warning to arrestees. The common law and archaic British procedure still prevailed in Virginia courts. Many case-law precedents went back to Colonial times and the old British law forms dating from the 1600's. It was a tough business, I don't mind telling you.

As I became more a prominent practitioner, I continued to agitate on behalf of Friel Allen. Gave interviews and speeches all over the state, buttonholed legislators, wrote letters. The Richmond Times-Dispatch took up the controversy and published a damaging editorial, "Who's Lying," that questioned Bill Baldwin's otherwise spotless reputation and forced Governor Mann to publicly disavow him and any 'deal for Friel.' Yet Mann did it in such a clumsy way that it increased the public doubts instead of laying them to rest. If the two men hated me before the editorial, they really hated me after it was published. They both knew they were lying, as a letter from Baldwin to Mann proved when it was discovered in the archives many years later.

***

Now, the controversy over Friel Allen's conviction has a bearing on what happened to me next, and I strongly believe — though I can't prove — what happened to Floyd and Sid Allen's brother Jack, father of Friel.

Jack Allen had been making a huge nuisance of himself, hounding the Agency and publicly embarrassing Bill Baldwin and Tom Felts about Friel's promised five-year sentence. Someone — and I'm making no specific accusations — someone decided he had to be eliminated. He was a formidable man, as I've indicated. Lots of folks were more afraid of him than they had been of Floyd.

Jack had traveled from Fancy Gap to Mount Airy to sell a load of lumber. On his way back, he stopped with his wagon and team to spend the night at Widow Martin's boarding house at the foot of the mountain, just inside the Virginia line. It was late afternoon and evidently he wanted to wait to make the hard trip up the Gap in daylight. It was also rumored that Mrs. Martin's establishment was a house of ill repute, and that Jack had stopped there for the presumed purpose. I honestly can't say if that's true. In those days widows had few ways to support themselves after the death of a husband and breadwinner. Providing room and board to travelers was a respectable livelihood, although it may be the services provided sometimes went beyond lodging and a meal. But even if Mrs. Martin's was a part-time bordello, it doesn't justify what happened next, assuming we know what happened. The Baldwins and their allies put out so many conflicting stories that we'll never know.

No need to repeat all the theories or try to sort through them. But these facts are not in dispute. On the night of March 16, 1916, someone shot and killed Jack Allen as he sat in the downstairs parlor warming by the fire. A Carroll County coroner's jury convened and named one Willie McGraw as the killer. He was another guest — or client — at the boarding house. McGraw maintained the shooting was in self-defense. He claimed he and Jack had gotten into an argument about the guilt of the Allen clan over the courthouse massacre, that Jack became irate, drew his pistol and advanced in a threatening manner, and that McGraw had no choice but to open fire. The coroner's jury either willfully or in ignorance overlooked the fact that Jack's fatal wound was in the back of his head, and that his sidearm was still in his saddlebag upstairs in his room.

I suspected at the time that the killing was ordered. I'd learned by bitter experience how the Agency used violence and intimidation to protect its reputation, justifying such acts as 'protecting the public.' Willie McGraw turned up a few days later in the West Virginia coal fields as part of the Baldwins' army to suppress striking miners. When I heard that, my suspicions hardened into certainty.

At the time I was living in Roanoke and working on a case to defend some of those same miners. I'd been in Mingo County, West Virginia and had returned to Roanoke to see Emma and draft a pleading. Byrd Marion, a close friend of the Allen family, came to see me in Roanoke and told me the story of Jack Allen's death. He also told me about the, ah, anomalies, in the official story. I didn't just take his word for it but checked out the details on my own. When I was satisfied, I wrote a guest editorial for the Roanoke Times, "Was Jack Allen Murdered?" It made no actionable libels or allegations — I was already too good a lawyer for that — but it did highlight the questionable findings of the Carroll County coroner's jury. It suggested no Allen could ever get fair treatment from the Hillsville courthouse, and led the reader to wonder if Jack Allen had been shut up permanently because Baldwin and Felts had refused to honor their promise to Friel.

Feeling quite satisfied with myself with having caused such a stir, I was sitting at home one night late in March 1916 when the telephone rang, one of those old-timey ones with separate earpiece and mouthpiece. The voice on the other end whispered hoarsely and set my heart to racing. I hung the receiver on its cradle and went to get my hat and coat.

Emma eyed me narrowly and said, "Where do you think you're going on a night like this?" It was freezing and blowing. Winter hadn't yet relinquished its iron grip on the Blue Ridge.

I told her, "Love, I just got a call from someone claiming to know about the Friel Allen case. Says he has information that might prove my claim. I'm going to meet him at the River Tavern." She was young and oh-so lovely then, and why I would ever have been tempted to leave her side on such a night... Well, I was young and oh-so foolish.

"This is no night for honest men to meet at a tavern," she said. "Why didn't he come here and give you his information?"

I replied, "Love, I didn't ask and can't say. Perhaps he wants to remain inconspicuous. Everyone knows what the Agency tried to do to me. Can't blame anybody for wanting to avoid the same treatment."

"Well, I don't like it. I wish you wouldn't go," she argued.

I patted my .45 in its shoulder holster under my overcoat. "I'll be all right," I said.

"That's supposed to reassure me? If you need to go armed, then you shouldn't go at all. Please stay," she practically begged.

She had a feeling, she told me. I should have listened. I didn't. Fueled by my own righteous indignation and shame and a welter of other emotions, I put on my coat, hat, and gloves and stepped out into the night.

We kept a Packard touring car in the stables behind the house, where two of the horse stalls had been converted. With an oil lantern in my left hand, I rolled open the double doors with my right and stepped inside. The flickering lamp barely revealed two hulking shapes that lunged at me from the darkness. Utterly astonished, yet with well-honed reflexes, I threw myself backwards out the door, flinging the lamp wildly at one of the assailants. The other one fetched me a heavy blow on my right knee. Down I went in the snow, in agony. But I rolled and rolled and rolled, making a poor target as the two thugs struck at me. In the corner of my eye I caught the image of a heavy logging chain, swinging mightily. What the first man was armed with I can't say.

They managed to land a few hits on my back and shoulders, painful as all hell but short of a crippling blow. As I rolled, I struggled desperately to retrieve my pistol from the layers of heavy clothing. Finally, after what seemed an eternity, I had it in both hands. Lying still for an instant on my stomach while the blows rained down, I racked the slide and chambered a round. As they drew back to strike again, I rolled over, sat up facing them, and opened fire. I fired wild and am sure I didn't hit anything. I was in terrible pain, breathing violently, it was dark, and blood was pouring into my eyes. But the sudden gunfire was enough. The attackers bolted.

Emma rushed onto the back porch and fired two shotgun rounds at their disappearing backs for good measure, then dropped it and dashed to my side. I was conscious, but just barely. I have no memory of half-crawling and being half-dragged back into the house. All I remember is the throbbing agony of the shattered right knee.

Since then I've walked with a limp. I recovered fully from all the other injuries, including a broken clavicle and rib fractures, except for the knee. The kneecap and the entire joint were badly damaged. I was lucky to be able to limp.

Was it the Baldwins? What I think and what I know are two different things. It could have been garden-variety thieves whom I surprised in the act. Or it could have been rogue Baldwin men. The assault came soon after Jack Allen was killed and my column appeared in the paper, which made me suspicious. The phone call might have been genuine, or maybe a setup to lure me out. But if the attackers planned to catch me by surprise, they evidently didn't plan to kill me, which they could easily have done with gun or knife. Not that the Agency was above killing someone who provoked them badly enough. Someone like Sid Hatfield, for example, who shot Lee and Albert Felts in the famous gun battle in Matewan, West Virginia. He was gunned down in turn by Baldwin men. In sum, I think but can't prove it was the Agency, and the plan was to administer a bad beating, to warn me off or disable me enough to stop my meddling.

***

Although the knee injury was permanent, I recovered enough to take part – a very small part – in the First World War. Evidently I didn't learn my lesson in the Philippines in 1901. The Great War is what we called it then, until an even greater one came along twenty years later. It seemed like a pointless conflict to me. No one really knew why we were fighting, except to win. But I went anyway.

The war broke out in Europe in the summer of 1914, but the U.S. didn't get drawn in until 1917. I was no war lover. I'd seen war's horrors and follies in the Philippines. And I was skeptical of the official rhetoric justifying our entry into a European conflict that served no American national interests as far as I could tell. I had learned from experience that in war the first casualty is truth.

Nevertheless, everybody was in a frenzy of whipped-up patriotism and war fever. The Germans were fools and overplayed their hand with the sinking of the Lusitania and the Zimmermann telegram to the Mexican government. Something in me responded, too. I simply couldn't sit back while good men enlisted and went off to the training camps.

I was not a child eager for some desperate glory; but… but war is a paradox. It holds a lure despite its horrors and follies. Perhaps it's the deep emotion, the adventure, the sense of being fully alive and part of some great enterprise. In war everything is intensified. Even simple courtesy and kindness that might pass unobserved back home in peacetime seem like miracles of the human spirit when they transpire in war. Was this what called me? Was I simply rationalizing that I could be of service? Even now I don't know. All I knew then was, my contemporaries were going off to fight and risk all. In spite of myself, I had to be one of them.

Arriving by train in Washington, DC, I went to Marine Corps headquarters at 8th and I Streets. Surely a VMI grad and Marine veteran of the Philippines would be given a company command at least. But one look at my limp and the personnel officer shook his head. Sadly, I might add.

"Mr. Hayne," he said. "We certainly could use someone with your training and combat experience. But I'm afraid you wouldn't get to first base on the physical. Combat leaders have to be totally fit."

"I am totally fit," I said. "I just limp. But I can out-hike any man here." Frankly, that wasn't the least bit true. But in those days a man was expected to tell such lies to show his courage and motivation.

"Yes, but can you run?" the Marine captain asked.

"Run? Marines never run," I said, caught up in my own bravado.

He regarded me with an expression I hoped was sympathy and not pity. "I mean, run toward the enemy," he said. Then he proceeded to write something on a slip of paper and handed it to me. "I see in your file you're a lawyer. Go to this address. The Army is recruiting officers for the Judge Advocate General Corps and they're waiving many of the physical requirements. If you really want to go to France, this is probably the only way."

"The Army!" I wailed. And that's how I ended up in the Army, as a military lawyer and JAG major.

Actually, it turned out not so bad. The Army has less esprit de corps than the Marines, as everybody knows. On the other hand, when I signed up there was far less spit-and-polish nonsense, fewer martinets. And if I had gone into the Fifth Marines as I wanted, I probably would have died in the wheat field at Belleau Wood, along with three-fourths of the officers and much of the regiment.

My war was relatively comfortable, far from the front at Division headquarters, mostly handling courts martial or defending some poor private who'd had enough of it all and shot off his toes to get out of combat. But I suffered greatly being separated from my Emma. After only a few months in France I reproached myself bitterly for allowing the pull of martial glory to outweigh my desire to remain with her, which I could have done without public censure. After all, I'd served in my war, and as everyone knew, I was a virtual cripple.

I was 'over there' in France when she... when she died.

Even now it's hard to talk about it. There was no one like her. We'd gathered as much joy as our hands could hold. Like two thieves in the night, we had furtively stolen a bit of happiness from the orchard of that great bully and tyrant called Life, who does his best to keep it from us. When I received word it was the evening of November 11, 1918. Armistice Day. The day the war ended.

Earlier in the day I'd gone forward to interview some soldiers of the 323rd Infantry, a National Guard regiment from the Baltimore area. They'd been charged with mutiny — mutiny! — for refusing to attack a German strongpoint on the morning of November 11. Every soldier in the AEF knew the Armistice was to go into effect at 11:00 AM on the eleventh day of the eleventh month. There was utterly no point in throwing their lives away in a war that was already over. But their battalion commander, a newly arrived Regular, wanted to win laurels for himself before it all ended; and he was willing to risk his men needlessly to advance his career. The troops quite sensibly balked, and he had them arrested and charged with what can be a capital crime under the old Articles of War. I went forward to conduct the initial investigation.

By this time I was a lieutenant colonel, same rank as the battalion commander, so it was easy for me to rip him to shreds. I vowed to make his name a curse and byword in the AEF if he didn't withdraw the charges at once. Which he did, I'm glad to say. When I returned to my dugout that evening, there was a long letter from Mother with the tragic news.

After living so long, I still don't know how we humans do it, how we live with such loss. The loss that leaves an aching hole in the heart. Though it's empty space, it carries such insupportable weight. I drained the dregs of anguish to the lees. Not a day goes by when I don't remember and grieve for her. Sometimes I wonder if God has given me this long a life just to test how much sorrow the human heart can hold.

Strangely enough, it was a riding accident. Emma had wanted to open a riding establishment in Little Washington where you could board your horse, get your horse trained, or get yourself trained in all levels of horsemanship. This kind of full-service stable is common today, but was a novel concept back then. With her reputation and Mother's connections, she had every reason to believe it would be a successful business. But it turned out no one in the area wanted to be associated with the renegade and turncoat Carter Hayne, or his wife. The business never got off the ground. She lived with my parents and cared for our daughter Eleanor, who was born in 1918 while I was in France. But she wanted to continue an equestrian career of some kind, any kind. Next to me and Eleanor, riding was her very life. She was reduced to traveling some distance and taking students wherever she could. In a way, indirectly, you might say she was a fatality of Hillsville, too.

She'd been with a group of young students on a trail ride near Leesburg and was on a Thoroughbred, which is a hot-blooded breed, excitable and skittish. Their temperamental nature is always lurking below the surface; and if spooked, they can bolt and propel you into a nearby obstacle without warning.

The trail narrowed through a section of old hardwood forest. Nobody knows exactly how it happened, but evidently one of the young women riding abreast in the narrow passage bumped a hornet's nest from its lodgment in an ancient red oak. As the cone hit the ground, hundreds of angry hornets came swarming out with vengeance on their minds. The two students immediately spurred their mounts and passed out of the danger zone, leaving Emma and her Thoroughbred in the path as she brought up the rear. Both horse and rider suffered too many stings to count. The maddened animal, impossible even for the most accomplished rider to control, careened into a low-hanging limb. We never knew if she died from the blow or from the poison of so many stings.

She was buried in the Hayne family plot near Sperryville, as was her wish, rather than in South Carolina. It's where I'll be buried, too. Very soon, I would say. All I had of her when I came home from the war were memories, memories that bless and burn down all the long years. And her monument, as simple and elegant as herself. The epitaph reads:
'Now who holds thee?'
'Death,' I said.
And there the silver answer rang,
'Not death, but love.'

***

Now I come to the final chapter of the world-famous Baldwin-Felts detective Agency. Their story reminds me of the old Medieval concept of the wheel of fortune. One day you're up, and the wheel turns and brings you down. Well, after all the Allens and Edwards were safely dead or behind bars for long terms, Baldwin-Felts was at the height of its notoriety and power. Bill Baldwin and Tom Felts were lionized, consulted by police agencies all over the country, not just in Virginia. They became extremely wealthy, celebrities in their own right. You might say they were the Wyatt Earp and Bat Masterson of their era.

Bill Baldwin remarked to me once that his men were the Knights Templar of the 20th Century. Like me, he was a Romantic, which was one source of our connection until the break came. And yet, as with the Templars, the wheel of fortune turned and within a few years after Hillsville they were brought low. They grossly overreached their legitimate role and abused their power in two episodes in particular, Ludlow, Colorado and Matewan, West Virginia. After those incidents the world suddenly began looking at them aghast. People began to question the wisdom of allowing powerful and unaccountable private corporations to unleash an army of 'shoot-first-ask-questions-later' gunmen on poor, exploited miners, including their helpless women and children. Folks began calling the Baldwins 'gun thugs' instead of 'detectives.'

First Ludlow. It happened in the heyday of the industrialists called the Robber Barons. They were the wealthiest men in the country, and they controlled the news and public opinion even more than now. So the full horrors of Ludlow only came out in bits and pieces, which helped the murderers — that's a harsh word, but it fits — avoid accountability.

In fairness, it must be noted that these industrialists created valuable companies that employed millions, raising the standard of living of the whole country. But they also believed they were above the law and could act with impunity. This sense of entitlement, combined with such ideas as Social Darwinism and the so-called 'Iron law of Wages,' proved an inevitable formula for exploiting their workers. The coal companies especially regarded their workers as mere commodities. I've seen mules and draft horses treated with greater dignity than the coalminers in Southwest Virginia and the state of West Virginia. And it was as bad or worse in Ludlow, Colorado in 1914.

Coal mining was – still is -- dangerous, dirty, back-breaking work. Hundreds of miners died every year from cave-ins and explosions from the build-up of methane gas. To save money the bosses ignored basic safety practices or failed to provide safety equipment. They paid their people poorly, and often in company scrip that could only be spent at the company stores with artificially jacked-up prices. If a miner complained he was summarily fired, and his family evicted if he happened to live in company housing. It's no wonder that such exploitation and inhumane conditions drove miners to despair, and to seek redress through unions like the United Mine Workers.

Now I'm not a particular fan of labor unions. I've seen them exploit their members as badly as the mine owners. But at least the unions spoke for the miners at a time when no one else would, and many unions sincerely represented their members' interests. When driven to the wall, miners naturally agitated or went on strike for the right to unionize. They believed it was their only defense from the bosses' grinding exploitation. Such efforts ignited the crisis in Ludlow,

Colorado in 1914, and later in Matewan, West
Virginia.

Mine owners routinely used Baldwin-Felts strong-
arm men to evict striking miners from their homes,
even those who merely spoke to a union representative.
Their destitute families had to subsist somehow in the
open, in tents if they were lucky. The strikers were
harassed in every conceivable way. Since they were
human beings, not saints, some of them responded
with violence.

Toward the end of 1913 the UMW called a major
strike against Rockefeller-owned mines in Colorado.
This gave the mine bosses the pretext they needed to
use overwhelming force. They ordered the Baldwins to
step up harassment of the strikers under the guise of
protecting the mines and the 'scabs,' non-striking
workers. Violence escalated, which is exactly what the
owners wanted – it justified their calling in the
Colorado State Militia. In April 1914 the tensions
boiled over into tragedy.

Many of the striking Ludlow miners were Greek
immigrants, and they lived in makeshift tent cities with
their families. The bosses wanted the embarrassing
tents removed, and when the militia went in, the
miners fought back. It was a real battle and lasted all
day. The militia and Baldwins used machine guns
against strikers armed with clubs, a few Springfield
and Winchester rifles, and scattered handguns. It was
no contest. Finally the miners broke and fled. Forty
strikers were killed, and thirteen of their women and
children burned to death as they huddled terrified in
their tents, which were set ablaze by machine-gun
tracer rounds. Louis Tikas, a leader of the strikers, was
captured and summarily executed — murdered —
along with two other miners, their bodies left exposed
for three days as a warning.

For several weeks the bosses were able to control the news of the atrocity. Their narrative became the official version: violent strikers, many of them Bolsheviks or barely civilized immigrants, tried to destroy the property of honest, God-fearing Americans and had to be restrained when they resorted to unjustified violence.

Well, you get the picture. But there was a photographer there who also got the picture, many pictures. His photo images trickled into the news bit by bit, along with scathing reports of eyewitnesses, many locals who had no part with the UMW. Americans everywhere became rightly indignant, and the Agency took a real plunge in public confidence for the first time since its founding.

Then came the Matewan battle in 1920 in Mingo County, West Virginia. It was a repeat of Ludlow on a smaller scale, except this time it was the Baldwins who got massacred and not the striking miners.

After the Ludlow atrocity, coalminers everywhere felt a particular grudge toward the Agency. Where before it had been feared, now it was hated more than feared. The tough Scots-Irish of the West Virginia hills — people much like the Allens, by the way — burned with a spirit of vengeance toward the Baldwin men who came into Matewan to evict the families of miners striking the Stone Mountain Coal Corporation.

The Baldwins assigned the task were under command of my old colleague Lee Felts, younger brother of big boss Tom. Another Felts brother Albert took part, and C. E. Cunningham, who'd replaced me the day I was re-directed to Hillsville back in 1912.

By all accounts — and they may be biased, I can't say one way or another — the Agency conducted the first day's evictions with special arrogance and brutality, dumping the precious few belongings of the hapless families unceremoniously into muddy spring streets. It was as if the toxin of hubris had accumulated in the Agency's bloodstream to fatal levels over the years. At the same time the level of hatred of the Baldwins in the community was building up to fatally explosive levels.

The next day's actions took place within the city limits of Matewan, not in the county. Matewan Mayor Cabell Testerman and Police Chief Sid Hatfield were staunch supporters of the miners, and these evictions fell within their jurisdiction. Sid Hatfield was a relative of 'Devil Anse' Hatfield, a name made nationally famous by the Hatfield-McCoy feud. That is to say, Sid Hatfield was not a man to be trifled with. Along with Mayor Testerman he confronted Albert Felts and demanded to see proper eviction orders authorized by the City of Matewan, which of course Albert didn't have. Hatfield promptly put Felts under arrest. But in the arrogant complacency typical of the Baldwins, Albert thought he held the trump card. Totally underestimating his adversary, he produced a warrant for Sid Hatfield's arrest issued by a Mingo County judge known to be in the pay of the coal corporations.

No one knows exactly what happened next, since the three parties to the exchange are all dead. But as best I can reconstruct, Mayor Testerman and Sid laughed off the Agency arrest warrant as fraudulent, which it was, as shown later by competent legal authority. Felts was a brave man and cool customer. Did he draw his pistol to enforce the warrant? Did Sid Hatfield simply draw unprovoked and open fire? Certainly neither was willing to cede the advantage of the first shot. In any event, Hatfield shot Felts. Albert fled, badly wounded, to hole up in the Post Office, where Hatfield hunted him down and finished him off.

In the first chaotic exchange of gunfire, Albert's wild shots mortally wounded Mayor Testerman.

Unbeknown to the rest of the Baldwins, dozens of armed angry miners had quietly taken up ambush positions in the streets and surrounding buildings. Many were armed with rifles, giving them the advantage of range and accuracy over the agents, who had pistols. When Lee Felts saw his bother fall, in grief and anger he fired on Sid Hatfield, who had advanced shooting, his fighting blood at a boil. Simultaneously the rest of the miners opened up from their protected positions on the rest of the Baldwins. Lee was hit several times and fell dead. Some of the agents fought back bravely, C.E. Cunningham, especially. Some ran in panic. Cunningham, the two Felts brothers, and four other agents died. Another was badly wounded, and two managed to escape. In addition to Mayor Testerman, two miners were killed.

The escaping agents brought word of the shocking debacle to the outside world. To the mine owners, the dead Baldwins were more than heroes; they were martyrs in the cause of law and order. To coalminers and their families, they were villains who'd finally gotten a taste of their own medicine. Thomas Felts was of course grief-stricken and beside himself with rage at the death of his blood kin. Two months later several of his men exacted revenge on Sid Hatfield, shooting him down in cold blood, without warning and in broad daylight as he stood on the steps of the McDowell County courthouse.

But this time, this time the Agency didn't succeed in putting its spin on things. The revenge killing of Sid Hatfield and other outrages finally began to catch up with Baldwin-Felts. Ludlow had undermined its moral authority, and Matewan destroyed its reputation for invincibility. The Baldwins' public standing dropped like a rock, and while they continued to perform legitimate and useful security services, on the railroad, for example; they were no longer used as an army-for-hire by the 'malefactors of great wealth.'

***

Well, now, I've come to the end. And in retrospect I wonder if perhaps I err in seeking some higher meaning in it all. Does the suffering of a solitary soul teach us any transcendent lesson? Is this bizarre story merely an interesting episode but without lasting significance? Or is it an act of the universal drama in which we all play a part?

To be sure, there will always be criminals who have to be dealt with, sometimes harshly. Yet the search for justice must always be accompanied by the need for mercy. This was what the Carroll County Courthouse Ring forgot, along with the state of Virginia and Baldwin-Felts. They triumphed, or so they thought. Floyd and his son were executed. Sid Allen, Friel Allen, and the Edwards brothers were put away for long prison sentences. But they hadn't counted on my transformation through my connection to the event. When I heard Claude laughing with his father on death row, when I heard his reply to the scorn of the prison guard, I saw Claude in his apotheosis. I felt I was in the presence of something both transcendent and permanent. I was transformed.

As different as I was from the Allens in background, education, social caste, and even temperament, from then on something of them — their independence, their fierce pride, their courage — was born in me even as they passed from the scene. I became their champion after the fact. I did what I could for my vision of law and justice, and for those who needed the advocacy they might have otherwise been denied. So you might say the Allens won the final victory after all over politicized justice, which is just a form of injustice and oppression. For this the High and the Mighty called me a renegade, just as they called Patrick Henry a traitor in his day. Like Patrick Henry, I flung it back in their teeth and said, 'Make the most of it.'

But this brings me to another point I must make as I conclude. The focus of the story has been the fate of Floyd and Claude and their kinsmen. That's as it should be. But I've never forgotten the other five that died that grim March morning in 1912 in Hillsville. They were innocent, too. Judge Massie, a decent man whose tragic flaw, if it was a flaw, was an excess of fair-mindedness. William Foster and Sheriff Webb. True, they had it in for the Allens and they overstepped the bounds of their office. But they were doing their duty as they saw it. And poor Gus Fowler and Betty Ayers; good, simple, homely people who never did anyone harm and wouldn't if they'd lived a hundred years. Weep for them, too. They are worth our tears.

Now 56 years have passed. The tumult and the shouting have long since died, the captains and the kings long since departed. I'm an old, dry, cracked, vessel — an empty vessel now that I've poured out this strange, sad tale. I'm bowed down under the accumulated weight of memory and loss, for the Hillsville tragedy reminds us of the tragedy of the Fall and man's loss of innocence. I was just one foot soldier in the old story of the oppression of man, which flows from the Fall co-equally with man's greatness. It's a pageant of woe as long as our existence on the planet. I was called to wage a fight that never ends because it must be fought and won in each generation. Now others who hear this tale must catch the falling flag of the struggle for reason, of the duty to stand against the lynch mob, to reprove the mass hysteria that mankind is so frequently subject to.

I couldn't save Floyd or Claude Allen, though I helped others avoid a similar fate. But I spoke for Floyd then, as I do now, for all his faults. I tried to speak for the least of them — the plain folk, faceless and voiceless, struggling in a world governed by giant corporations and big banks, by money power and corrupt politics, by social status and empty celebrity. I tried to speak for the neglected little people on whom our daily lives depend — the coalminers and dirt farmers and truck drivers without whom we would go through life cold, hungry, and in darkness; yet who are ill equipped to resist the limitless powers of the modern state. Too often they end up crushed and mangled by a soulless, indifferent bureaucracy, by rogue cops and arrogant judges, by a system of justice dominated by oligarchs and plutocrats, in which the perversion of the law becomes a principle. I pray my poor efforts will be entered to my credit in the Great Ledger; for as Christ himself said, "If ye have done it unto the least of these, my brethren, ye have done it unto me."

The rich and powerful and politically-connected have plenty to speak for them. They own the government, the courts, the news media, the corporations, the banks. These mighty ones care little for the poor and the powerless. But the poor and powerless are still men. They possess the sovereignty all men possess inherently — they have their choice. They can submit dumbly like sheep, which is what the corporate-state system demands. Or, if the embers of courage and dignity still smolder, which are the essence of our humanity, they can look the system squarely in the eye and declare on behalf of all freeborn men in defiant, ringing words that still echo today, "Gentlemen, I ain't a-goin'."

— The End —

Draper, Virginia, 2011

PROSE PRESS
The origin of the word prose is Latin, *prosa oratio,* meaning straightforward discourse.

Prose Press is looking for stories with strong plots.

We offer an affordable, quality publishing option with guaranteed worldwide distribution.

Queries: E-mail only.
proseNcons@live.com

CPSIA information can be obtained at www.ICGtesting.com
Printed in the USA
LVOW080243200212

269471LV00004B/2/P